Teamworking and Quality Improvement

TEAMWORKING
AND
QUALITY IMPROVEMENT

LESSONS FROM BRITISH AND NORTH AMERICAN ORGANIZATIONS

Edited by

**RICHARD TEARE
EBERHARD E. SCHEUING
CYRIL ATKINSON
CLIVE WESTWOOD**

CASSELL

Cassell
Wellington House
125 Strand
London WC2R OBB

PO Box 605
Herndon, VA 20172

First published 1997

British Library Cataloguing-in-Publication Data

A catalogue record for this book is available from the British Library.

ISBN 0-304-338-389 (paperback)

Printed and bound in Great Britain by Redwood Books, Trowbridge, Wiltshire

Contents

PART 1: THE UK MICHELIN AWARD

Single problem/management promoted team projects:

Continuous improvement/self-directed teams:

Editors and contributors

EDITORS

Richard Teare PhD is the Charles Forte Professor of Hotel Management, Department of Management Studies, University of Surrey and a Non-Executive Director of the NSQT, UK. He is also Research Director of the HCIMA's *Worldwide Hospitality and Tourism Trends* CD-ROM project. He is Editor of the *International Journal of Contemporary Hospitality Management*, Editor of Cassell's *Resource-Based Series in Hospitality and Tourism Management* and a member of the Editorial Advisory Boards of six international journals. He has co-written and edited fourteen books on service industry management.

Eberhard E. Scheuing PhD is Professor of Marketing, Director of the Business Research Institute & Director of Executive Education at St. John's University, New York, USA. As Founder and President of the *International Service Quality Association* (ISQA), Eb co-chairs the prestigious series of international conferences on *Quality in Services* (QUIS) and is co-editor of *The Service Quality Handbook*. To date, he has published more than 500 articles and 25 books on aspects of purchasing management, customer service, new product management and strategic partnering.

Cyril Atkinson was until recently Executive Director of the National Society for Quality through Teamwork (NSQT) with the challenge of providing continuous support to the society's members in their strategic development and promoting the culture of quality through teamwork in the UK. He joined the NSQT in 1989 having previously held the position of Vice President, Quality International with International Computers Limited (ICL). He has extensive quality management experience with previous senior appointments in design assurance, reliability and manufacturing quality.

Clive Westwood is a Quality Consultant mainly working with the NSQT where he used to co-ordinate their conferences, seminars, special events and news letters. He trained as a Production Engineer then worked as a Unit Manager at Mullard South-ampton. He then joined Philips, Southampton as Central Inspection Group Manager which included responsibility for Quality Circles and the role of Facilitator for the com-pany's Total Quality Culture programme. He is a Chartered Engineer and a Member of the Institute of Electrical Engineers.

CONTRIBUTORS

Andy Anderson was a founder member of the first quality improvement team at Perkins in 1985 and since then he has been involved in the development of the total quality philosophy and teamworking activities in the Perkins Group of Companies. In 1987 he was appointed to the role of Teamwork Co-ordinator and for the past nine years he has also been actively involved with the NSQT at regional and na-tional levels. As a qualified and licensed trainer, assessor and verifier of NVQ com-petences, Andy is committed to the concept of enabling people to achieve their full potential.

John Bicheno is Reader in Operations Management at the University of Bucking-ham. He is the author of four books in the area of Just-in-Time Manufacturing and Total Quality, both fields with strong links to teamworking. He has run a public course on Self Directed Work Teams at Brunel University for a number of years. Prior to his current post he was a practitioner in the field of operations management and he has also held the post of Associate Professor of Industrial Engineering at the University of the Witwatersrand, South Africa.

Jackie Brander Brown is a Senior Lecturer and Research Co-ordinator, Depart-ment of Accounting and Finance, The Manchester Metropolitan University, and she has also taught at Cornell University, USA. Jackie is an associate of the Institute of Chartered Accountants in England and Wales and of the British Association of Ho-tel Accountants. Her research interests include the impact of organizational culture on the effectiveness of organizations and she is currently completing a PhD degree at Oxford Brookes University.

Nancy Burzon is Team Leader – Competency Development for GTE Corporation where she is responsible for the direction and development of educational pro-grammes for GTE's executive staff. She also directs the quality education curricu-lum for all GTE management employees, guides the marketing/sales management educational curriculum and leads GTE's international educational curriculum de-velopment effort. Nancy is a Director and Treasurer of the International Service Quality Association and is a contributing author to *The Service Quality Handbook,* published in 1994.

Carole Congram PhD is an Associate Professor in the Department of Manage-ment, Bentley College, Massachusetts, USA where she teaches operations man-agement. Carole has 20 years of consulting experience in services marketing and among other publications, she edited and contributed to *The AMA Handbook of Marketing for the Service Industries,* published by AMACON in 1991. Carole is a member of the American Marketing Association, the American Society for Quality Control, the International Service Quality Association and the Decision Sciences Institute.

Ian Fryer is Statistical Process Control Co-ordinator at Albright & Wilson's Oldbury site. He joined the company as a trainee chemist in 1985 and after graduating with an honours degree in Chemistry in 1990, became Group Leader of the site's Quality Assurance Department. In 1992, he took up his current role and spends the majority of his time working on process improvement initiatives.

Frank Gleeson has been involved in the technical/quality function at Wellman International for the past 20 years. After college he spent a short time in the petrochemical and mining industries before joining Wellman International Ltd in 1973. He was appointed Quality Control Manager in 1975 and took on both production and product development roles before taking up his present post as Quality Development Manager in 1992. This involved the introduction of ISO 9002 and the subsequent Continuous Improvement process.

Richard Gray began his engineering career at Perkins where he served his apprenticeship and later moved into technical support. After two years working with Rockwell International producing printing presses, he returned to Perkins and in 1989 was appointed Supervisor in the Technical Services department where his involvement in the teamworking programme began. Richard has since acquired a broad base of experience in quality engineering, quality audit and test and production machining.

John Green is Quality Facilitator in a Severn Trent Water operational district. Prior to his current role he worked in the central Quality Support team at Severn Trent's headquarters in Birmingham, providing support to 27 facilitators. He holds a Master of Education degree and previously worked with systems houses and in education.

Chris Guymer is a Chartered Mechanical Engineer who has spent the past 20 years working in the oil and gas industry on a number of onshore and offshore projects. During this time his career has centred on project engineering and project management. Chris has seen six years' overseas service, including a two and a half year period spent working on a major offshore project for Petrobas in Brazil. He has also spent several years working on field conceptual design studies. For the past two years he has been working on the Britannia Topsides Project.

Roger Hallowell is a Doctoral Candidate at Harvard Business School, USA where he is researching the delivery of customer value and competitive advantage in labour-dominant services. Roger has served as Research Associate to the Service Management Interest Group at Harvard Business School in which capacity he researched and wrote case studies on service companies and contributed to several academic and practitioner books and articles. He holds an AB and an MBA from Harvard University and has worked in service industries as diverse as banking and industrial uniform rental.

Derek Harwood is a Chartered Chemical Engineer who has been active in the oil and gas industry for 20 years, working on both onshore and offshore projects. Derek began as a process engineer, moving into project engineering and thence to project management. He has worked mainly in the UK but also served three years in Saudi Arabia. Derek has worked for AMEC for seven years and his recent experience includes the Shell/Enterprise Nelson Field development. Derek has spent the last two years on assignment with Britannia and is accountable for engineering, materials and quality assurance.

Anthony Ingold PhD is Reader & Director of Research at Birmingham College of Food. Tony trained as a medical biologist, specialized in microbial ecology and later diversified as he became interested in the application of research methodologies to a variety of problems. Tony has worked with Land Rover before and has co-authored work relating to their CQI programme. He has an interest in aviation and flying light aircraft and he is currently co-authoring a book on yield management that draws on the practices of airlines.

Hadyn Ingram graduated from Middlesex University and worked as a manager in luxury hotels in London and Yorkshire before taking on the running of a busy pub in the suburbs of London. In 1993 he was awarded his MSc at Oxford Brookes University and worked for four years as a Senior Lecturer at Bournemouth University. He now owns a sixteen-bedroom hotel in Salisbury and teaches hospitality management in the Department of Management Studies at the University of Surrey. His publications and research centre around teamwork and performance in the hospitality industry.

Shelagh Iwanowicz began her Civil Service career working in a District Office, later transferring to the Regional Directorate Training Organization where she became a Senior Executive Officer and Customer Services Manager for Fylde Benefits Directorate. Shelagh was also given line management responsibility for the Benefit Enquiry Line (BEL) project, assuming full-time responsibility for BEL in 1992 and leadership of its TQM programme. She is trained as a validator for the Benefits Agency Quality Award and recently completed assessment procedures training for the European Quality Award.

Nick Johns PhD is a Reader at the City College Norwich, a Regional College of Anglia Polytechnic University where his writing and research focuses on quality and productivity in service operations. Nick has participated in numerous conferences in the hospitality management field and at present, he is developing a service quality assessment model for small hospitality enterprises. He is an Associate Editor of the *International Journal of Contemporary Hospitality Management* and his forthcoming book addresses the application of research methods in service industry management.

Conrad Lashley is Head at the Centre for Hospitality Management in Nottingham Business School at Nottingham Trent University. He joined the University in 1986 having had industrial experience in both consumer goods marketing and human resource development. He has extensive research and consultancy experience in service quality management and employee empowerment and has written more than twenty conference papers and journal articles on the topic. He is a Vice-Chair of the Council For Hospitality Management and Co-ordinator of the Fifth Annual Hospitality Research Conference.

Andrew Lockwood is a Senior Lecturer in Hotel Management, Department of Management Studies at the University of Surrey, UK. He graduated from the University of Surrey in 1974 and his industrial experience includes working for international hotel companies both in London and the provinces in a range of managerial positions before running his own 40-bedroom hotel. Andrew has written four books and many articles, chapters and conference papers on the management of hospitality operations and his research interest lies in the field of quality management, the subject of his PhD work.

Brenda McDonnell is a Senior Lecturer in the School of Financial Studies and Law at Sheffield Hallam University. Prior to entering academia she gained several years' experience working as a management accountant in service businesses. Her current research interests are in the areas of performance measurement including the use of non-financial measures, the balanced scorecard and empowerment and its consequences for the management control system.

Martin R. Mariner is Director, Quality, Corning Incorporated, USA with responsibility for quality strategy, direction and leadership. A founding member of the Executive Committee of the New York State Governor's Excelsior Quality Award Task Force, Martin also trained the New York State Board of Examiners and served as an examiner, Malcolm Baldrige National Quality Award for six years. He is a judge for the Federal Quality Institute, Federal Quality Award and a member of the American Society for Quality Control, the US Quality Council and The Total Quality Forum Advisory Council.

Vaikalathur S. Mahesh is Course Director (Service Management) at the University of Buckingham, UK. His research, teaching and consulting interests span human motivation, business ethics and service management. He has twenty years of senior managerial experience in diverse industries – automobiles, hotels, information technology, medical systems, consumer products and financial services. His book, *Thresholds of Motivation: The Corporation as a Nursery for Human Growth*, published by Tata McGraw Hill in 1983, won the Escorts Book of the year award.

Sally Messenger was a Lecturer in Hotel Management at the University of Surrey where her research and publishing interests lay in education and training and organizational change management. Sally holds a Master of Science degree and prior to her current appointment she worked for City and Guilds of London Institute where she was responsible for designing new competence-based qualifications for the hospitality industry. She later became Divisional Manager of the Curriculum Development Department and has also worked for the National Council for Vocational Qualifications.

Dave Rusk is currently Quality Manager (Corporate Office) for Royal Insurance Life & Pensions and he is based in their Liverpool Head Office. He joined Royal from University and spent some years working for their general insurance operation in a variety of branch management and head office roles. He is a Fellow of the Chartered Insurance Institute and in 1995 acted as an assessor for the UK Quality Award and as senior assessor for the North West Quality Award.

Ray Sprason is the Co-ordinator for the Discussion Group Programmes at Land Rover Vehicles and has been involved with the training and development of the Group since their beginnings in 1988. He joined the company in 1971 and worked in many divisions of the company, ranging from logistics to personnel. Previously a member of the NSQT organizing committee, he is currently responsible for co-ordinating Land Rover Vehicles' Recruitment Programme. Ray is also a member of the TQM/FE Facilitation Team for the Rover Group.

Peter Stannack is a Senior Consultant with Project North East, a non-profit consultancy and economic development agency supporting organizations across the UK and in India, Africa and Eastern Europe. He has worked in a number of industrial and service sectors in the areas of marketing, supply chain management and human resource management. The author of several papers and books on supply chain and human resource management, he has most recently supported the first public–private sector revenue partnership in the UK and assisted the partnership in securing a £3.5 million contract.

Kevin Starling is the Business Implementation Manager at Anglian Water Plc, UK where he is responsible for information technology, strategy and implementation. Kevin's main interests lie in customer services and in particular, strategic development and service quality. In 1995 he was awarded an MSc in Service Management with distinction by the University of Buckingham, UK.

Mark Thompson is Total Quality Facilitator at RHP Bearings, Ferrybridge, where he is responsible for assisting the management team in determining and implementing the appropriate total quality strategy and plans for the site. He graduated from Sheffield Hallam University in 1990 with an honours degree in Engineering with Business Studies and achieved Chartered Engineer status in 1994. He previously worked for British Rail Engineering in Doncaster and prior to his current appointment he was a Manufacturing Engineer at RHP Bearings, Ferrybridge.

Philip Welton-Cook MInstFT was educated at Worcester Technical College where he received an HNC in Mechanical Engineering. He served his apprenticeship with Rockwell International. He joined Garringtons in 1992 as a consultant on Quality Systems and compiled their quality manual. In late 1992 he became TQI Facilitator and in early 1993, with the Garringtons Management Steering Committee, launched a TQI programme. He is now Light Forgings TQI Facilitator with responsibility for two sites in the British Steel Forgings Group – Garringtons and Smethwick Drop Forgings.

Nigel Williams is a Continuous Improvement Advisor with Britannia Airways based at Luton Airport. Nigel joined Britannia in September 1991 and he is currently a member of a small team responsible for the design and implementation of the Continuous Improvement Programme throughout the company. This involves designing and delivering training courses, and the subsequent facilitation of teams at all levels. Prior to joining the company Nigel had fourteen years' experience in the Royal Air Force where he served as an Airframe Technician.

The companies

Albright & Wilson Plc was founded in 1851 at Oldbury near Birmingham and is now a leading multinational chemical business with manufacturing sites in fifteen countries and sales offices in a further sixteen countries. A recent highly successful flotation has seen Albright & Wilson's return to the London stock market after sixteen years as a wholly owned subsidiary of the American-based Tenneco Inc. Employing more than 4000 people worldwide, the company's main manufacturing focus is in the areas of phosphates, surfactants and speciality chemicals. This includes making chemicals for the food, soft drinks, toothpaste, and pharmaceutical industries among others.

Benefit Enquiry Line (BEL) is a national, free telephone advice and information service for people with disabilities, their carers and representatives. BEL advisers give advice on all Social Security Benefits. BEL also has a free Claim Form Completion Service, Braille Service and Textphone Service. BEL has developed a strong teamwork programme and is committed to increasing empowerment and customer satisfaction levels. It was one of the first areas in the Benefits Agency to attain the Benefits Agency Quality Award; BEL has also attained Charter Mark status and *Investors in People* accreditation.

Britannia Airways started operating in May 1962 as Euravia, flying three Lockheed Constellations from Luton Airport where it still has its headquarters. In 1964 the current name was adopted and in 1965 Britannia became part of the International Thomson Organisation (now the Thomson Corporation). Britannia has led the way in introducing new aircraft into its fleet; in 1968 it became the first European operator of the Boeing 737-200 and in 1984 it became the first operator in Europe to introduce the Boeing 767 wide bodied aircraft. Currently Britannia carries eight million holiday makers from seventeen UK airports to more than 100 destinations worldwide.

Britannia has grown to become Britain's second largest airline and the world's biggest charter company.

Britannia Operator (BOL) Ltd is owned by Chevron and Conoco (acting as a single operator) along with Union Texas, Santa Fe, Phillips and Texaco, providing a single identity for the development of the North Sea Britannia natural gas and gas condensate field. The Topsides Division of the Britannia Project is an innovative integrated project team, made up from BOL and AMEC, the engineering and management contractor, who are supported by various fabrication and hook-up and commissioning contractors. Together they are responsible for the design, fabrication and installation as well as the hook-up and commissioning of the Platform Topside facilities.

British Steel Forgings Garringtons has been based at Bromsgrove, Worcestershire since 1946. Originally part of GKN and later UES Ltd, the company has recently been taken over by British Steel PLC. The Garringtons site specializes in a wide range of high volume forged and machined components for automotive and engineering applications. As the largest forge in the UK and with its continuing programme of technological development, it has the reputation of being one of Europe's most advanced forging companies. Garringtons' commitment to the concept of continuous improvement through teamwork is inextricably linked to the company ethos of exceeding customer expectations in quality, cost and delivery.

Corning Incorporated, a *Fortune 500* company, is a diversified company with a strong tradition of technological innovation. Although historically a glass and speciality materials manufacturer, today Corning concentrates on the three key global markets that account for 60 per cent of its revenues: optical communications, life sciences and the environment. In addition, Corning continues to be a leading manufacturer of such speciality materials as glass for eyewear and plastic for labware. The company's quality journey, which began in 1983 with a quality awareness initiative, has evolved in four phases. Today, Corning employees are integrating quality into their business and personal lives by using quality tools to build customer relationships, develop new products and improve processes.

GTE Corporation is the largest single provider of local telephone services in the USA, where the firm provides local telephone services in numerous geographically disparate markets across the country. GTE also provides cellular telephone services to its local markets, manages all telephone services in Venezuela and the Dominican Republic, and owns subsidiaries that publish telephone directories and provide telephone services to governments. In 1994, GTE had 111,162 employees and earned profits of $2.5 billion on revenues of $20 billion.

Land Rover, based at Solihull in the Midlands, is part of the Rover Group, recently acquired by BMW. It is the home of Rover Group's 4×4 vehicle production which includes the world-famous Defender, Discovery and Range Rover models. Since 1990, the company has doubled its production and, reversing the general trend, has employed thousands of new staff over the past few years. Multiple winners of the coveted IIP Award, Land Rover is now in its sixth year of a cultural change programme that recognizes people as its greatest asset and extraordinary customer satisfaction as its mission.

The Varity Perkins Group, a world leader in diesel engines, was founded in 1932 since when over thirteen million engines have been built. Today, more than 300,000 Perkins engines are built in thirteen countries and sold in 160. They power more than 3000 different applications from 600 major equipment manufacturers, ranging from 5–52,500 bhp for use in construction, power generation, materials handling, auto-motive, agricultural, marine, rail and defence industries. Major customers include Caterpillar, Chrysler, JCB, Hanomag, F. G. Wilson, Linde, Agco, Volvo Penta, Ingersoll-Rand, GKN, Renault, ERF and Vickers. Around 70 per cent of products built at the group's three UK manufacturing plants in Peterborough, Shrewsbury and Stafford are exported. Engines are also assembled in Argentina, Brazil, China, Indonesia, India, Iran, Mexico, Pakistan, Peru, Poland, South Africa and Turkey.

RHP Bearings was formed in 1969 and in 1990 the world's second largest bearings manufacturer, NSK of Japan, acquired the company. NSK employs around 18,000 people and operates 25 manufacturing sites with worldwide sales of £2.6 billion. NSK-RHP Europe consists of seven RHP manufacturing sites, five of which are in the UK. In addition there are sales companies in France, Germany, Holland, Italy, Spain and UK with annual sales of £300 million and approximately 4000 employees, 2700 of whom work in RHP Manufacturing. The markets served are very broad based and include automotive, aerospace, machine tool and general industrial with such customers as Ford, Rover, Rolls Royce, Pratt & Whitney, British Aerospace and Bearing Services Ltd among others.

Royal Insurance Life & Pensions is part of the worldwide Royal Insurance Holdings Plc which transacts business in over 90 countries through some 900 offices, employing more than 22,000 people. In 1995, the Royal celebrated its 150th Anniversary and since 1845, it has become one of the largest truly international general and life insurance companies in the world. It provides a complete range of pension, investment, protection and mortgage-related products through three distribution channels – direct sales, tied agents and independent financial advisers. In recent years, it has successfully maintained its level of long-term profit while at the same time achieving a reduction in its expenses.

Severn Trent Plc is one of the world's largest companies specializing in water services and waste management. It is among the 100 largest listed companies in the UK and employs over 10,000 people serving a total population of more than eight million customers. In the five years since privatisation, the Group spent over £2.6 billion on capital investment and improved efficiency and customer service. Severn Trent comprises fifteen districts, each responsible for supplying water and waste water services. The organization has become a market leader in handling and treating waste products and it is currently developing other specialized non-regulated businesses.

The Slag Reduction Company is a Division of Faber Prest Plc. Its 'core business' is the loading, management and unloading of the raw materials involved in steel processing. Fifty-three 'core' staff operate a range of unloading and raw materials handling equipment. The Slag Reduction Company works in partnership with British Steel at the Redcar Terminal on Teesside. British Steel's Teesside Works is one of three integrated steelmaking sites with an annual liquid steel production of 3.75 million tonnes, accounting for 30 per cent of the total output.

Wellman International Limited is a subsidiary company of Wellman Inc. based at Mullagh in the Republic of Ireland. The parent company is a large manufacturing organization producing a range of polyester and nylon products from its operations in the USA, Holland and Ireland. Wellman Inc. is also the world's largest recycler of post-consumer plastic soft drinks bottles. The main product of the plant in Ireland, trading as Wellman International Ltd, is fibrous polyester material used, for example, in domestic furniture, clothing, carpeting, geotextiles, abrasives and roofing felt. Its second main manufacturing activity is in the recycling of post-consumer soft drinks bottles made from a long-chain polyester molecule called Polyethylene Terephthalate or PET. Every year, three hundred million such bottles are processed initially in the plant in Holland prior to being transferred to Ireland for integration into the normal polyester raw material stream.

The National Society for Quality through Teamwork

With a pedigree stretching back to 1884, when its roots were formed out of the 'Co-operative movement', the National Society for Quality through Teamwork (NSQT) can be said to be well established. The recorded Cooperative minute called for an Association to develop the involvement of people in the workplace and led to the Industrial Participation Association (IPA) being formed.

Within the IPA, almost 100 years later, a number of member companies struggling to develop and sustain 'Quality Circles' as a means of participation formed a small sector to network their activities and develop the Circle philosophy together. That sector became known as the National Society for Quality Circles (NSQC).

The sector grew as more companies adopted Quality Circles, and in 1989 was established as a company owned by its corporate members and given Charity status. The development of teamworking in the UK in many forms, but rooted in the Quality Circle approach, led to a change of title for the Society.

The NSQT's aim was, and still is, to encourage mutual support of its member companies who are each seeking to enhance their business by utilizing the creative ability of their total workforce. In addition the Society endeavours to assist and support companies that wish to explore the opportunities available to them in the Teamworking field. To do this the NSQT provides: facilitating workshops for management teams so that they evolve the best possible continuous improvement programme; training in implementation for management and their staff; conferences and workshops to expand understanding and awareness; and regular networking of experience meetings throughout the UK.

A main development has been the introduction of 'award' schemes which are designed to provide the UK business world with the opportunity to compare themselves against the best in class, in the jargon to *benchmark themselves*. The Perkins Award, a scheme sponsored by Perkins Engines, was launched in 1987, and the

Michelin Award, sponsored by the Michelin Tyre Company, started in 1990. The awards address two different team-related areas, but they complement each other.

The Perkins Award is given to the management teams who have demonstrated that they have achieved a highly successful programme of change which results in effective people involvement and teamworking. The judging criteria are designed to measure the management team's progress during the immediate past years.

The Michelin Awards are given for excellence in teamworking in two forms. Firstly, awards for teams who, like Quality Circles, identify problems to be addressed themselves, seek effective solutions and implement those solutions in their own area of responsibility. They are applying a continuous process of improvement. Secondly, awards are given to teams who were formed to address and solve problems, or to identify improvement opportunities, which are identified and given to the team. They are a single project team which usually disbands on completion of the given task.

A third award, sponsored by Josiah Wedgwood and Sons, encourages teamworking in the National Health Service and uses the same judging criteria as the Michelin Award.

Recognition of achievement, and measuring by benchmarking against the best, are two ingredients in the NSQT's 'ingredients for change'. The Perkins, Michelin and Wedgwood awards are a way of satisfying both needs.

The National Society for Quality through Teamwork is a registered charity dedicated to facilitating companies in all sectors of British Industry to achieve their goals in continuous improvement, people involvement and customer service. NSQT members represent many different industries and vary in size from small regionally based companies to major multinationals. For membership information, write to: NSQT, 2 Castle Street, Salisbury SP1 1BB.

The Award Sponsors:
Perkins Engines Limited and Michelin Tyre PLC

We at the NSQT are very pleased to bring to you a record of the achievements of companies participating in the 1995 Perkins Awards and the 1995 Michelin Awards. Each story is different but together they give a good overview of the variety of approaches which can be adopted to the benefit of the organization. All the enterprises demonstrated, in different ways, their commitment to quality through teamwork and the beneficial effects on their organizations.

We are also particularly pleased to be able to include in this book the case studies on two US enterprises. It is of course important that we widen the net of knowledge to include the world's best, and the inclusion of the US stories is a step in that direction.

The Award sponsors, Perkins Engines Limited and Michelin Type Plc, have highly developed team-based programmes themselves.

The Perkins total quality programme includes several hundred working teams within the group which are engaged upon change for improvement in the organization. Their total quality approach, by focusing on processes and bringing together representatives or process owners has, and is, fundamentally changing the way the organization works, crossing functional boundaries and acting directly upon the process flow towards the customer. A sample of the Perkins teamworking approach in included in the book as a Michelin award finalist.

The Michelin teamworking programme has evolved over the past fifteen years and included within its past achievements the Perkins finalist award. Their programme has been heavily based on maximizing people involvement and their ownership of the work processes. Many forms of teamworking are used, and they are in the vanguard of operations developing self-supervising teams. They are regularly held up as the company to benchmark against in this field. Market share growth to be the world's No. 1 tyre manufacturer indicates the extent of their success.

Teamwork is the driving force for improvement and change – and change is now recognized as an essential element in the continuance of Perkins' and Michelin's success. They are both committed through change processes to offer competitive products and services, developing at an ever faster rate to remain ahead of competition and to attract new customers.

In the United Kingdom the importance of competitive wealth creation is now well understood and the majority of businesses are seeking to gain competitive advantage by utilizing the knowledge and experience of their people. It is clear from the entries for both the Perkins and Michelin Awards that diversity in teamwork is wide but that the application is universally growing at a high rate.

We believe that the stories in this book of the award winners from 1995 and the enhancing US stories will help to show the way forward.

Myles Coleman, Manufacturing Director, Perkins Engines (Peterborough) Ltd
Bob Bell, Head of Personnel & Training, Michelin Tyre Plc

Foreword

For two reasons it gives me great pleasure to be associated with this book which records the achievements of a number of organizations who are pre-eminent in the field of Total Quality.

First, because for the past fifteen years I have passionately believed in the philosophy and have taken every opportunity to promote the principles and practices of Total Quality. As a nation we are, I believe, too ready to under-value our achievements and on occasion only to pay lip-service to the new ways of working without fully understanding their implications and challenges.

As President of the NSQT it has been my privilege over a number of years to meet with and hear the success stories of many people and organizations who have embraced the practices of continuous improvement and of teamworking. Truly great progress has been made in understanding the importance of customer requirements and of the ways in which we can harness the knowledge and commitment of everybody to deliver those requirements. Some of these successes are celebrated in this book and I commend them to you.

Secondly, as Personnel Director of Blue Circle Industries I am pleased that my Company is committed to and active in the practice of Total Quality. Over the years we have come to understand the benefits which it brings to the business and to all who work in it. Starting in the mid-1980s with the introduction of a multi-skilled workforce we have seen a change in the mind-set of employees throughout the businesses. There has been a desire to be involved and to contribute coupled with a growing sense of self-confidence and pride.

I hope that in these case studies you will find encouragement and understanding which will enable you to start this journey of discovery. For those who have already started I hope you will benefit from the experience of others and realize that you are part of a growing movement which is vital for our future success as individual businesses and as a nation.

Whichever group you belong to I wish you every success for the future.

Peter Mutter
President, NSQT and Personnel Director, Blue Circle Industries Plc

Preface

The book aims to provide case examples of teamworking, quality improvement and innovation drawn from fourteen British and North American organizations. It seeks to provide a practical guide for practitioners and a versatile resource for teaching and learning by providing illustrations, ideas for class discussion and for case study work. The material is grounded in the experiences of the participants so as to provide an accessible style and a realistic view of the issues involved in planning, implementing and evaluating a quality improvement strategy. Specifically, the case illustrations examine *how* quality improvement impacts on the organization as a whole and/or team performance. The twelve UK organizations are national finalists in the 1995 Michelin and Perkins Awards organized by the National Society for Quality through Teamwork (NSQT) and sponsored by Michelin and Perkins respectively.

The pursuit of quality has been an all-consuming passion for American businesses for more than a decade. In 1987, the Malcolm Baldrige National Quality Award was created as a public–private partnership to encourage and recognize world-class quality in American companies. The framework for this award has become a model for quality awards across the United States and around the world. It is no accident then that the two American companies represented by chapters in this book are global industry leaders who have either won or qualified for the Baldrige Award. They have long been known and respected for their strong commitment to quality. In fact, GTE was a founding member and early sponsor of the International Service Quality Association (ISQA). GTE has twice co-hosted International Quality in Services (QUIS) conferences at its magnificent GTE Management Development Center in Norwalk, Connecticut.

While their journeys have necessarily been quite different, Corning and GTE are characterized by an extraordinary passion for quality that has been relentlessly driven from the top. While they both have corporate quality offices, these offices are deliberately kept small to emphasize their role as facilitating resources, rather than as drivers of quality processes. Responsibility for quality performance rests with the operating units which all receive quality education in a cascading approach, starting with senior management. Further, both companies are global players with presences on several continents, making quality their basic business principle, regardless of where they operate. They do so because they define quality as meeting customer requirements. It is from this perspective of being customer-driven and customer-focused that they keep on reinventing their organizations to remain customer-responsive and enhance competitive advantage.

The Michelin Excellence Awards are given each year to up to three teams who have demonstrated excellence in the way they have identified a problem, solved it and then implemented an effective solution. Accordingly, the six chapters in Part 1 concentrate on 'the project and the result' so as to bring out the most interesting aspects of the project work undertaken in two categories – (i) single problem/management-promoted team projects and (ii) continuous improvements made by self-directed teams.

(i) Single problem/management-promoted team projects are:

- *The Potassium Phosphates Improvement Team* (Albright & Wilson UK Ltd, Warley, UK). This team undertook a project with the aim of increasing output and yield from a critical process while at the same time reducing waste emissions and their visibility.

- *The Hub Run-Out Team* (UEF Garringtons, Bromsgrove, UK). A multi-discipline/cross-functional team sought to tackle a problem with 'run-out' in the machining and assembly of front wheel hubs supplied to a leading UK motor manufacturer. The team achieved process improvement and a product design change which resulted in a permanent solution to a reoccurring problem.

- *The Goscote Team* (Severn Trent Water Ltd, Birmingham, UK). A project drawing on a multi-functional team of six people who were set up to resolve a problem in a refurbished water treatment works while at the same time maintaining compliance and throughput.

(ii) Continuous improvement/self-directed team projects are:

- *Quality Street* (Britannia Airways Ltd, Luton, UK). A multi-skill/multi-trades voluntary team drawn from the Britannia Engineering Department based at Manchester Airport. The team sought to make a design improvement to aircraft interiors so as to make passenger cabin servicing easier to perform.

- *New Star Trekkers* (Land Rover, Solihull, UK). A discussion group team that identified and resolved a problem relating to paint damage that was occurring during the rear floor panel assembly of Land Rover's Defender vehicle.

- *Dyane Team* (Perkins Engines, Peterborough, UK). An inter-departmental team that came together to resolve a set of reoccurring problems associated with obtaining replacement honing heads for diesel engine production lines.

The Perkins Quality Improvement Award is presented to the organization which best demonstrates its continuing commitment to a programme of total involvement, with quality and employee activities as key elements. Perkins criteria include: (a) the quality journey; (b) the deployment of quality improvement throughout the organization; (c) quality education and training; (d) the systems of measurement applied; (e) achievements as recorded by the measurement system; (f) management commitment and the recognition process; (g) future continuous improvement plans. The featured organizations are:

- *Benefit Enquiry Line* (BEL), Preston UK. BEL is part of the Benefits Agency and it provides a national, free telephone advice and information service for people with disabilities, their carers and representatives. BEL provides advice on all Social Security benefits and among others, Braille and Textphone services.

- *Britannia Topsides Project, London.* As part of the wider Britannia Field development project, it creates facilities to produce gas and condensate from a UK North Sea field. Three companies, contractor AMEC and oil companies CONOCO and CHEVRON, form an 'alliance' to jointly develop the offshore facilities.

- *RHP Bearings Ltd, Ferrybridge.* RHP's parent company NSK, the world's second largest bearings manufacturer, employs 18,000 people worldwide. Ferrybridge is one of seven RHP manufacturing sites, with a workforce of 620 people.

- *Royal Insurance Life & Pensions, Liverpool.* Royal Life is part of the worldwide Royal Insurance Group and it provides a complete range of pension, investment, protection and mortgage-related products. It is one of only a few companies to sell its products through the entire range of distribution channels.

- *Slag Reduction Company Limited, Redcar,* is the industrial service division of Faber Prest Plc on Teesside. The company offers a comprehensive service to British Steel section, plates and commercial steels including the operation of an ore terminal at Redcar.

- *Wellman International Ltd, Kells.* Based in Ireland, Wellman is a premier supplier of polyester and polyamide fibres to customers in Europe and beyond. Wellman's products are designed for use in the non-woven, filling, automotive and carpet markets.

The fascinating stories of corporate and team renewal in the fourteen organizations are told in these pages by teams of experienced academic writers collaborating with some of the people who made quality improvement happen. We would like to thank both the writers and the companies for their willingness to share tools, experiences and insights so that others may benefit from them.

Richard Teare, Eberhard E. Scheuing, Cyril Atkinson, Clive Westwood

PART 1

THE UK MICHELIN AWARD

ONE

ALBRIGHT AND WILSON, OLDBURY, UK

Group sublimation for quality

VAIKALATHUR S. MAHESH,
KEVIN STARLING
AND
IAN FRYER

ONE

Albright and Wilson, Oldbury, UK:

Group sublimation for quality

INTRODUCTION

A leading UK Chemicals company, when faced with a multiple crisis – fundamental shifts in market demand, loss of a major customer, pressures from the local community to reduce pollution – successfully responded to the crisis in a manner that is well worth reporting as a case in participative management. Some essential principles of quality management get highlighted in this example. Creation of a dedicated team formed of members with diverse managerial and technical backgrounds, generation of team commitment to overcome a perceived threat, and a way to allow *group sublimation* to take place are but some of the learning that emerges from this case.

PART I

The company

Albright and Wilson is a leading multinational chemical business, employing over 4000 people. The plant in question is the production facility at Oldbury, UK, covering 55 acres and employing over 450 people, which has production plants manufacturing in the phosphate and speciality chemical areas. The potassium phosphate plant's products are used in such diverse products as pet foods, toothpastes, spray polishes, paints and dishwasher detergents.

Background

The potassium phosphate plant at Oldbury was originally designed to produce a finished product predominantly in liquor form. The plant operated with a solid to liquor ratio of 40:60. Total output per annum of solid was 6500te.

Over the years Albright and Wilson have seen a decrease in customer demand for liquor and an increase in demand for solid output. Satisfaction of this demand was being impeded primarily by the inappropriate design of the plant which had hitherto focused on liquor output. Besides, there were a number of operational problems which contributed to low output figures. In addition, the company faced continued pressure from a local Residents Association concerning a highly visible steam plume which emanated from the plant.

The final blow was delivered by one of the company's major consumers of potassium phosphate liquor who reformulated their process, no longer requiring liquor.

PART II

Case for action

The culmination of all of these problems forced Albright and Wilson's management team to seek a radical solution. They created a multi-skilled team to examine the problems and empowered them to address the following objectives:

1. Output – total output of the process was to increase from the current 6500te per annum to 10,000te per annum.
2. The solid/ liquor ratio was to change from the current 40:60 to 85:15 in order to meet the changing demands of customers.
3. The visible steam plume, currently considered unsatisfactory by the Residents Association, was to be considered satisfactory by the end of the project.

It was imperative that these changes were made in the shortest possible time frame. The alternative to this was the eventual relocation or closure of the plant as production would become increasingly uneconomical.

The team

A team of cross-functional experts was formed in March 1994 to address the problems. Everyone was made aware of the severity of the problem and understandably, from the outset, the commitment to change the process was very high as there was, quite simply, no other alternative.

The team consisted of the following personnel:

Ian Fryer	Statistical Process Control Co-ordinator
Sean Matthews	Project Engineer
Niven Price	Technical Support

Nick Price   Process Supervisor
Process Operators   Eight-man team who operate the plant 24 hours/day, 7
                          days/week:

                          Dave Attwood
                          Lee Bevington
                          Shane Bissell
                          Bill Coulthard
                          Richard Daly
                          Steve Foster
                          Zam Hussein
                          Ken Pratt

The relationship of this team within the overall site structure is shown in Figure 1.1.

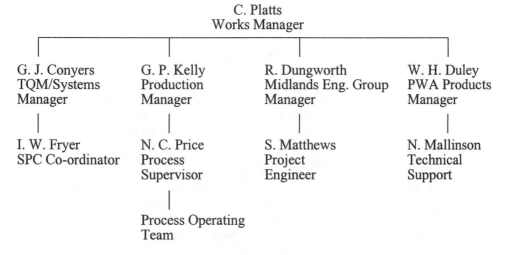

Figure 1.1   Team structure

PART III

The early stages

The main team members realized from the outset that the success of the project would be determined by the way in which they operated as a team and in particular how well they worked with the eight-man team of process operators, who were after all the real experts.

The team commenced the task by ensuring that the fundamentals of the project were firmly established. First, all of the main team members and the process operators were appraised of the task in hand. Secondly, the main team members ensured that they fully understood the plant, its constituent parts and the process of creating the finished product. This was done over a period of two weeks with members of the main team working alongside the process operators. To ensure that continuity and clear communications were maintained, the main team members worked a twelve- hour shift from 7 a.m. to 7 p.m. This overlapped with the process operators' shifts of 6 a.m. to 6 p.m. and allowed for main team members to be present at the shift handovers and for an additional hour to fully appraise all their colleagues of the problems and actions of the preceding shift. An additional advantage of this overlapping shift system was to enable main team members to meet and discuss the process with both shifts.

The third element that was set in place right from the outset was the introduction of a process log book. This book was used initially to record all of the main problems that were perceived with the process to date. The information was gleaned from all of the process operators. The log was then used to capture all of the problems that were encountered as and when they occurred. Comments professed and decisions taken throughout the duration of the project life-cycle were duly recorded in this. Details were logged when a problem occurred along with its root cause, if identifiable, frequency of occurrence and, most importantly, suggested solutions to the problem. The log also contained the telephone numbers of the main team so they could be contacted 24 hours a day.

Early wins

The gelling of the team was achieved very quickly as small improvements to the process were identified and implemented. Minor operational problems were solved, such as the removal of redundant control valves, correction and updating of the control system computer graphics and the installation of catchment trays for minor powder leaks from the kiln. While none of the quick wins solved the main objectives of the team, they nevertheless demonstrated the power of teamworking and the commitment of management to improving the process.

As the improvement process started to accelerate, a major boost for the process team came during the commissioning of a new cooled screw that was to be used to transfer the solid product. The existing system for this part of the process involved an air-lift where air was sucked by a fan through a tube and the solid was dropped into an air-flow which in turn transferred the product and cooled it at the same time. The system was a poor performer with regular blockages and a high level of breakdowns.

Prior to the commissioning of the new cooled screw system a number of alternatives were considered with all members of the team involved in detailed discussions as to the best solution. The objective was to overcome the problems of regular breakdowns and develop a system that could have the capability of increasing the output of the plant. Engineering experts were called in to discuss a mechanism for transferring the solid product and how this could be incorporated into the existing process with the minimum of disruption.

Options considered included having two separate solid handling systems – one working via the problematic air-lift and one working via a mill and cooled screw conveyor. The mill was common to both options and was responsible for ensuring oversized solids were converted to the correct particle size. Disadvantages of the dual system included leaving a system in place that was known to cause a high level of operational problems. The advantage of this approach lay in the fact that if there was a breakdown of one system the other could still run, hence maintaining some output from the process.

The alternative to using two solid handling systems was to use only one: the mill and the cooled screw conveyor in combination. A distinct advantage of this system was a much higher level of reliability of the equipment, leading to a higher level of 'on-time' and hence increased output. A disadvantage was that as a single stream system, any equipment failure would immediately reduce solid output to zero. The process operators were naturally concerned; yet, as they were well aware of the criticality of the problem, they accepted that such risks needed to be taken. Indeed, the then existing air-lift system had also been breaking down often, resulting in zero output.

As part of the decision-making process it was decided to review the structure of the old system. This is shown diagrammatically in Figure 1.2 (not to scale). Several plant meetings were held to discuss all of the alternatives. In total eight different configurations were considered. All of these had one area of commonality – complete removal of the air-lift and associated equipment as all agreed that this could no longer be economically supported. Each of the eight options was discussed at further plant meetings, exploring them in much more detail than had been done previously. Such details included how best to operate the system, facilities for maintenance and cleaning, trip sequences, alarms and maximum operating rates. No stone was left unturned.

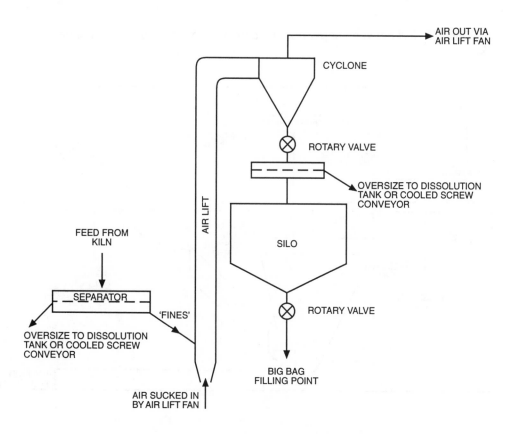

Figure 1.2 Sketch flowsheet for old system

To help the team with their decision, extensive trials were undertaken between June and July of 1994. The trials successfully proved to all of the team members that the proposed cooled screw system would work. By mid-August the team reached a decision and option number seven was chosen. This is shown in Figure 1.3 (not to scale). The net result was to have a much simpler layout and one that was much smaller, approximately one-quarter the size of the existing air-lift system. The complete proposal was put to senior management in early September and authorization for the capital outlay was given immediately.

A detailed implementation plan was developed, culminating with a complete plant shutdown for installation of the new mill and cooled screw conveyor, as well as the removal of the redundant equipment between 17 and 25 October 1994. Following a successful installation of the new equipment, the system became fully operational, under normal plant production rates by 29 October. Quite naturally a feeling of elation swept through the team who realized what could be achieved if they really put their minds to it. Visible results were to be seen immediately with the change of liquor to solid ratio from 60:40 to 40:60 – and through a much more reliable process at that. The team had moved some way towards achieving their objectives, yet there was quite a way left to go.

Option 7: Mill between separator and conveyor to maximise hopper capacity

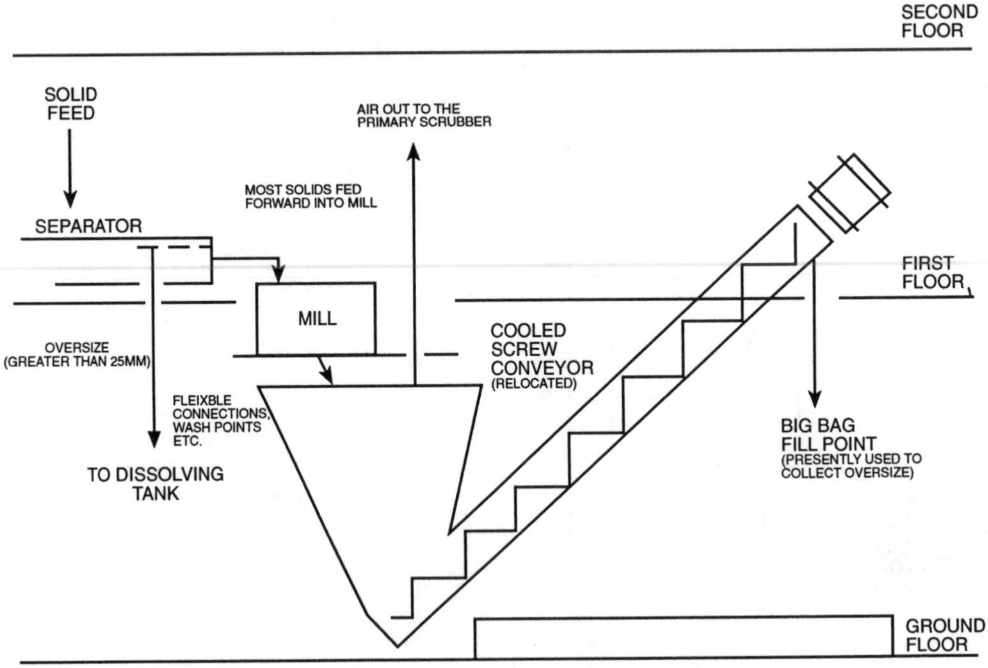

Figure 1.3   Sketch flowsheet for new system

The kiln

While the introduction of the cooled screw improved the total product output, there was still more to be done. The next area for the team to address was the kiln. The 40 per cent of solid material that was not leaving the kiln was actually leaving via the gas exhaust system, as a very fine dust. This dust was subsequently captured and scrubbed (cleaned) via a dual water scrubbing system, thus producing liquor as a finished product.

Theories abounded on ways to recover some of this 40 per cent. Alterations in kiln operating temperatures, feed solution strengths, spray bar arrangements and spray nozzle sizes were all suggested. The most common themes, however, were all related to the spray bars and spray nozzles. The spray nozzles are of the flat fan type, that is, they produce a 'V-shaped' spray pattern of negligible thickness. One of the many suggested solutions involved experimenting with the angle of the spray nozzle – the Spray Angle. Another was to experiment with the Nozzle Rating. This is the size of the hole in the nozzle through which the feed liquor flows. A third parameter investigated was to examine the effect of altering the Inclination Angle of the spray bar. This concerns how steeply, or shallowly, the spray nozzle points to the floor of the kiln. The aim of these alterations was to produce larger spray droplets in the kiln but not so large that they would impede the process by being unable to be properly dried by the end of it. Indeed, the failure to get the spray at exactly the right size and angle would result in the formation of *dams* within the kiln itself. A dam is a build-up of material on the kiln surface that resembles a doughnut. Dam formation would very rapidly lead to lower output levels and ultimately plant shutdown. The current method produced much smaller droplets which correlates to a higher dust output and low solid output. Experiments to get the right balance of spray angle and size of spray confirmed this correlation.

To study the effects of each of these parameters, identifying criticality and best operational levels, it was decided to perform a set of Robust Design Experiments, based on the techniques developed by Dr G. Taguchi.

During the period 16 July to 19 August, the Robust Design Experiments were conducted. Of the eight experiments performed, all eight led to the eventual formation of dams and resulted in plant shutdown. Despite this, the experiments themselves were successful – the best result obtained indicated a solid to liquor ratio of 80:20 – almost the desired target level. However, the consistent formation of the dams was a concern. It was a time of excitement. The team had got so close and all were determined to find a resolution to the problem. They established that whatever was being done wrong was consistent and must therefore be there to be found. Intermittent problems are generally a great deal harder to find.

The team members were determined not to be beaten. They obtained one of the spray bar set-ups and knocked it completely to pieces. They measured every angle, length and width that was possible to measure. The spray bar set-up is one of four spray nozzles individually fed with liquor through a stainless steel tube. These four tubes then join a main feed line. What the team discovered was that the Inclination Angle of the individual bars is not always consistent. Where spray bars diverge slightly there is no problem but where they converge, the spray droplets interact forming oversized spray droplets. Since these do not dry properly before they hit the kiln floor, they attract other solid material within the kiln, which subsequently leads to creation of a dam.

To prevent dam formation the spray bar set-up had to be built with each individual bar/nozzle at a divergent angle from its neighbours. The team had done it. In fact they had exceeded their targets. Implementation of the team's idea resulted in an immediate solid to liquor ratio of 90:10. In turn, the improved performance meant minimal shutdowns resulting in an increase of the annual production output to over 10,600 te.

Stack plume

The team had one more objective to meet. This involved improving the stack visibility from an unsatisfactory to a satisfactory condition. The criteria for this would be to use neighbourhood complaints as a measure, the target being zero complaints.

Visibility of the plume was diagnosed as being largely dependent upon the prevailing atmospheric conditions at any given time. The plume essentially contained a consistent amount of water at all times yet it was more visible in certain conditions. The challenge to the team related to how they could influence this visibility without unnecessarily impeding the production process of the plant itself.

The effect of the atmospheric conditions on the plume actually provided the key to the solution. During cold, damp, drizzly conditions the stack plume was highly visible and often in excess of 150 metres in length. On warm, dry days the plume would perhaps be as little as 30 metres in length. So duplicating warm, dry conditions seemed to be the answer.

The way this was accomplished is shown diagrammatically in Figure 1.4. By utilising the warm air at 40 °C in the roof space (generated from radiant heat from the kiln) and using the redundant fan from the air-lift solids transfer system, this warm and comparatively dry air was pumped into the plant stack. This had two beneficial effects.

First, the volume of air coming out of the plant stack is increased, but as the total water load is constant, the unit water content goes down; this decreases the visibility of the plume.

Secondly, as the injected air is warm, the overall temperature of the stack plume gases rises. This also decreased the visibility of the plume.

Both of these effects in combination with modifications to the plant's scrubbing systems had the effect of approximately halving the plume length.

Since the complete installation and operation of the system, there have been no complaints about the stack plume visibility from the local community up to the time of writing up this case study.

PART IV

Achievements

By November 1994, the team's achievements had exceeded its targets as shown in Table 1.1.

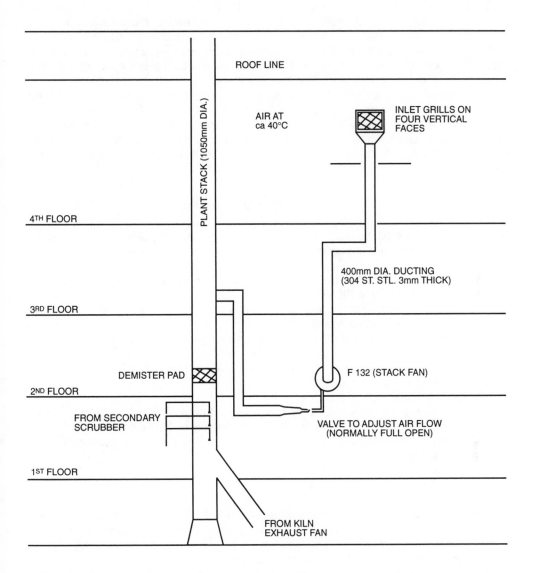

ROOF LINE

PLANT STACK (1050mm DIA.)

AIR AT
ca 40°C

INLET GRILLS ON
FOUR VERTICAL
FACES

4TH FLOOR

400mm DIA. DUCTING
(304 ST. STL. 3mm THICK)

3RD FLOOR

DEMISTER PAD

F 132 (STACK FAN)

2ND FLOOR

FROM SECONDARY
SCRUBBER

VALVE TO ADJUST AIR FLOW
(NORMALLY FULL OPEN)

1ST FLOOR

FROM KILN
EXHAUST FAN

Figure 1.4

Table 1.1   Achievements

Parameter	Target	Achieved
Output	10,000te	10,600te
Solid/Liquor Ratio	85:15	90:10
Visible Plume	Satisfactory	Satisfactory

This has resulted in a much higher profile for the plant and significant recognition for the team, both internally and externally. Externally, the team entered the Michelin Excellence Awards 1995 and, as A&W's first-ever entry, made it successfully to the final round of the Awards. Internally, the team were put forward for the Ted Lowe Award, a site competition where teams from all areas make entries describing their improvement work in a specific work area.

The Potassium Phosphates Improvement Team were successful in winning the award for 1995 and have since appeared in an edition of the Company magazine *Albright World*. This magazine goes to all the Company's sites worldwide and, as a result of this publication, the team have received communications from their sister site in Cincinnati, USA who wish to know details of the team's highly successful work.

PART V

If one were to describe, in general terms, what has so far been described in specific terms in this case, what happened at A&W was this:

1. A series of crises had led to the entire organization's energies being galvanized to overcome a common threat.
2. The challenge implied in the attempt to overcome the common threat was for the team to prove themselves against the odds.
3. The objectives, or goals, were clearly and unambiguously enunciated.
4. The team leaders, or the members of the core group, were visibly and totally involved, and were leading from the front – by being on the shop floor all the time, in two twelve-hour shifts.
5. The risk of failure was indeed high.
6. There was an immense sense of personal commitment, driven by a strong intrinsic motivation to succeed, with no thoughts whatsoever for personal rewards.
7. There was a small team of close associates with free flow of information, trust and camaraderie.
8. There was very little time to achieve results.
9. Inherent in the event was tremendous scope for learning.

This is exactly the set of criteria that has been described in *Thresholds of Motivation* as the universal pattern observed when groups of people combine to produce 'quality' in the purest sense of the term. Crises that appear to overwhelm an organization can be converted to opportunities for organizational members to *sublimate* their energies in a combined effort of superior achievement. This is what happened at Albright & Wilson.

GLOSSARY

Solid to liquor ratio   Split of production as solid or liquor – all liquor figures are expressed as solid.

Air lift   Transfer/cooling system for solids using moving air as conveyor.

Oversize solid   Solid material with diameter greater than 4 mm.

Spray Nozzle   Used to break a liquid stream into a spray of droplets.

Spray Bar   An arrangement of three or four spray nozzles.

Dam   A large doughnut-shaped solid built up in the kiln.

REFERENCES

Mahesh, V.S. (1993) *Thresholds of Motivation*, Tata McGraw-Hill, New Delhi, pp. 268–69.

TWO

GARRINGTONS:

The hub run-out team at British Steel Forgings

JOHN BICHENO
AND
PHILIP WELTON-COOK

TWO

Garringtons:

The hub run-out team at British Steel Forgings

INTRODUCTION

This chapter discusses the successful application of teamwork, both internally and between a supplier and assembler, to solve two related problems in the machining of a front wheel hub supplied to a major car assembler in Britain. The car assembler, in an effort to reduce the potential risk of brake judder, was working with all of their suppliers of front wheel components to reduce run-out tolerances. There was an urgency to finding a satisfactory solution. A core team at the supplier, Garringtons, was appointed under the overall leadership of the Quality Co-ordinator of the Machining Department. The core team split the problem into two parts, each of which was investigated by a multi-functional team. Both teams used data-based problem solving techniques which were agreed between Garringtons and the car assembler, ensuring that supplier and customer 'spoke the same language'. The first team carried out an investigation which led, via the use of fishbone charts, to a considerable improvement in the machining capability index. The second team worked system-atically with the car assembler in investigating a number of design and process modifications, leading to one being accepted and successfully implemented.

The chapter highlights a number of important features: the commitment of management, use of a multi-functional team, the systematic use of data based problem solving, the determination to solve the quality and safety problem without undue consideration to cost constraints, and the benefits of forming open customer-supplier partnerships.

THE COMPANY AND THE PRODUCT

Garringtons, a part of British Steel Forgings, has for a number of years manufactured a wide selection of high volume forged components for automotive and engineering applications. The Machining Department of Garringtons was formed in 1988/89 to provide dedicated machining facilities to manufacture high volumes of fully machined high volume wheel hubs and spindles for vehicle assembly. Since its formation the Machining Department has added further fully automated machine lines, so that today Garringtons is one of the largest suppliers of finished machined wheel hubs in Britain.

Two points are of significance. First, the hubs are machined from forgings which is a business still considered by many outside the business to be a 'black art'. The case conclusively demonstrates that a systematic data-based approach is an effective strategy, overcoming resistance to change and prejudices that still persist towards quality. Second, an automated line is not without problems, and team-based improvement by people with a deep familiarity with the process remains necessary.

The product on which the team worked is a car front-wheel hub, onto which locates the wheel assembly. Garringtons are responsible for forging, machining, the drilling of four holes and the placement of four studs (supplied by an outside supplier). A diagram of a wheel hub, excluding the studs, is shown in Figure 2.1. A wheel hub needs to be machined to a high level of accuracy and consistency, with 'total run-out' tolerance having reduced from around 60 microns to the current requirement of 48 microns. 'Total run-out' is defined as the measurement taken at a specified point or surface while revolving around a specified datum.

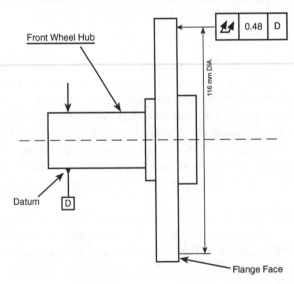

Figure 2.1   Understanding run-out

Forged hubs are supplied to a fully Automated Machining/Stud Assembly Line consisting of the following:

Op.10:	Lathe	Rough turns front side of forging and rough/finish turns the bore.
Op.20:	Broach	Broaches the bore.
Op.30:	Lathe	Rough and finish turns the reverse side of the forging and finish turns the front side.
Op.40	Drill	Drills the Stud holes in the flange.
Op.50:	Grind	Grinds the Bearing Diameter/Radius and Bearing Shoulder.
Op.60:	Wash	Cleans the component.
Op.70:	Paint	Paints the Wheel Location Diameter.
Op.80:	Oil & Dry	Covers the part in a protective film.
Op.90:	Stud Press	Locates and Presses in Studs.
Op.100:	Audit	100% Run-out and Vital Characteristics Quality Control Check.

Figure 2.2 Understanding the process

The product is made on an automated machining line as shown in Figure 2.2. The line is dedicated to the machining of one type of wheel hub for one customer. At each stage, except drilling, as parts move along the main line they are picked by robot and placed in the relevant machine. The final operation before packing involves the insertion of the four studs, which are power-pressed into the machined forging.

THE PROBLEM

In line with practices which are becoming the norm in the car industry, Garringtons are expected to deliver wheel hubs Just-in-Time and 'right first time' to the customer assembly line without the need for receiving dock inspection. The customer, a major car assembler in Britain, wished to reduce the risk of wheel judder under heavy braking. In a concerted effort with their suppliers they had highlighted run-out within their front wheel assembly as an area where improvement would be beneficial. The customer requested that Garringtons reduce the tolerance but was anxious that this should be achieved as a permanent solution without requiring major expenditure. To this end, the customer requested feasibility trials to establish if a 20 per cent reduction on the total flange face run-out was possible.

In order to avoid the necessity for receiving inspection, the customer expectation is that the process demonstrates a capability index Cpk of at least 1.67. (This index measures the ratio of the distance from the average point of the process variation to the nearest tolerance limit, divided by half the natural variation of the process.)

Before the project began it was felt that further reduction in run-out tolerance was simply not possible with the existing tools and equipment, and that a tightening of standards by the customer could only be met by greater investment and more rigorous inspection.

TEAM FORMATION, INITIAL INVESTIGATION, AND SUPPORT

To address the problem, Garringtons management gave permission for the establishment of an investigation team. The core team comprised three people having direct responsibilities within the Machining Department. The members were Neil Payne, the Quality Controller, Keith Thomas, the Process Engineer, and Peter Ward, the Production Engineer. The selection of this core group enabled the exercise to draw on three key skills people with intimate knowledge of the product and the line.

Significantly, all three had attended quality improvement problem-solving classes run by the customer as part of their supplier education programme. Probably also significant was the fact that the customer believed in a 'hands-on' approach to monitoring supplier processes, frequently visiting the plant to ensure and discuss product quality. Thus, from the start, there was a good understanding and a common language of problem solving between customer and supplier.

The first stage of the project involved a senior-level meeting between Garringtons staff and representatives from the customer's company. The outcome of this meeting was an agreement between Garringtons and the customer on the timing and approach to be used. Significantly this included agreement by the customer to participate in possible design modifications, something that had not previously taken place.

The next stage of data-based investigation was aimed at understanding the build-up of run-out variation. This revealed that total run-out variation was made up of two factors: first, distortion of the flange face itself and second, distortion resulting from the insertion of the studs. These two factors each contributed approximately the same amount to total run-out variation. This is shown diagrammatically in Figure 2.3. Notice that in the majority of cases the post-stud variation is in the same direction as the pre-stud, but that sometimes pre-stud variation was being cancelled out, indicating that there was significant variation in both stages. This important finding allowed the core team to decide that the solution to the overall problem would best be achieved by having two investigative teams, one on each of the two contributing factors. Conveniently, stud insertion is the last step in the process and therefore the two teams were set up to tackle the pre-stud process and the post-stud process.

Once again a pragmatic approach was adopted, with the belief that the best people to contribute to each team were the people actually concerned on a day-to-day

Example of graph Showing Pre / Post-Stud Runout

HUB PRE-STUD AGAINST POST-STUD

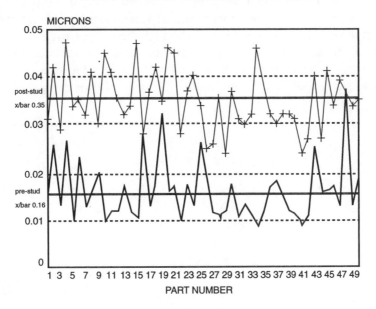

Figure 2.3   Hub pre-stud against post-stud

basis with pre- and post-stud operations. The core team members also contributed to each team, thereby ensuring a consistent approach between the teams. Each team comprised eight people, including the core team. All team members worked part-time on the problems. The commitment and support of the Department's manager, Bob Parker, was an important factor. The investigations were conducted over a period of some four months. Formal meetings were held regularly, but perhaps more important were frequent informal communications between all team members. Staying in contact, frequent updating of progress, maintaining enthusiasm, and keeping the pace of investigation going were probably key to the eventual success-ful outcome of the project.

During the project period normal production, of course, had to be maintained. This meant that, in order to experiment, extra work using extra materials was re-quired. (The experimental parts could not be passed on to the customer, and in most cases had to be scrapped). Here, the support and commitment of management was important. Authorization to undertake extra work with extra materials was given without reservation. This allowed both the pace of experimentation and enthusiasm to be maintained; both key factors.

INVESTIGATIONS BY THE PRE-STUD TEAM

The pre-stud team began their work with an investigation of run-out Cpk values. These are shown in Figure 2.4. Notice that the variation is 'spiky' indicating inconsistency in the process. Notice also that although the process is generally above the customer target value of 1.67, occasional dips make it unsatisfactory. The team therefore concentrated their attention on this variation, beginning with a brainstorming session about contributing causes. These are shown in Figure 2.5.

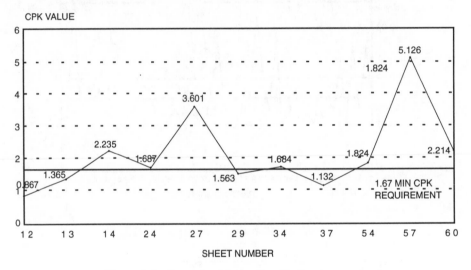

Figure 2.4   Example of data collated before improvements

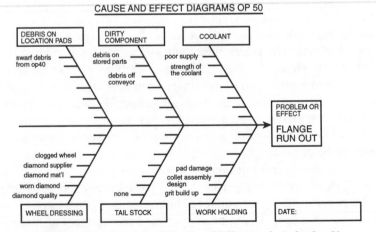

Figure 2.5   Example of Cause and Effect Analysis for Op. 50

The possible causes of variation were investigated systematically over a period of two months. As a result of the investigations, six areas were identified as being the most significant. These were :

1. Tool life
2. Cleanliness of the work holders
3. Wear and damage on rotalocks handles
4. Gauge probes sticking or set wrong
5. Coolant strengths and supply inadequate
6. Gauge wear and damage.

Before the investigation, it had been assumed that the automatic monitoring of the process and the regular procedures adopted would be sufficient. The investigation revealed unexpected variation in all six areas. The team considered the best way to address the problems and decided that they could best be tackled by instituting a regular preventative check, covering all six areas and all steps in the process, at the start of each week. The check sheet that has been adopted is shown in Figure 2.6. This is really an application of what in several companies is termed Total Productive Maintenance.

The effectiveness of this application of regular process inspection is shown in Figure 2.7. Not only is process capability vastly improved, but variation has been reduced. The levels of capability achieved are such that the customer need now have little concern for variation in flange run-out tolerance.

INVESTIGATIONS BY THE POST-STUD TEAM

At the onset of this investigation a brainstorming session was held which included representatives from the customer. This was useful because it established the boundaries of possible project work. In other words certain investigations, such as variations in the studs themselves, were excluded in as far as they were regarded as being entirely satisfactory from the customer's viewpoint. An important customer requirement was that the stud rotational torque test stipulates that, for end-customer convenience and safety, studs must shear before turning in the hole and for this there is a specified destructive test procedure.

Based on their experience of the process, the team brainstormed out a set of possible options of which, after preliminary discussion and exclusions, four remained. These were the hardness of the component, the stud press speed, the profile of the hub itself, and the hole diameter into which the studs were pressed. Once again the team set about a systematic data-based investigation of the four possible causes. Each of the four options could be further subdivided, each necessitating different courses of action.

WEEKLY PROCESS CHECKS							
LINE:							
DATE:							
PERFORMED BY:							
OPERATION 10	Chuck Jaws OK		Chuck Jaw Pegs OK		Swarf Removed from Chuck		Robot Loading OK
	A	B	A	B	A	B	A B
OP10 Comments:							

OPERATION 20	Air Sensors Working	Pot in Good Condition
OP 20 Comments:		

OPERATION 30	Check Rotalock Wear	Rotalock Run-out 30 microns or Less			
		Flange Run-out		Bearing Abutment Run-out	
	A	B	A	B	A B
OP 30 Comments:					

OPERATION 50	Coolant Strength	Adequate Supply to Dresser	Pads OK	Grit Build Up on Pads
OP 50 Comments:				

OPERATION 50 GAUGE	Probe Setting OK	Gauge Clean	Check For Damage
OP 50 Gauge Comments:			

Figure 2.6 Machining solutions

To undertake the investigative work, a team member was assigned responsibility for each of the four areas. The investigations involved experimental work, much of it requiring overtime working. Several tests were involved, but the team felt that this did not necessitate the use of an orthogonal array exercise.

A summary of the tests conducted is shown in Table 2.1. Here the benchmark tests refer to internal benchmarking necessary to establish the standards against which future measurements would be made. The results of each test were presented and discussed in detail with the customer. This established a fruitful source of ideas for further investigations. An example of the recommendations presented is given in Figure 2.8. and the systematic nature of the investigation is apparent.

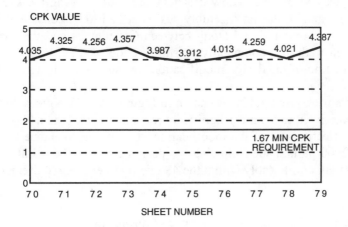

Figure 2.7   Hub run-out (pre-stud). CPK values after improvement

FRONT WHEEL HUB. POST STUD RUNOUT/DISTORTION IMPROVEMENT SUMMARY

NO	ITEM	OPTION	CONCLUSION	RECOMMENDATIONS
1	HOLE DIAMETER	INCREASE THE MEAN STUD HOLE SIZE BY CHANGING THE BORING TOOL ,TIP RADIUS. FEED PER/ REV & RPM. THEREBY INCREASING THE INTERFERENCE DUE TO AN IMPROVED SURFACE FINISH	INCREASING THE HOLE SIZE DOES REDUCE DISTORTION, BUT THIS OPTION DOES NOT ALLOW AN INCREASE IN HOLE DIAMETER, DUE TO A FAILURE IN TORQUE SECURITY ABOVE 13.965mm. THIS OPTION DOES IMPROVE STUD HOLE SURFACE FINISH. THEREBY IMPROVING CONSISTENCY AND REPEATABILITY OF MEASUREMENT AND DOES REDUCE THE VARIABILITY OF DISTORTION.	REQUEST FOR A CHANGE IN THE PROCESS TO. 0.4mm TOOL TIP RADIUS. AT 0.15mm FEED PER/REV. AND 4000 RPM. REQUEST FOR A DESIGN NOTE CHANGE IN STUD HOLE SIZE TO 13.925mm +/- 0.025mm.
2	HUB PROFILE	1) REDUCE THE SIZE OF THE FLANGE OUTSIDE FACE CHAMFER.	REDUCING THE CHAMFER DOES STRENGTHEN THE FLANGE FACE. REDUCED POST STUD RUNOUT/DISTORTION. GIVES CONSISTENT LEVELS OF DISTORTION. REDUCES THE EFFECT OF HOLE SIZE ON DISTORTION. CAPABILITY CPX VALUE OF 3.94. ESTIMATED MEAN 0.016mm at 116mm DIA.	REQUEST FOR A DESIGN NOTE CHANGE TO THE OUTSIDE FACE CHAMFER OF 45 DEG AT 120 DIA +/- 0.2mm REQUEST FOR A DESIGN NOTE CHANGE TO THE RUNOUT TOLERANCE OF 0.048 MAX AT 116mm DIA POST STUD.

Figure 2.8   The proposed solution. Example of the summary report format used

The data-based tests led to the conclusion that there was considerable scope for a modification to the hub flange profile, but that the other three possibilities offered less scope. The flange modification possibility involved retaining more metal on the flange than the design specified, thereby improving the strength of the flange and hence stud stability. The problem was that the original design had been specified in a particular way in order to allow easier manipulation during the subsequent assembly process and so the car assembly customer had to be consulted. Since there had been close co-operation all along between Garringtons and the customer, this issue was dealt with in a comparatively short period of time. Following assembly trials, confirmation of the design modification was subsequently agreed by the customer.

The results were remarkable, as shown in Figure 2.9. It is noticeable that the design modification led to the most significant reduction in variation. To complete and confirm the effectiveness of the modification, the run-out tolerance was measured on the first 2000 parts made following the design change. The results showed that all 2000 parts fall comfortably within the 48 micron tolerance requirement.

AFTER DESIGN CHANGE

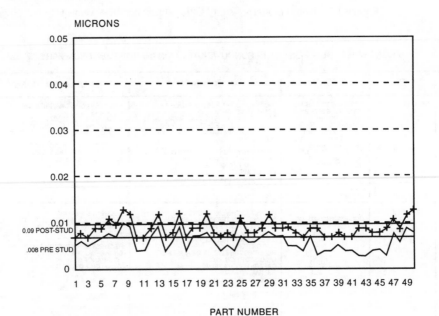

Figure 2.9   Hub pre-stud against post-stud

A SUMMARY OF METHODOLOGIES USED

In both the pre- and post-stud exercises the teams used collective brainstorming, meticulous project planning, and systematic data-based investigation. The pre-stud team used cause and effect (fishbone) diagrams to identify potential causes of variation, and the post-stud team worked on a specific test programme where data analysis and experimentation led to the identification of the problem and its solution. In both cases the Pareto approach of identifying the most significant contributor to work was used.

COST JUSTIFICATION OF THE PROJECT

It is not possible to quantify directly the size of the savings achieved as the level of scrap and rework was minimal at the start of the project, and an improved tolerance of 48 microns was under evaluation. However, the achievements can be judged against the costs that were considered necessary to achieve the improved standards required by the customer. It is estimated that, based upon variation figures obtained during the project, the extra costs of scrap in Garringtons would have amounted to some £34,000 per annum plus some £20,300 on further inspection. These figures exclude savings made by the customer, and the unquantifiable improvement in end-customer satisfaction.

THE ACHIEVEMENTS AND LESSONS LEARNED

The projects led the team members to feel that they had

- achieved a permanent solution to the problem
- used and demonstrated a standard and logical approach to problem solving
- developed an understanding of the need to use data to make decisions
- demonstrated the need to investigate all ideas and solutions
- developed a better understanding of fellow team members, other people within the department, and with their customers.

The success of the projects can probably be attributed to the following:

- The enthusiasm of the team leader, and his willingness to participate in continuous informal discussions with team members, thereby maintaining a high level of interest and commitment amongst team members.
- The selection of an appropriate core team with the necessary blend of quality, process engineering and production engineering skills.

- The commitment of senior management to the project, especially of the Department Manager, and in particular their willingness to fund and support experimentation.
- The active participation of the customer.
- The selection and use of front-line staff as team members, thereby ensuring that the combined experience of such people was made use of.
- The speed with which the customer provided feedback on recommendations made.
- The teams selecting the right tools and techniques to suit their problems.

Probably the greatest benefit was the successful demonstration of a joint customer and supplier approach to problem solving. This showed that the oft-heard-of approach to supplier partnership is a reality which can bring benefits both parties.

ACKNOWLEDGEMENT

The authors would like to express their thanks to members of the team, particularly Neil Payne, Keith Thomas and Peter Ward.

THREE

SEVERN TRENT WATER LTD:

Working for quality – a practical application

SALLY MESSENGER
AND
JOHN GREEN

THREE

SEVERN TRENT WATER LTD:
Working for quality – a practical application

INTRODUCTION

Severn Trent Water Ltd was formed in 1989 when the water authorities were privatized. By area it is the second largest of the UK's water companies – serving a population of over eight million people. The company is made up of fifteen districts, each responsible for supplying water and waste water services. The focus of this chapter is Goscote Sewage Treatment Works which is located within the Tame district. Goscote Works was commissioned in 1974 and treats domestic sewage and industrial waste. During the period 1991/92, in anticipation of stricter control limits being imposed upon the works, refurbishment work was undertaken. Shortly after the commissioning of the refurbished plant a technical problem was identified in the form of a thick scum ('mousse') which began to appear on the final tanks. This mousse resulted in a continuous threat to consent compliance and therefore required ongoing remedial action in order to maintain quality levels. Significant resources were involved in an attempt to treat the symptoms, maintain compliance and discover the root cause of the problem.

Approximately nine hours per day were involved in hosing the scum from the surface of the final tanks and recirculating it to the head of the works. Not surprisingly the morale of the workforce was low. Little progress was achieved in finding a solution to the problem despite the investment of considerable resources. From April 1992 to May 1993 the manpower cost of hosing was in excess of £23,000. The introduction of the company's 'Working for Quality' programme provided an ideal opportunity, therefore, with which to explore the potential benefits of a multi-functional team approach to problem solving using 'Working for Quality' tools and techniques. In January 1994 a team of six people was established and provided with a short in-house training programme. The team members were drawn from a variety of disciplines, positions and locations within the company and their objective was:

'To investigate the performance of the Goscote sewage treatment works over the period 1986 to 1994, with particular regard to changes in: operating practices, plant and sewage composition.'

PROJECT ORGANIZATION

As has been stated the project was originally designed to study performance over an eight-year period, however, this was subsequently considered to be too ambitious due to the large volume of data involved. The investigation was therefore shortened to cover the period 1/1/92 to 31/12/93. The project criteria encompassed resource requirements, restrictions and evaluation. The resources provided took the form of a quality Facilitator at the meetings and support for additional trials plus extra laboratory analyses. Reconfiguration of the works floor/operation was supplied by the Sewage Treatment Manager. The main restrictions imposed were that the output of the works should be maintained for 24 hours per day and that no specific budget would be allocated – any expenditure incurred was to be achieved through flexibility within existing resources. With regard to the monitoring of progress it was agreed from the outset of the project that data should be both quantitative and qualitative.

A project plan was drawn up in which the various stages of the work were identified and a target completion date of 31 October 1994 was established. The first stage in finding a solution to the operational problems at the Goscote works was familiarizing the group with the works itself, the nature of the problem and sewage treatment principles. This initial step resulted in the production of a 'Cause and Effect Diagram' which identified the possible areas of investigation as: plant design, plant operation, manpower and influent. The historical information was collected for the period 1/1/92 to 31/12/93 and included physical dimensions of the plant, pump rates, flow and biological data.

All team meetings were held on site, enabling operational problems to be viewed 'first hand' by the team. This approach reinforced the learning of the team and focused attention on the practical problems being experienced at the works. A problem definition sheet, which took the form of a wallchart, was displayed at every team meeting. The problem definition sheet included the current and desired situation and sought answers to questions such as: Who is affected? When does it occur? and What are the potential benefits? This regular presentation of the problem and desired situation reinforced what the team was attempting to achieve. The displaying of 'Problem Solving Discipline' wallcharts ensured the team followed a structured procedure as well as prompting possible tools and techniques. The procedure adopted was as follows: define the problem, analyse the root causes, generate solutions, plan and implement, measure and standardize (Figure 3.1). Progress, together with the tools used, was recorded on the charts at every meeting.

At the early meetings of the team it was agreed that important factors in the investigation were the accurate measurement of flow through the aeration bays and final settlement tanks together with the quality of treatment achieved by the individual tanks. No data of this nature was available but it was agreed that it was essential for such data to be obtained if progress was to be achieved. The only practical way of acquiring the data was to reconfigure the flows through the works, while at the same time conducting a series of tests, samples and laboratory analyses. The performance of this work involved 'streaming trials' which meant running the works as six separate 'streams' over six weeks plus a further two weeks for sample analysis. The requirement of a

Step   1   Define the problem

- Learn the process together, so all are equally aware
- Define the area of improvement
- Need to monitor progress regularly

Step   2   Analyse for root causes

- Brainstorm all the possible causes and issues surrounding the problem
- Use a cause and effect diagram to help see patterns and assist with analysis
- Shortlist the most likely root causes using discussion as a prioritization technique

Step   3   Generate solutions

- A solution may have complete or part impact on the problem
- There may be a number of solutions to a problem
- A Solution Matrix/Solution Effect may prioritize them
- Trial each solution one at a time

Step   4   Plan and implement

Step   5   Measure

Step   6   Standardize

Figure 3.1   Problem solving process

project extension was discussed with the project owner together with the funding of additional sampling and analysis. Both resources and the adjusted time-scale were agreed. As a result a separate plan was constructed, identifying times, dates, frequency, sample type and responsibilities agreed by the team. In order to maintain the momentum of the project wallcharts illustrating the stages of the Problem Solving Discipline were displayed at every meeting and progress was noted on them. Notes of all meetings were kept and distributed to all group members and the project owner at the end of each meeting. Actions arising from these meetings were allocated to members of the team together with 'delivery dates'.

TEAM DEVELOPMENT AND EFFECTIVENESS

The team induction programme took the form of tasks which were designed to break down barriers and to generate mutual respect amongst the group members. The different backgrounds and levels of experience within the group ensured that a wide range of ideas were generated whenever a particular aspect of the problem was examined. The positive atmosphere led to ideas being fully explained and analysed from a variety of viewpoints. With constructive input confidence grew at both the individual and group level (Figure 3.2).

Where appropriate, individual group members introduced external advisors to assist with particular technical aspects of the project. The opportunity was also taken to visit areas of the plant under discussion to clarify issues, thereby bringing the group closer to the problem. The mixed backgrounds of members meant that the group had access to many different types of information associated with the problem. Whenever this information was assimilated for meeting purposes, copies were made available for each group member which once again ensured full discussion of a particular topic and enabled members to highlight trends, or revisit data sets at their own pace, if time permitted.

The volume of data available to the group, coupled with the unique individual skills, meant that the tasks were evenly distributed amongst the group members. Data assimilation often involved certain members gathering the raw data and passing this to other members for interpretation and presentation at meetings (Figure 3.3). This resulted in a greater appreciation of the problem and improved communication between group members who were often situated at different locations throughout the company.

The ongoing nature of the problem required the gathering of historical data as well as documenting current performance. The team members who were located on-site were involved in providing detailed 'up to the minute' facts and figures, while other members related these to historical situations and wider aspects.

The complex nature and volume of data generated meant that progress was slow at times. In order to improve group morale during such phases, posters were displayed to illustrate progress to date and to generate a positive attitude (Figure 3.4).

Throughout the duration of the project there was a conscious effort to inject an element of fun into the proceedings. This was further embellished by visits from senior management to group meetings and the participation in company videos to promote the discipline of Working for Quality. The Team Leader also had a set of T-shirts produced for the group as a gesture of thanks for their work during the year of the project.

- Keep building the team
- Keep listening
- Keep involving
- Compliment and encourage
- Spread the workload
- Keep checking
- Ensure others are informed, keep communicating successes
- Bring in other experts as needed
- Liaise with project owner for adequate resources
- Have fun

Figure 3.2   Good team leading

- Obtain current facts and information
- Draw up graphs, flowcharts, schematics, Pareto
- Avoid collecting too much or too little data
- During the problem-solving process it may be necessary to return to the definition stage
- Data gathering may represent 75% of the whole project

Figure 3.3   Data gathering

- Appropriate training
- Meet regularly
- Record the outcomes of meetings
- Ensure action points are followed up
- Maintain enthusiasm
- Keep questioning and challenging

Figure 3.4 Team facilitation

THE SOLUTIONS

The solutions developed were the result of team brainstorming and this was facilitated by the acquisition and analysis of up-to-date factual information, the introduction of process experts who provided technical advice and the site visits. All the solutions were implemented as part of the normal day-to-day operation of the works. There was no sudden improvement in quality as such, but improvements in stages, as solutions were trialled and left in place. The major exception to this was the streaming trials, which involved detailed planning and co-ordination of actions.

Following the implementation of the solutions the Goscote Works experienced stability with regard to effluent quality and operational problems. A series of recommended future actions were identified by the team, the majority of which have been adopted. While the management of the sewage treatment function within the district were well pleased with the successful outcome of the project, the operators at Goscote Works were equally pleased. No longer are they required to stand for up to three hours from 5.30 a.m. each morning hosing the scum off final settlement tanks. They appreciate that time and resources were spent to their benefit and they readily accept the solutions, as they had a direct input into the implementation.

The main benefits of the project were identified as being:

1. The threat of consent failure has been significantly reduced.
2. Performance of the works has been improved.
3. Significant financial savings have been made in analysis, tankering and hosing the final tank costs. During the periods of excessive scum formation three extra tankers a day were required to transport the increased volume of sludge. This situation was arising approximately two days in each month. The result was an annual saving of approximately £7,200.
4. Improvement in morale.

REASONS FOR SUCCESS AND LESSONS LEARNED

In reviewing the success of the Goscote project a number of reasons can be identified. Firstly the composition of the team is critical. It is important to involve individuals who are actively involved in the operation. Having established a team the next stage concerns building and leading the group. This requires an even allocation of the workload. Good facilitation is an integral part of this process. Such a role requires the maintenance of momentum, ensuring regular meetings are held and questioning and challenging the outcomes at every stage of the project. Data gathering is another critical step which involves obtaining up-to-date facts and information and ensuring that not too much or too little data is collected.

A number of lessons were learned as a result of the project. For example, the team leader needs to be trained and to have experience in managing meetings. Wallcharts proved to be a very effective tool for communicating and reinforcing the message. A valuable lesson learned was that everyone has something to contribute and that there are times when team members become disheartened and need encouraging. It is also important to act only on facts and not on assumptions. Finally, the process takes time and patience is required.

FOUR

BRITANNIA ENGINEERING AND MAINTENANCE:

Who needs ashtrays?

CONRAD LASHLEY

AND

NIGEL WILLIAMS

FOUR

Britannia Engineering and Maintenance:

Who needs ashtrays?

Britannia Airways is part of the Thomson Tour Operations which also comprises of Thomson Holidays and Lunn Poly. Britannia started operations in May 1962 as Euravia, flying three Lockheed Constellations from Luton Airport where it still has its headquarters. In 1964 the current names was adopted and in 1965 Britannia became part of the International Thomson Organization (now the Thomson Corporation). Britannia has led the way in introducing new aircraft into its fleet, in 1968 it became the first European operator of the Boeing 737-200 and in 1984 it became the first operator in Europe to introduce the Boeing 767 wide bodied aircraft. Currently Britannia carries eight million holiday makers from 17 UK airports to more than 100 destinations world-wide. Britannia has grown to become Britain's second largest airline and the world's biggest charter company.

INTRODUCTION

This chapter reports on the process of continuous improvement based on Action Teams at Britannia Engineering and Maintenance. Britannia Airways is the UK's second largest airline and the world's largest charter flight company. It has a substantial involvement in the UK's package holiday business. Engineering and Maintenance is one of seven divisions within the company. It was the first division to introduce a continuous improvement programme and its Action Team approach is now being used as the model for the rest of the company.

The approach to continuous improvement began to develop in 1990 when a newly appointed Technical Director in the Engineering and Maintenance division felt that organizational effectiveness could be improved by a more participative approach to management of the division. In particular, the approach recognized that organizational members at all levels could contribute to the continuous improvement of the operation and there was deep reservoir of ideas and experiences which were not being fully utilized. At around the same time, Europe-wide standards of operational auditing were beginning to apply within the British airline industry.

Amongst other things, this European initiative required organizations to develop operating standards on which to work. After initial training the preparation of these procedures and processes provided the focus for more employee involvement. Later the first Action Teams were set up to provide a mechanism for continuous improvement. Since that time the number of Action Teams in the Engineering and Maintenance division, and latterly in the rest of the company, has grown steadily. This chapter describes the processes used through the experience of one Action Team operating at the division's Manchester base.

THE CONTINUOUS IMPROVEMENT PROGRAMME AT BRITANNIA AIRWAYS

Britannia Airways has made an organizational commitment to continuous quality improvement through Action Teams backed up by a continuous improvement network outlined in Figure 4.1. Each Action Team has the responsibility of identifying and solving their own work-related problems, and through this it is intended that employees will assume ownership of quality and operational improvement.

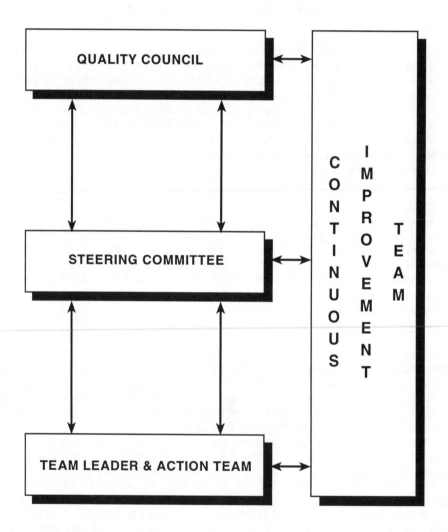

Figure 4.1   The continuous improvement network

The Action Teams are made up of 4–8 people who work in the same area of the organization. Membership is voluntary and in the long run it is intended that all employees will have the opportunity to become members of Action Teams. Currently each team meets in company time and works with a trained team leader and continuous improvement advisor who guide them through the processes involved in problem identification, analysis and resolution. Once the team has investigated a problem and identified a solution, they make a presentation to senior management outlining their findings and plans for implementation.

Through the Action Teams, it is intended that employees develop a sense of involvement and commitment to organizational objectives, particularly as these relate to quality improvement and cost reduction. The role of the advisor is fundamental in acting as a facilitator, mentor and expert to assist the team in its progress through the processes of problem solving. In addition, the team leader needs to understand the philosophy of the approach and encourage a style of working in which employees participate in the investigation of problems and accept responsibility for tasks chosen by them. The team leader has a number of responsibilities and duties in his or her relationship with the team. Chiefly these responsibilities and duties are associated with encouraging and assisting the team to identify problems and then providing the necessary organizational and co-ordinating backup to help the team. For example, it is the team leader's duty to plan, convene and organize regular Action Team meetings, and to ensure that appropriate records and minutes are produced. Training of both Action Team members and team leaders features problem solving techniques. The team leader is the team's link with wider continuous improvement activity through the continuous improvement advisor. Where needed this link can provide further access to wider resources and expertise for the team.

The continuous improvement network

Figure 4.1 shows how the departmental Action Teams integrate with the continuous improvement network. The Action Teams, based largely on departments, can be inter-departmental where it is deemed necessary, such as where one or more departments service each other in the operational sequence and improvements in their relationships can be achieved. The Action Teams drive the process of continuous improvement from a 'bottom up' process, though communications throughout the organization are crucial to the network's success. Overall direction and policy are provided through the Quality Council. The Quality Council involves senior divisional managers, a director of the company and the continuous improvement manager for Britannia Airways as a whole. It is the Council's responsibility to ensure that the Continuous Improvement Programme is implemented across all aspects of the division and acts as a final decision-making forum. This provides a direction and impetus which is 'top down', complementing and giving direction to the 'bottom up' flow of ideas and suggestions from the Action Teams.

The Steering Committee provides a decision-making and evaluative function. They both consider and approve quality improvement proposals, and report on team recommendations to the Quality Council.

Alongside this structure a group of specialist advisors make up the Continuous Improvement Team. This team constitutes the advisors who support the Action Teams and generally act as a conduit for spreading expertise, advice and training through the network. Through this organizational commitment and co-ordination of continuous improvement, and the flow of improvements from the Actions Teams closest to the problems, it is intended that overall organizational performance be continually improved.

QUALITY STREET AND PROBLEM SOLVING

Quality Street is the name which team members chose to call the Action Team at Britannia Line Engineering based at Manchester Airport. Team membership includes eight personnel covering a wide range of expertise and engineering skills. The full work group includes 40 personnel working a twelve-hour shift with a four days on, four days off cycle. The operation extends through 24 hours per day over 365 days per year which creates some logistical problems for the interaction of all members within the workforce. Given the rotating nature of shift patterns, some personnel do not see each other for weeks on end. At the beginning of the process none of the members had been previously involved in Action Teams.

A Code of Conduct for the Quality Street Action Team was devised as a guide to team and team member performance and expectations. The team decided on a programme of monthly meetings and the code of practice laid down standards for the team's conduct during and between meetings. The code includes items such as the frequency, organization and attendance at meetings, together with member responsibilities and individual conduct when dealing with criticism and actioning decisions taken by the team. Minutes of the meetings are produced after each meeting and show that attendance by team members averaged over 80 per cent during the project under discussion in this chapter.

The team used a problem solving model which is highlighted in Figure 4.2. Essentially this involves phases of 'brainstorming' at various stages of the process, followed by phases of investigation and subsequent evaluation.

At their first meeting the team went through an initial problem identification phase. They identified some 50 items on the 'problem list', that is, items which might provide suitable cases for improvement. Before taking the investigation further, each item was judged against the degree to which the item was within the team's span of control. Each item was then given a rating (T = totally in the team's control; P = partially in the team's control; N = not in the team's control). The team prioritized those items which were totally or partially in their control for further consideration. After discussion the team reached a consensus view that three projects should be investigated in parallel. This chapter reports on just one of these topics, namely the investigation of the costs of continuing to include, service and repair cigarette ashtrays in *all* passenger seats even though the 'smoking permitted' section of the aircraft represented only a small proportion of total seating on the aircraft.

The project began soon after the first phases in the model outlined in Figure 4.2 had been completed. They had identified opportunities for improvement, they had prioritized and selected the problem, and they had appraised the issues to be investigated. The following section details the processes involved in investigating the problem further and making suggestions for improvement.

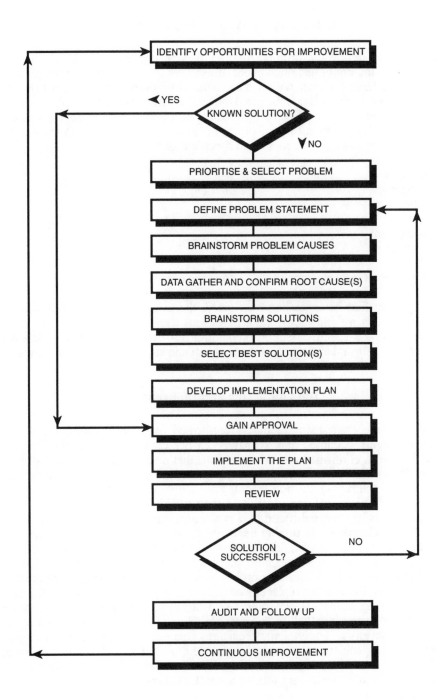

Figure 4.2 The problem solving process

ASHTRAYS – WHO NEEDS THEM?

In attempting to define the problem, the team were concerned with potential costs associated with the continued attachment of ashtrays in all seats on passenger aircraft irrespective of their location within the cabin. Thus despite the designation of the majority of seats in the aircraft for non-smokers, ashtrays had previously been fitted, cleaned and maintained in all passenger seats. During their brainstorming session the team identified the following list of potential 'hassles' associated with the continued inclusion of ashtrays in all passenger seat specifications:

- cleaning time
- breakages
- stockholding
- costs
- chewing-gum
- repair time
- availability
- the break point between smoking and non-smoking areas

Having identified issues to be investigated, the team allocated responsibilities for information gathering and fact finding to various team members. Each was charged with investigating a specific issue in preparation for their next meeting which would help to inform their understanding of the problem and suggest possible outcomes.

Data gathering and root causes

The reports back from team members confirmed that the smoking areas on the majority of flights occupied approximately 25 per cent of seats on the Britannia's aircraft. They also confirmed initial impressions that all ashtrays in the aircraft needed cleaning during the 'between-flight' servicing. Indeed discussions with the cleaners had shown that ashtrays in the non-smoking areas not only represented an unnecessary additional task, they added considerably to their workload, because the debris in non-smoking ashtrays was more difficult to remove. Smokers' litter is more easily removed with a vacuum cleaner or by tipping the contents on to the floor and then vacuuming, whereas the ashtrays in non-smoking sections were often used to deposit sweet papers, chewing-gum and other passenger litter, all of which were more difficult to remove.

In addition to the extra cleaning problem which the team had first identified, the team discovered that ashtray replacement represented a significant cost to the airline. In the year ending January 1995 some 537 ashtrays had been replaced at a material cost of £10,200 per year. Much of this cost was generated by passengers removing the ashtrays for souvenirs, though some breakages also occurred. Inventory costs further compounded the problem as the company needed to hold a stock of ashtrays so as to feed the turnover and loss of ashtrays. Thus what had started out as an investigation of a time-wasting and inconvenient job for aircraft cleaners, had unearthed a substantial cost to the company.

Further information included in the team's review related to the proportion of seats devoted to smoking areas. This varies between seasons, cities and aircraft use. Fights from Glasgow tended to require the largest number of seats for smokers, and some charter flights may require ashtrays in all seats. There was a need therefore to further investigate the optimum number of seats required for smoking and the marketing implications of restricting the number of aircraft seats to be fitted with ashtrays.

Brainstorming and selecting the best solutions

Having identified the problem, the team then considered possible solutions so as to limit the cleaning of ashtrays not used for smoking and reduce the costs associated with ashtray replacement. Further investigation showed that the Civil Aviation Authority would not allow the removal of the ashtrays without some means of covering the hole left behind. Some suggestions focused on disabling existing ashtrays by either gluing them or riveting them shut. After discussion and debate, the preferred solution was the removal of the ashtray and the fitting of a blanking plate to cover the ashtray recess. This solution met the criteria of safety, low cost, flexibility and simple installation. The team used a Solutions Effect Diagram so as to identify the implications, departments and individuals involved. Team members were again individually charged with following up on the identified information needs or initiating the actions highlighted by the team. One team member decided to video the aircraft cleaning process so as to confirm the time and inconvenience associated with emptying ashtrays in non-smoking areas.

Further observation revealed that the turnaround time needed to clean the aircraft could be cut if the ashtrays were removed from the non-smoking areas of the cabins. It was estimated that some passenger debris in seating areas might increase, though additional cleaning activity arising from the removal of the ashtrays might take less time to complete. Similarly, extra work in dealing with chewing-gum left on arm rests or trodden into the carpet might also be minor. One team member was able to show that extra savings might be generated by a reduction in aircraft weight achieved by removing the ashtrays. Though relatively small in comparison to total fuel usage, it was shown that annual fuel usage might be reduced by 2000 kilos due to the projected weight saving.

Through the potential savings generated by reductions in aircraft servicing time, the savings in fuel used and the reduced costs of ashtray replacement, it was estimated that savings would pay back the cost of removing ash trays and fitting the blanking plate within three years. Subsequently the airline would make an ongoing saving of over £13,500 per annum.

Gaining approval

Once the team had assembled the evidence in support of their proposal, the team prepared a report and gave a presentation to the Steering Committee. The team recommended that the ashtrays be removed and replaced with a blanking plate in all seats in the non-smoking areas. The Steering Committee received the team's presentation and raised a series of detailed questions in relation to the safety aspects of the proposal, the cost savings, the potential problems associated with additional refuse and the disposal of chewing-gum if the ashtrays were removed. Subsequently the Steering Committee approved the team's proposals and congratulated the team on their convincing presentation.

Implementing the plan and reviewing the results

In a heavily regulated industry such as aviation it is not feasible to replace components without careful planning. The proposals would need to be approved by the Civil Aviation Authority and the blanking plates installed by properly trained personnel. As soon as the modifications had been carried out on one aircraft, the team was charged with monitoring and evaluating its proposals. The measures they used were informed by a need to evaluate the practical application of their proposals 'on site'. Specifically they were to investigate the reductions in cleaning time, the turnover in ashtrays and the stock holding of ashtrays. Apart from direct observation and the review of the operational statistics, the team were to gain feedback from flight crew, cleaners and engineers together with feedback from passengers.

Project benefits

As a result of the Action Team's investigation, a number of potential benefits and cost savings have been identified for the organization. A reduction in aircraft turnaround time achieved by through a reduction of cleaning time facilitated earlier access for subsequent checks made by crew and engineers. The time saved could also be used to carry out a more in-depth clean, or allow cleaners to pay more attention to detail, thereby improving the quality of the service. The selected blanking plate design is easy to replace with an ashtray if required and the seats are also interchangeable for maximum flexibility. In addition there was a less visible cost reduction by means of a reduction in the inventory and the need to purchase replacement ashtrays or to handle, store and fit them.

Direct cost savings accrue because of the reduction in losses and the need to replace them. The project also delivers payback on the costs of installing the blanking plates within three years and is likely to produce an estimated saving of almost £90,000 over ten years. Again, when set against overall operating costs, the savings made are relatively small, but when taken cumulatively with savings from other Action Teams they can generate significant reductions in total operating costs.

BENEFITS OF ACTION TEAMS

The case study has shown how Britannia Airways has been able to gain from establishing Action Teams drawn from personnel who are familiar with the operational details of the business. By enabling and empowering teams to identify and take ownership of problem solving and continuous improvement, the organization has been able to benefit from the detailed knowledge and experiences of shop floor personnel. It is unlikely, for example, that senior managers would have identified the potential waste associated with the location of ashtrays in the non-smoking sections of aircraft in the fleet. Change, if it had not occurred, would have followed from another organization's recognition of the problem, perhaps in the form of feedback from suppliers or cleaning contractors. The Action Team approach has helped to ensure that innovations occur sooner and more quickly.

Apart from the speed of innovation, the organization has benefited from a potential increase in employee commitment and morale. Involving people in this type of process produces a greater sense of worth and involvement in the organization's objectives. In the long run, successes such as this provide a good benchmark for other organization members, and in so doing, encourage continuous performance improvement.

FIVE

LAND ROVER:

'Enterprising' solutions

ANTHONY INGOLD
AND
RAY SPRASON

FIVE

Land Rover:

'Enterprising' solutions

HISTORY OF LAND ROVER

Worldwide recognition

Since the beginning of 1948, one of the greatest strengths of Land Rover has been the ability to recognize a global need and respond to it. Early Land Rovers, now Defenders, are durable, multi-purpose vehicles that are able to adapt to all kinds of situations. Initially, the vehicle was seen as a short-term solution to the post-war vehicle shortage but worldwide demand boosted sales and further development of the vehicle.

A milestone in the development of the company was the launch in 1970 of the Range Rover. It was not the luxury vehicle in production today but it was useful for day to day transport and capable of off-road usage.

In the early 1980s, Third World markets went into rapid decline and Land Rover responded by diverting its market towards its more up-market clientele in order to take advantage of a desire in developed countries for more sophisticated vehicles. The mid-1980s saw the opening up of the personal transport sector. It was discovered that there was a growing number of people who use their vehicle in support of an active leisure life. The Discovery was developed to satisfy this need. It was an instant success and outsells its closest UK rivals by two to one.

The New Range Rover shows a marked improvement on the original. It is slightly larger with more head room, more leg room, a larger rear seat compartment and 50 per cent more luggage space. Burr walnut and leather in the interior give the refinement, comfort and luxury.

THE SOLIHULL SITE

Location of the site

Land Rover is situated in Lode Lane at Solihull in the West Midlands. The site is 308 acres in size with 14 miles of roadway and 4,200,000 square feet of floor space. At Land Rover the world famous 4×4 wheel drive vehicles are manufactured, namely the Range Rover, the Discovery and the Defender. Defender is the name given to the vehicle previously known as the Land Rover.

History of the site

The Rover company took over the Solihull site in 1946. Land Rover is a major part of the community in Solihull. Employing over 10,000 people, it is the second largest
employer in the area after the local authority. Production at Solihull has doubled over the past five years as new products have been developed and launched into new market places. The site is also unique in that it contains what has come to be known as the Land Rover Jungle Track, land set aside within the plant to demonstrate the all-terrain capabilities of the vehicles. The Jungle Track is used to teach the skills of off-road driving to individual owners as well as to the emergency services.

Rover have been able to achieve this success because at every step along the way they have gained the commitment and co-operation of all the people at Land Rover and in some of the practices they are amongst the best in the world. While the new Rover plant represents one of the finest production facilities of its type, the working practices and philosophy developed by the people who operate it are also breaking new ground in participation and involvement.

THE PRODUCTS

Defender

The Defender was launched at the beginning of 1991 and is based on the Land Rover 90 and 110 range. The four wheel drive Defender is known throughout the world as a tough workhorse able to venture into areas impassable to other vehicles. The original Land Rover was launched in 1948 and although similar in appearance has been constantly developed over the years. The 1.5 millionth example of this model, which has been sold in every country in the world, recently rolled off the production line. The new 300 Tdi engine produces 111 bhp and 195 lb ft torque at a very low 1800 rpm, making this engine ideal for off-road and towing work. Models are also available with the powerful V8 3.5 litre petrol engine or 2.5 litre petrol and the naturally aspirated diesel. Land Rover places a great importance on its range of Defender optional equipment and accessories to ensure that customers can tailor their vehicles to their exact requirements.

Discovery

The award-winning Discovery is sold in more than 50 countries. It is available in three- and five-door variants and is fitted with the 111 bhp, 195 lb ft torque, 300 Tdi engine or two fuel-injected petrol units - a 2 litre and a 3.9 litre V8. The ingenious interior has unusual features such as heater temperature controls for both driver and front-seat passenger, storage pockets in the roof lining above the rear seating area, and fascia-mounted radio controls. A raised roof line means that the head room and luggage capacity is spacious. Driver and front-passenger air bags are also available. The Discovery was launched in the USA in April 1994. To cope with the expected demand and substantially increased sales worldwide, weekly production was increased from 900 to more than 1050.

New Range Rover

The new luxury flagship model not only surpasses the current Range Rover's legendary off-road capability, but also has greatly improved on-road ride and handling characteristics to compete with the world's best luxury cars. The original Range Rover, launched in 1970, has gained a worldwide reputation for its classic and elegant style. It is the only vehicle in the world to have been exhibited in Le Louvre in Paris as a work of art. The 4.6 litre unit produces 225 bhp and takes the new Range Rover from 0–60 mph in 9.3 seconds with a top speed of 125 mph. There are three models in the range starting with 4.0 V8 or 2.5 diesel versions, followed by SE derivatives in petrol or diesel, leading to the flagship HSE model with the 4.6 V8 engine.The new Range Rover, the result of a £300 million investment programme, is not only aimed at traditional loyal customers, but also at people who buy other luxury models and performance cars. It is now more than 25 years since the Range Rover was launched. Since then it has become a 'Classic' due to its unique design and Land Rover's policy of continual improvement. It remains virtually unchallenged at the luxury end of the four wheel drive market. During the past five years, an extensive development programme has seen changes in all areas. The new Range Rover Vogue LSE went on sale in the autumn of 1992.

DISCUSSION GROUPS AT LAND ROVER

Throughout the company there is a programme of Continuous Quality Improvement, CQI. This philosophy is at present being cascaded down throughout the total workforce. Forming an integral part of this quality programme are quality circles, which Land Rover call Discussion Groups. The discussion group programme currently has over 215 discussion groups investigating work-related problems with the aim of improving the quality of product and level of service to all customers both external and internal. Groups have the opportunity to meet once a week for two hours. The initial training for discussion groups is considered to be very important.

The first six meetings are attended by the Discussion Group Facilitator. During this formative period the group obtains its identity and members learn how to run effective and efficient meetings. It is also important that the group is able to achieve accountability from those outside the group such as managers and other employees. When the group is firmly established (usually around the six-month period), members have the opportunity to attend a two-day course on leadership, teamwork and problem-solving skills, held off-site at the Rover Group Marketing Institute.

A BRIEF HISTORY OF NEW STAR TREKKERS DISCUSSION GROUP

The group was formed in June 1988 and called Land Rover No 2 Discussion Group. The original members were then chosen from the shop floor and had a manager as the group's chairman. They took on all types of problems from Quality issues to the toilet blocks. In April 1990 the group was asked to represent Land Rover in the Michelin awards.

The group had undergone a change of chairman. The new incumbent had a great interest in Star Trek and so decided to devise a presentation around the Star Trek theme, hence the new name, 'The Star Trekkers'. The group has had a total of 31 members during the seven years it has been together. The group, now called the New Star Trekkers (Next Generation) have taken on and resolved many problems and represented Rover on a number of occasions.

They still have the same goal: 'To go where no group has gone before'.

THE NEW STAR TREKKERS DISCUSSION GROUP

Group members

There were eight members of the team who contributed to the project outlined here. They include Phil Harmon, Chairman of the group; Mick Aplin, Secretary; John Timbrell, Deputy Secretary; Steve Bradbury; Steven Archer; David Chambers; Geoff Shannon; Wayne Hodgkiss, Mentor. Wayne is a Land Rover Defender manager. The New Star Trekkers discussion group call Wayne to the meetings every once in a while for his professional advice on matters relating to projects in hand. Other than this, Wayne has no outside connection with the group. The group invite him to presentations they give at events outside Land Rover.

Group objectives

The group are given a 'hit list' of the most pressing problems that are crucial to the performance of the business, by management, but they also take on problems that they have identified themselves from other sources. The group usually take on one major problem from this hit list and several others of their own finding. More than one project is needed in hand at any one time as they may be waiting for contacts or meetings with other members of staff in that particular field, or may need to speak to a supplier or even prepare line trials or special jigs or tooling changes. The group can quickly switch between problems while such requests are being met.

Problems need thorough analysis and monitoring by the group to establish the extent of the problem before involving a senior member of staff. They need to know the costs of the existing means of protection, and to find better means as an alternative, over a period of time. They need to speak to their own shop floor members for ideas on how to combat general problems with the least expense. They take into account that as shop floor workers, they sometimes create the problems accidentally or unintentionally, so they try to find the answers to self-generating problems. This is indicative of Land Rover's to empowering their associates as part of their policy of continuous quality improvement.

INTRODUCTION TO THE 'MICHELIN' PROBLEM

When the Defender is being manufactured, the rear floor panel needs to be covered to prevent damage and scratching to the body and paintwork. Prior to Group action wooden boards were used for this purpose. Following a Vehicle Quality Audit, it was noted that the floor was scratched and damaged. The audit was carried out on a finished vehicle ready for sale to a potential customer, and therefore the damage was seen as a major problem for the business. The manager of the Vehicle Rectification Department approached the Discussion Group to assist him in solving this problem.

INITIAL OBSERVATIONS

As a Discussion Group, the first task was to visit the Defender body area to view the problem at first hand. It became obvious to the Group that the wooden protection boards in use at the time were badly fitting and did not cover the whole of the rear floor panel. The group followed a vehicle from the beginning of the build to process completion and then returned to their meeting to brainstorm every possible cause of the problem.

BRAINSTORM OF INITIAL PROBLEM CAUSES

To brainstorm the problem each group member took it in turn to provide an idea – if a member did not have an idea they would 'pass'. The group recorded all ideas put forward and did not criticize or debate suggestions at this stage. From this, the group highlighted problems related to both material used and bad practice by associates.

Disadvantages of present protection boards

- All of the rear body is not covered by the present floor boards
- Boards continually broken – but still in use
- Contamination – Brake Fluid, Swarf

Cause and Effect diagram (Fishbone)

The Fishbone or Cause and Effect Diagram is one of the methods used in evaluation. Ideas from the brainstorming were placed under each category or branch; this helped the group to see the cause and effect relationship and decide how to tackle the problem (Figure 5.1).

FURTHER INVESTIGATIONS

The Group decided to monitor the damage to rear panels on vehicles over a four-week period. The survey showed, both diagrammatically and graphically, the extent of the damage on a daily basis. Figure 5.2 shows the results of the survey for Week Four.

The group also felt they needed to understand the cost of maintaining the current protection covers and the purchase of new covers to replace broken and damaged boards.

Costs of Current Protection Boards

With the help of the Finance Department the following was discovered:

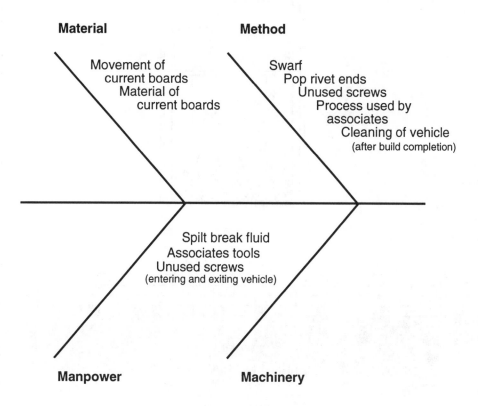

**The New Star Trekkers
Discussion Group**

Material

Movement of
current boards
Material of
current boards

Method

Swarf
Pop rivet ends
Unused screws
Process used by
associates
Cleaning of vehicle
(after build completion)

Spilt break fluid
Associates tools
Unused screws
(entering and exiting vehicle)

Manpower

Machinery

Figure 5.1   Causes of paint/panel damage on Defender rear floors

Current protection boards renewed every quarter at a cost of:	£396
Giving an annual total of:	£1,584
Two operators take approx. *20 man hours per quarter to adapt the boards:	£230
Making a total of:	£2,504 per year

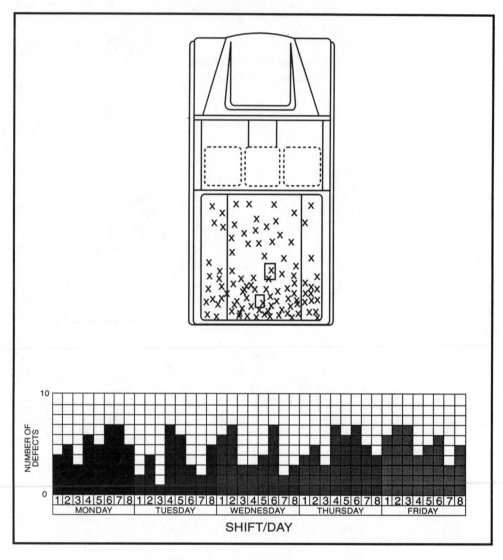

Figure 5.2   Outcome of initial survey, Week Four

In addition to the cost incurred to repair the boards it costs approximately £75 per vehicle to repair a damaged panel and repaint.

IDENTIFYING A SOLUTION

The group believed the current boards were expensive, not very effective and not user friendly. They were a main cause of paint damage. The group brainstormed possible solutions to the problem (Figure 5.3).

The New Star Trekkers Discussion Group
Defender Rear Floor Panel Protection
Solution Brainstorm

Item	Score	Item	Score
Foam		Fibre glass	5
	17		
Vacuum	17	Carpet	24
Newspaper	6	Lino	12
Plastic sheets	17	Tissue	0
Bubble pack	18	Rice paper	0
Brush	8	Leather	5
Brown paper	13	Rubber mat	26
Cling film	9	Moulded rubber	30
Air blower	7	Canvas	14
Hard board	21	Felt	13
Card board	14	Vax	2
Cloth	7	Bakelite	3
Underfelt	8	Flotex	14
Magnet	6	Wood	2
Velour	12	Carpet slippers	1
Masking tape	1	Cotton sheet	6

Scores out of a maximum 30
Top Ten

Moulded rubber	30
Rubber mat	26
Carpet	24
Hard board	21
Bubble pack	18
Vacuum	17
Plastic sheets	17
Card board	14
Canvas	14
Flotex	14

Figure 5.3   Defender rear floor panel protection solution brainstorm

With the brainstorm list the group converted the data into a Solution Effect diagram, which enabled the group to choose the most realistic solutions to their problem (Figure 5.4).

Although there were various solutions the group could implement, they decided to run a line trial on two realistic proposals, the NAS (North American Specification) floor mats and the use of bubble pack to protect the vehicle; both proposals are already used within the area for protection of different parts of the vehicle.

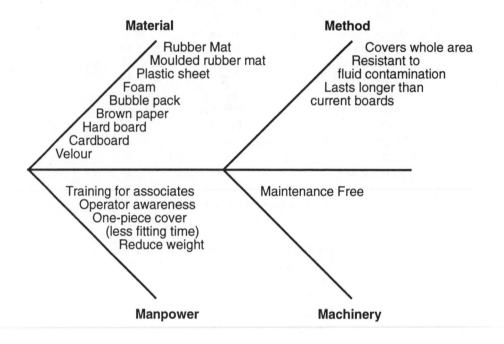

Figure 5.4   Solution Effect diagram

ADVANTAGES/DISADVANTAGES OF SOLUTIONS

The group then highlighted the advantages and disadvantages of both solutions, as follows:

- **Benefits of NAS rear mats**
  - More durable material

- Better all-round protection for the body floors
- Easier for all operators to lift into and out of Defender vehicles
- Suited to all types of Defender vehicles and little or no contamination during use
- **Disadvantages of NAS rear mats**
  - Expensive to use
- **Benefits of bubble pack**
  - Better all-round protection for the body floors
  - Easier for all operators to lift into and out of Defender vehicles
  - Suited to all types of Defender vehicles and little or no contamination during use
- **Disadvantages of using bubble pack**
  - Not recyclable
  - Expensive to use

Line trials

Line trials were then carried out for four weeks. The line trials highlighted the best possible solution – the rubber mats currently used for the Defender NAS (American market) and sold in the UK as optional extras. The rubber mats are specially prepared to cover the whole of the rear floor area and the wheel arches.

IMPLEMENTATION

Costing the rear mats

The group contacted the Engineering Department to obtain costs for the NAS rubber mats and found that each mat costs £25.00 to purchase. The group felt that this was expensive and decided to contact the supplier direct, with a view to purchasing mats without the Land Rover logo at a reduced cost.

Unexpected bonus

Because they encountered some initial problems with the rear NAS mats and the supplier had experienced moulding problems, there were some rejected rear body mats. This prompted an idea to re-negotiate the piece price and to buy back these rejected mats, thereby bringing the cost down by £8 per unit. The next step was to involve engineering to line trial the mats, and monitor for any improvements in the rear floor paint quality.

FINAL STEPS

The group were confident that the rubber mats would solve the problem of paint and
panel damage in the rear floor area. The group decided to approach the Defender manufacturing manager with their proposals:

> To purchase enough mats to give a total stock of 120, then to conduct a three-month line trial to validate the complete process, and therefore justify not only the time spent on this project, but also any capital outlay against the inevitable savings.

Immediate savings

The group felt that before their presentation to their management team they had to understand the financial saving to the business as against the cost of implementation.

The group contacted their Purchasing Department for advice on how they should proceed.

After investigation the initial savings were shown to be:

Yearly cost of old type protection boards:	£2,504
Projected yearly cost of new mats:	£1,500
Saving = £1,004 per year (minimum) on existing boards	

The estimated savings to the business could amount to more than £50,000 if the need to rework damaged vehicles was eliminated. The presentation to the management team was very successful, the group was well prepared and had to hand all of the facts concerning the project. This resulted in the group being granted financial approval for the project. The mats were purchased and the project implemented on the line.

Further savings

The group contacted Purchasing to place the order for 120 rear floor protection mats (the original scrap mats). Purchasing contacted the supplier and re-negotiated the cost of the scrap mats. A further saving of £5 per mat was achieved, allowing Land Rover to buy the mats for a cost of £12.00.

PROBLEM SOLVED

The group took delivery of the rubber mats and arranged for the training of the as sociates line-side. The operators now have to fit and remove mats from the vehicles. Although the initial boards had to be fitted and removed the group arranged for a time and motion study to be conducted. This enabled the man assignments to be changed so that the operators could work to the new process.

SUMMARY

The problem of paint and panel damage on the rear floor no longer appears as a finished vehicle audit issue. The groups solution of fitting rubber mats to all vehicles during assembly has totally eliminated the need to rework vehicles for rear floor paint damage. The Vehicle Rectification Department confirmed that their department no longer has to rework vehicles for this condition. Previously it would cost approximately £75.00 per vehicle in labour and paint.

Statistics suggest that before implementation of the solution (the rubber mats) the Vehicle Rectification Department were reworking in excess of fourteen vehicles per week. Fourteen vehicles at £75.00 each calculated over 46 weeks of production gives a saving in excess of £50,000 per year. After deducting the cost of the new protection covers the group has achieved a saving of £48,000 in the first year. Following their success, the group exclaimed:

'We await our bonus in anticipation!'

SIX

PERKINS ENGINES,

PETERBOROUGH:

TQ Dyane: A new technical process and procedure

RICHARD TEARE,
ANDY ANDERSON
AND
RICHARD GRAY

SIX

Perkins Engines, Peterborough:

TQ Dyane: A new technical process and procedure

INTRODUCTION

Perkins Engines (Peterborough) Limited specializes in manufacturing diesel engines ranging from 5 BHP to 1500 BHP. Its annual production is around 200,000 fully built engines with a further 100,000 being produced in kit form for final assembly overseas. Perkins power encircles the globe, with a comprehensive manufacturing, distribution and service base supporting the needs of over 600 equipment customers worldwide. Perkins is also a total quality (TQ) organization and views its suppliers, customers, distributors and end users as part of a continuous value chain. Training and employee development, teamwork and benchmarking against other world leaders are some of the ways that it seeks to improve its operations and adds value. For example, all five Perkins business units qualified for ISO 9000 certification in a single year and at the first attempt.

The TQ Dyane project was set up to address the problems of supply and to reduce the costs and delivery cycle (or lead time) relating to the reconditioning of honing heads – expensive items of equipment used to finish the engine cylinder bores. The honing head (or hone) is used to create a precision bore in the cylinder liners fitted to cylinder blocks and the team focused initially on honing heads fitted to a Citroen honing machine (Figure 6.1).

The cylinder liner, once pressed into the cylinder block, has to be machined to a particular size. The first operation is to fine bore the liner. The surface produced by fine boring is not suitable for operation of the engine. The finished surface is produced by a honing process, which leaves a controlled surface with the required finished characteristics for engine function.

This chapter outlines the problems that the team faced and the approach they took to design and test a new process and procedure that saved £42,000 on hone reconditioning costs in 1994 and produced inventory savings of £50,000.

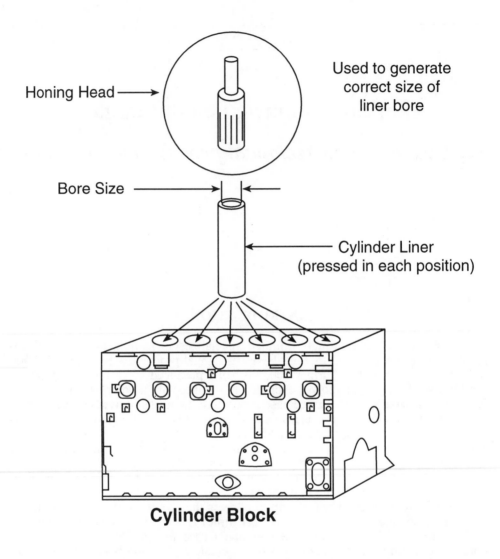

Figure 6.1   A diagram showing the relationship between the honing head, the cylinder liner and a Perkins diesel engine cylinder block

Technical terms:

Honing head:	A tool used to generate a particular size and finish bore diameter in a cylinder block liner.
Cylinder liner:	A cylindrical insert pressed into a cylinder block. The piston inside this liner reciprocates in the completed engine.
Cylinder block:	One of the main parts of a Perkins engine.

THE TQ DYANE PROJECT

The TQ Dyane team came together in order to solve a reoccurring set of problems relating to the servicing (or reconditioning) of honing heads. This particular, silicone carbide honing process is relatively new to Perkins as the Citroen honing machine was introduced in the mid-1980s. Around five years ago the machine operators noticed that the hones were starting to show signs of wear and this meant that they had to be sent away for reconditioning. Prior to despatch, the hones were sent to the site Tool Room where they were stripped down. The hone itself was then sent to an external supplier for reconditioning while the Tool Room stored the respective component parts. As the Tool Room technicians didn't have a dedicated storage area for the hone component parts, smaller items were occasionally mislaid.

To authorize the reconditioning work each hone had to pass through the Perkins' order and despatch system. This involved some 27 transactions and accompanying paperwork, further complicated by the fact that different business units had Citroen machines and were using the hones, but they didn't want to pay for someone else's usage. So, it was necessary to track back and identify who had incurred the wear on the hone, raising the necessary paperwork and getting it signed off by the appropriate person prior to raising the dispatch papers. After this, each hone had to be packaged ready to send away and these procedures had to be dealt with in reverse when the hone arrived back from the external supplier. The reconditioning process itself often took between 4–6 weeks and it was necessary to set up and maintain the contract with the external supplier. In the first year, 27 hones were sent out for reconditioning at a cost of £1,000 per hone. The combined problems of the out-of-service delays, the paperwork involved and keeping track of each hone coupled with the high cost of servicing, prompted a decision to review the existing arrangements and resolve the sense of frustration experienced by all concerned with the reconditioning process.

The TQ Dyane team initially drew its membership from among end-user operators, the Tool Room and from all departments involved in processing the hone reconditioning work. The project sponsor's role was to enable the team to form in such a way that it could reflect on the specific problems experienced by different departments. For example, the 'opportunity for improvement' was readily identified by the process owner who frequently commented on the difficulties he was experiencing in maintaining quality, while the project sponsor had concerns about the financial implications of delays and lost production time.

TQ Dyane: Project team members

Team member	Team role
Richard Gray	Production Supervisor and Team Leader
John Willis	Process Owner
John Rickards	Tool Room Technician
Doug Shaw	Tool Room Technician
Alan Purdy	Production Engineer – Projects
John Thornburn	Production Engineer – Tooling
Peter Nicholas	Production Manager and Project Sponsor

The first few team meetings confirmed that all the contributing departments were experiencing difficulties with the existing arrangements and in bringing the groups together to consider what could be done, it soon became apparent that a complete solution rather than a 'quick fix' would be needed.

The solution would need to address the various kinds of logistical problems that were affecting the supply of honing heads. As they are used in several factory areas, it was proving difficult to monitor and stock check the actual locations of the 32 honing heads in use and at £10,000 each, the team felt that it should also devise a better system for returns and issues so that the exact locations of all hones in use could be verified. Despite regular stock checks, team members involved in monitoring the hone supply found that there were almost always two or three hones unaccounted for. This situation was exacerbated by the fact that operators were able to take a honing head whenever they needed it and if there were two of the correct size available, operators would often take two so that they had a backup. This practice made it difficult to take accurate stock takes and it also meant that with four or five hones out for service at any given time and with no clearly defined responsibility for keeping the honing heads under review, the 4-cylinder and 6-cylinder block production lines would periodically stop because the hones in stock were the wrong size for the machine needing a replacement.

THE DYANE TEAM APPROACH

The team used a brainstorming technique to identify the scope of the problem and to begin to explore possible solutions (Figure 6.2). Team members felt that the major source of frustration related to the volume of transactions needed to process the work – sometimes as many as 30 separate activities – and the fact that the external supplier was tied to little more than a servicing exchange with a long and variable turnaround for completing the work. Further, the Tool Room were not informed when a consignment of hones were due to be returned and some of the delays seemed to be occurring because the supplier had been sourcing carbide replacement strips for the hones in France, requiring a separate and occasionally discontinuous chain of supply.

The team began to examine the administrative procedures linking the chain of paperwork to see whether the number of transactions could be reduced and handled more quickly. The aim was to shorten the lead time by streamlining the paperwork but it soon became apparent that improvements here wouldn't solve the problem of loss of control and accountability once the honing head left the premises. A source of frustration stemmed from the fact that the reconditioning work was handled by an agency, so telephone messages and instructions were relayed from here to the workshop. Discussions with the workshop technicians failed to achieve much improvement in the turnaround time, nor could the workshop guarantee a faster lead time in the future. Some consideration was given to sourcing an alternative supplier, but in fact there were very few that could do the work. So, after three or four meetings the team realized that the ideal solution would be to undertake the reconditioning 'in-works'. Interestingly, the Dyane project didn't follow the typical Perkins section-based TQ style as it needed a cross-departmental team. Yet the team was able to function with fewer members once the in-works solution had been agreed, as it could be implemented without a lengthy administrative procedure.

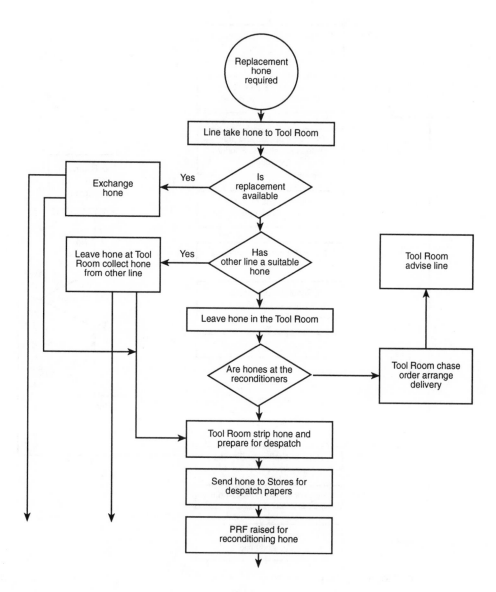

Figure 6.2 A flow diagram showing the existing sequence of events for reconditioning and supplying honing heads

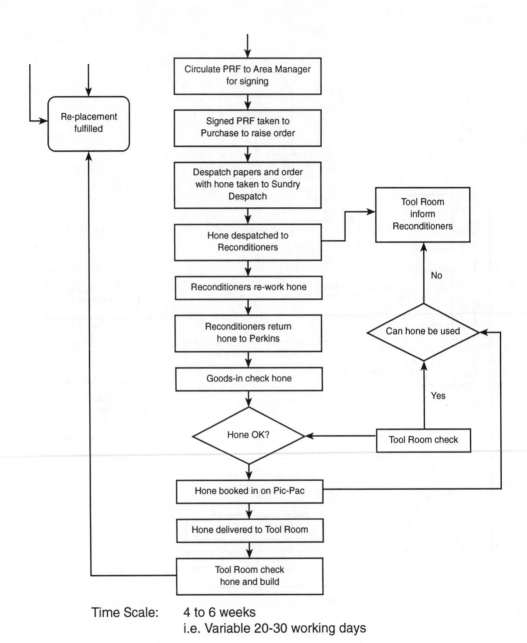

Time Scale: 4 to 6 weeks
i.e. Variable 20-30 working days

Figure 6.2 (*continued*) A flow diagram showing the existing sequence of events for reconditioning and supplying honing heads

TQ Dyane: Project team dynamics

Team roles and involvement:	Each team member had a different role with shared problem-solving responsibility and full involvement in decision making throughout.
Team continuity:	The initial project ran for a total of 24 months (with trials for six months) during which the team held 20 formal meetings. The team continues to meet to discuss refinements to the hone reconditioning process.
TQ style:	The team adhered to a full total quality cycle with experts in particular fields co-opted onto the team for short periods.

After agreeing its goal, the team started to focus on how to address the technical challenges it posed and 'low key' exploratory trials were undertaken so that the team could be sure that it could handle the work prior to announcing the in-works solution more widely. It is also seemed feasible to prototype the Citroen honing head reconditioning process and then to use the same approach to bring other types of honing heads in the factory under process control. In fact, all the honing heads in the factory were either reconditioned or stripped down by Tool Room technicians and trials confirmed that they were capable of handling the entire process. Further, the Tool Room actually did a better job with lead time reductions from 4–6 weeks to three days. The Tool Room were also willing to act as a storage and distribution point for honing heads so that wear and usage records could be easily maintained and, having set this up, the honing head stock for two new product introductions can be added in to the system.

THE PROBLEM-SOLVING APPROACH

As the project team sought to address the different problems encountered by participating departments, brainstorming among other TQ techniques helped the team to explore widely, especially in the formative stages. All Perkins employees receive training in the use and application of a range of TQ techniques, supported by the Perkins TQ techniques manual. The Dyane team drew mainly on brainstorming, process mapping and action planning and the Perkins TQ circle diagram provided the necessary planning framework for the project (see Appendix 6.1). The agreed approach was to mount flipchart output from the brainstorming sessions on the office walls where the team met and by adhering to a non-judgmental approach, the ideas under discussion reflected the equal contributions of all team members. The team also refrained from criticizing an idea – be it process, technical or systems related – until it was up on the board, so that all the ideas and suggestions could be discussed in a controlled manner. In this way the unity of the team was maintained throughout the life of the project. It also helped that the team members knew each other well and accepted that finding a workable solution was more important than the views of any one team member. The team's decision to submit the project to an in-company TQ award scheme provided an added incentive and a sense of achievement in that the solutions that were tested, refined and implemented helped to resolve an ongoing problem (see Appendix 6.2).

When the 'ideal' solution emerged during a brainstorming session – that the Tool Room could take on the reconditioning work – the Tool Room team members were initially sceptical. The supplier had led them to believe that reconditioning is a highly specialized task and they didn't have the piece of equipment needed to undertake the work. In order to proceed with the trials it was necessary to buy the item of equipment (at a cost of £1,000) and to source and stock a supply of carbide strips. The team sponsor was able to provide some financial support but as everyone in the team had a role to play, it wasn't difficult to secure the necessary support needed to mount the trials. There were, in fact, quite a number of set-backs in the early stages, but once the project had reached the trial stage, it progressed smoothly to completion. In fact, project failure was not an issue, more the relative level of success achieved. The key decision revolved around how far to take the project and if the process design hadn't succeeded, the team had resolved to persevere as it was convinced that the Tool Room had the skills and capability to undertake the work.

PROJECT TRIALS AND IMPLEMENTATION

Prior to commencing the project trials, each team member had to complete different preparatory tasks and so action plans were drawn up as a means of co-ordinating the work within an agreed timescale. It was also important to brief supervisors and staff affected by the new in-works process and requisitioning procedure.

While the project was ongoing, team members were continuing with their normal jobs, so it was thought necessary to design and implement an interim system to keep the supplier 'on the ball' while working on the project. Scheduling meeting time was initially difficult until a routine had been established, as some team members came from departments operating two shifts and others three shifts a day.

The trials encompassed testing and refining the reconditioning process and setting up a system and procedures for storing, issuing, transporting and returning the hones to the Tool Room. To afford better protection, the hones were housed in individual cases and stored in a made-to-measure storage bench so that they could be used on a rotation basis. In all, the trials involved spending £6,000 on equipment and items to support the project. It was also necessary to buy a domestic oven in order to melt the honing head glue prior to stripping it down. The oven cost £99 and proved to be the most difficult item to obtain as it was necessary to persuade non-team members responsible for countersigning the order that it wasn't intended for domestic use!

Prior to TQ Dyane, Tool Room staff had to spend some of their time tracking down the honing heads rather than actually working on them. A three-day turnaround and the introduction of an effective requisitioning system has meant that the number of honing heads in use can now be reduced. For instance, there are fifteen honing heads used in conjunction with one type of machine and it is now possible to reduce the number of honing heads in service to nine. Figure 6.3 shows the new system.

PROJECT OUTCOMES

The advantage of teamwork is that it enables a group of individuals, each with a different piece of the same jigsaw puzzle, to come together to share insights and

TQ Dyane: Project implementation: Summary of the presentation to shop floor supervisors affected by in-works reconditioning of honing heads

Objective	• To improve the service for honing heads. • To reduce the cost of reconditioning honing heads by using in-works Tool Room personnel instead of an outside supplier. • To standardize a new process and procedure.
Key improvements	• The Tool Room now has the capability to service Citroen hones and is introducing a new returns and issuing procedure. They will also keep records on hone condition and current locations and offers improved cabinet/bench storage with an individual 'lin bin' carrier for each hone.
Implementation	• Start date is: 3 May 1994 with a review and feedback period of one month, after which refinements will be made as necessary.
Key features of the returns and issuing procedure	• A standard issuing procedure for all hones is to be introduced with a one-for-one exchange available during day and night shifts and during most overtime shifts. In case of emergency, contact Gate 5 Security. • Replacement hones must be signed for in the hone log book. • Tool Room hone storage cabinets have been clearly remarked so that hones are issued in rotation. • The lin bins for housing the hones should not be used for any other purpose and all operators should be briefed on the returns and issuing procedure.
How will it work?	• Start: Hone on machine requires replacing. Operator removes the hone and takes it to the Tool Room (in hone box). Operator sees Tool Room supervisor or any other Tool Room personnel and returns the used hone. Tool Room personnel unlock cabinet and issue replacement hone. Tool Room personnel fill out hone log: date, hone type, location and line operator signs. Operator returns to line with hone. Hone available for use.

suggestions. If any one member of the team had tried to take on this particular project in isolation from the rest, it wouldn't have succeeded as it needed a range of skills to achieve a breakthrough. The team had succeeded in designing a new process and procedure that saved time and money.

TQ Dyane: Cost savings

Comparative cost schedule	External supplier	In-works supplier
Reconditioning costs per hone	£1,000	£326
Cost of reconditioning 27 hones in 1993	£27,000 (actual cost)	£8,802 (estimated cost)

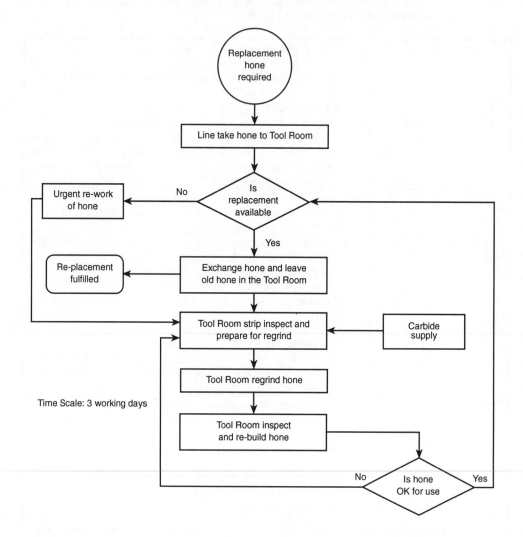

Figure 6.3   A flow diagram showing the new, in works sequence of events for reconditioning and supplying honing head

TQ Dyane: Financial summary

TQ Dyane project highlights	£
Project start-up costs	6,000
Project payback period	7 months
Cost reductions achieved in year 1 (1994)	12,198
Project cost savings in year 2 (1995)	18,198
Expected further savings per annum (in addition to year 2 savings)	3,500

Prior to TQ at Perkins, innovative solutions were rarely possible as 'solutions' were handed down rather than devolved to the people facing the problem to solve. The cultural change that has occurred now means that all employees are consulted and are able to specify what they want to achieve, based on their own ideas. For instance, the hone requisitioning system now uses a store cupboard with sliding doors so that a 'last in, first out' approach is used. This helps to ensure that the hones are subject to an equal amount of use and wear.

TQ Dyane: Summary of project team achievements

Cost and lead-time objectives	To reduce costs and improve lead time availability of honing heads to production areas. Achieved by in-works servicing giving total control over all honing heads and a reconditioned turnaround time reduced to 1 day if required. This solution offers the best financial payback and lead-time availability.
Improvement objectives	To ensure the accuracy and consistency of all reconditioning work. Reconditioned hones are now available from the Tool Room for use on honing machines on time, every time. The process and issuing procedure has been adopted as standard practice for on-site honing heads and all backup documentation is in place.
End-user satisfaction	The new process and issuing procedure is working effectively and all honing heads are now carefully monitored so that wear and eventual replacement needs can be assessed more accurately.

TQ Dyane also exemplifies the power of teamworking – six or ten people working and thinking together, rather than one individual delegated to solve a particular job. It means that people with different backgrounds and skills – technical and managerial – learn from each other and learn to respect one another's points of view. Six years ago, different concepts were introduced as 'flavour of the month' ideas at Perkins and between 80–90 per cent of the factory personnel were totally sceptical about the value they brought to the workplace. But since then, as many as 80 per cent of the workforce has completely changed – everybody wants to work together and it's a much more positive attitude and approach to problem-solving and continual improvement. Now, most people want to help and instead of ignoring problems or blaming others, people actually offer to help.

Prior to TQ, it was often difficult to make suggestions to others – especially if they had specialist skills or held more senior roles, but now it is commonplace to share, irrespective of a person's job role and status. This has helped to engender a sense of personal confidence and rapport with others. It also gives the individual licence to approach others with ideas and suggestions and since TQ was established, people have become much more available. TQ *does* make a difference – if teams, sections or departments are facing a problem and are unable to resolve it themselves, the response is to 'TQ it' by setting up a project team to address the problem. This provides a sense of team accomplishment which is now very strong at Perkins and which offers the potential for achieving very much more in the future.

APPENDIX 6.1
A summary of the main TQ techniques and applications used by the TQ Dyane project team

Action planning

An *action plan* is an outline of who will do what, when and with what resources, to achieve a specified objective. It forms the basis of 'getting it right first time'. Charts are commonly used to show an *action plan* in an organized way, typically with the following headings:

Objective

What to do	Resources	When	Who

Preparing an *action plan* helps to: decide priorities; establish any interrelationships; decide who does what; establish 'required by' dates; review and monitor progress.

Brainstorming

Brainstorming is a technique which encourages creative thinking and the generation of ideas. After agreeing on the participants, decide on group roles, explain the purpose of the meeting, allocate time to each step and encourage idea generation. After this, it is necessary to establish some initial classification, group ideas with a common theme and evaluate and select the most appropriate ideas.

Process mapping

A *process map* is a pictorial representation of a process, using basic flowcharting symbols. Process mapping helps to test the basic steps required to achieve quality output. Once completed, a process map can help identify weaknesses in the process and establish priorities for action. The symbols are shown in Figure 6.4.

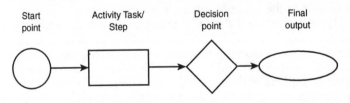

Figure 6.4

These should be large enough to count in terms of delivering quality output; small enough to map and understand; result in output which is aimed at meeting the requirements of a customer.

To use *process mapping*, assemble a team of people who collectively know the full range of activities that make up a process, establish the correct sequence of activities and challenge the complexity of the process. For example: Can the individual activities be simplified? Should customer–supplier agreements be established? Where should quality measures be used? After this, agree who the process owner should be and agree action plans for improving the process.

The Perkins Quality Improvement Cycle

Using a storyboard design, the Perkins Quality Improvement Cycle provides an overview of the total quality cycle and the techniques that can be used at each stage in the Cycle (Figure 6.5).

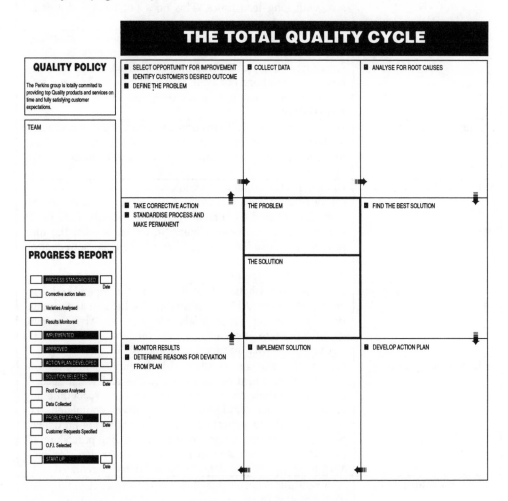

Figure 6.5   The Total Quality Cycle

APPENDIX 6.2
TQ Dyane: Project overview

Stages involved in ensuring the cost-effective supply of honing head tools for Citroen honing machines

Stage	Task definition
1. Opportunity for improvement	To ensure the availability of hones ready for use on honing machines.
2. Customers' desired outcome	A continuous supply of hones on demand, reconditioned in the most cost effective way possible.
3. Define the problem	Problem is: present supply of reconditioned hones is expensive with long lead times. This does not meet end-user requirements.
4. Collect data	Review the current process (process mapping); number of hones reconditioned during previous 12 months is 27; research how long current lead time is (charted at 4 to 6 weeks); how often was hone not available when required? (1 in 6 ratio failing to meet customers requirements; 1 in 10 ratio causing serious delays).
5. Analyse for root causes	Drawing on stage 4, brainstorm and prepare cause and effect analysis. Root causes identified as: supplier takes too long; process start-to-finish is too long; too many chances of hold-ups arising.
6. Find the best solution	Brainstorm for solutions. Possible solutions identified as: (a) rationalize system by reviewing process using process mapping; (b) find an alternative supplier, ideally Tool Room if capable; (c) recondition hone 'in-works' so that the total process and capability is kept in-works for maximum control; (d) make reclaim of hone a user-friendly in-works process with minimum lead time.
7. Develop action plans (AP):	AP1: ascertain whether Tool Room has the capability to undertake the work. AP2: if successful, Tool Room and production line to carry out trials and assess. AP3: prepare specifications to implement a new process, use force field analysis to identify the possible problems.
8. Implement solution(s)	(a) Benches/storage installed; (b) 'lin bin' containers obtained, colour coded hones exchanged as and when needed; (c) secure carbide stock needed for the hone reconditioning process; (d) hone supply and demand survey completed, records started (history sheet developed); (e) hone log introduced prior to implementing a new returns and issuing procedure; (f) project presentation arranged (with a repeat date for non-attendees); (g) start-up date agreed and details circulated.
9: Monitor results	(a) Lead-time reduced from 4–6 weeks to three days; (b) control improved (hone log gives location/date/hone number and is signed by operator); (c) internal customer feedback: so far

	all requests met, production panics eliminated; (d) quality improved: so far no reports of damage or rust since commencement of in-works hone reconditioning; (e) costs reduced.
10. Check for deviations	New process/procedure differs to that used for non-Citroen hone types. Standardization is needed so as to incorporate other hone types into the new system. Conduct trials to test whether hardened steel could be used to replace carbide for further cost reductions (estimated potential savings of £3,500 per annum).
11. Corrective action	New process/procedure gives improved control and accountability and should be adopted for all hones on site.
12. Standardize process	Process standardization across all hone types, supplied by the Tool Room. Evaluate the possibilities of using hardened steel rather than carbide, during the reconditioning process.

PART 2

THE PERKINS AWARD

SEVEN

BENEFITS AGENCY, UK:

Benefit enquiries, customer advice and quality improvement

JACKIE BRANDER BROWN
AND
SHELAGH IWANOWICZ

SEVEN

Benefits Agency, UK:
Benefit enquiries, customer advice and quality improvement

INTRODUCTION

Benefit Enquiry Line for people with disabilities (BEL) is an autonomous unit within the Benefits Agency, which itself is an executive agency of the Department of Social Security. This chapter tells their story: their rapid growth since their formation as a national service on 10 June 1991, their recognition of the need for a quality programme, the development of that programme through an empowered team approach, and their quality goals and plans for the future.

TOTAL CUSTOMER SERVICE

BEL is a free, confidential advice line offering general information on all Social Security and related benefits to people with disabilities, their carers and representatives. BEL also provides a free forms completion service, which can either give customers advice on completing benefit claim forms or alternatively will complete the whole claim form for a customer and then send it to them to check and sign. A free textphone service is also available for customers who are deaf or hard of hearing, while leaflets, claim forms and letters can be provided in Braille or large print for people who are blind or partially sighted. Information is also available to all customers on audio and video cassette tapes.

BEL was originally introduced in 1990 as a six-month pilot scheme just in the Berkshire area, with a view to extending the service nationwide in time for the launch of two new disability benefits – the Disability Living Allowance and the Disability Working Allowance – which were planned for April 1992. There were a number of significant reasons for establishing such a service. People with disabilities who need advice or information about Social Security benefits often find it difficult to visit their local Social Security Office in person. As a result of such difficulties, and many others which people with disabilities face, it is more likely that these customers will telephone the appropriate benefit office for help. However, telephone calls can prove expensive – especially when a customer needs to ring long distance for advice – and as many disabled people live on limited incomes this may deter them from seeking the help and advice they need.

In February 1991 the BEL service was extended throughout London, and then further throughout the south of England in April. On 10 June 1991 the national BEL service became operational, based in Preston, commencing with just eleven staff. However, from these somewhat modest beginnings BEL has experienced rapid growth, which in 1994 involved them in providing advice and information to over one million customers, issuing over half a million leaflets, letters and forms and assisting over 43,000 customers to obtain help with the completion of their benefit claim forms. To enable BEL to keep up with such a level of customer demand the unit has grown from the eleven staff in 1991 to nearly 200 today – as Figure 7.1 shows.

As they had developed at such a fast pace, it was vital that BEL identified how they could cope with the uncertainties of their rapidly changing workplace while continuously improving the efficiency of their services. Two areas were seen as being of crucial importance to achieving this: firstly, it was considered imperative that BEL's organizational culture was enabling, empowering, co-operative and team driven, and secondly, it was realized that BEL needed to involve in such a 'team' not only their own staff, but also their customers and their suppliers.

'TOGETHER EVERYONE ACHIEVES MORE'

BEL's vision

In October 1992 BEL held a 'Team Event' to allow everyone at BEL to have their say about the direction in which the organization should develop. The event helped to reduce uncertainties, to stabilize the team, to promote creativity and to encourage ideas which everyone at BEL could support. Also, as BEL had no specific role model to follow, a 'golden opportunity' was identified to build the BEL team on Total Quality Principles, demonstrating BEL's firm belief that 'together everyone achieves more'.

During the Team Event, BEL developed their vision for their future :

'To be the best benefit advice and information service available for people with disabilities, their carers and representatives'

Realizing that this would not be easy to achieve, the team began to develop a programme to enable them to progress towards their vision.

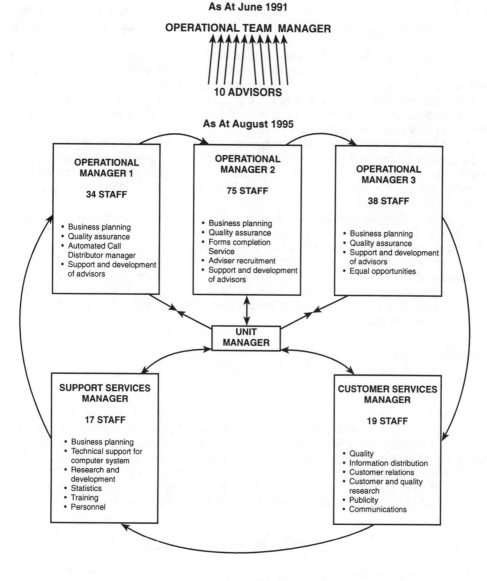

As At June 1991

OPERATIONAL TEAM MANAGER

10 ADVISORS

As At August 1995

OPERATIONAL MANAGER 1	OPERATIONAL MANAGER 2	OPERATIONAL MANAGER 3
34 STAFF	**75 STAFF**	**38 STAFF**

OPERATIONAL MANAGER 1 — **34 STAFF**
- Business planning
- Quality assurance
- Automated Call Distributor manager
- Support and development of advisors

OPERATIONAL MANAGER 2 — **75 STAFF**
- Business planning
- Quality assurance
- Forms completion Service
- Adviser recruitment
- Support and development of advisors

OPERATIONAL MANAGER 3 — **38 STAFF**
- Business planning
- Quality assurance
- Support and development of advisors
- Equal opportunities

UNIT MANAGER

SUPPORT SERVICES MANAGER — **17 STAFF**
- Business planning
- Technical support for computer system
- Research and development
- Statistics
- Training
- Personnel

CUSTOMER SERVICES MANAGER — **19 STAFF**
- Quality
- Information distribution
- Customer relations
- Customer and quality research
- Publicity
- Communications

Figure 7.1　BEL organization charts

Achieving the vision

To achieve their vision, the team believed it was essential that BEL employed caring, professional and fully involved people, who would actively listen to customers and give them time to fully explain their enquiry and to discuss their benefit needs. In particular, the team considered it crucial that customers were given time, rather than limiting them to a specific call length, so that each call can be tailored to the customer's individual needs.

The team also recognized that to achieve their aim BEL would need to ensure a high level of customer satisfaction through the provision of both a quality service and value for money. As BEL is a publicly funded unit, it is essential that it delivers quality services at the lowest cost to the taxpayer. The BEL team therefore decided that a strategic aim to underpin this was for BEL to work towards attaining Charter Mark status, which they achieved in 1994.

In addition, the BEL team recognized that in order to achieve their vision, they must remain committed to continuous improvement. This was supported by their quality programme, which was given further structure with the introduction of the Benefit Agency's own Quality Framework in 1993. BEL attained the Benefits Agency Quality Award in 1994.

Finally, if BEL was to achieve its vision, the team felt it was essential for them to continue their policy of openness and consultation with both internal and external customers. In order to manage this successfully the BEL team developed a communications strategy and an empowerment awareness programme, both of which will be discussed in more detail later in the chapter. Also, as the team believed it was vital for people to be encouraged to reach their full potential, the team set themselves a goal to achieve Investors in People accreditation within three years – a target which BEL achieved in 1995.

The team approach

BEL's team approach did not end with the event held in October 1992. In order to encourage team working and inter-departmental support all staff at BEL are involved on a daily, weekly, monthly and annual basis in the running of the unit through a variety of 'cross-grade' and 'cross-team' discussion and consultative groups – which are discussed in more detail later – including, for instance, the External Customer Focus Group, Team Talks and the Quality Focus Group. BEL firmly believes that all of its successes have been achieved through teamwork, and there are a variety of recognition methods to celebrate these successes.

BEL's achievements

BEL was one of the first areas in the Benefits Agency to attain the Benefits Agency Quality Award. As already noted, the BEL team has also succeeded in attaining Charter Mark status and Investors in People accreditation and has introduced a quality management system. In addition, BEL has developed a strong teamwork programme, is committed to increasing empowerment awareness and is achieving increasing levels of customer satisfaction – which were independently assessed at an outstanding 99 per cent in 1994. It should also be noted that this has all been accomplished within the funds allocated to BEL – there has been no additional funding for their 'Quality Programme'.

But just how has all this been achieved? For this to be fully appreciated we now turn to a detailed account of their quality improvement programme.

BEL'S QUALITY IMPROVEMENT PROGRAMME

BEL's quality journey

From the very beginning BEL has adopted total quality principles. For instance, BEL's customers, both external and internal, were consulted about their expectations and requirements of the service. Also, BEL's staff were consulted about their needs and BEL's service delivery was regularly monitored and revised accordingly to ensure continuous improvement. All of these principles are still employed at BEL today.

Furthermore, as the BEL team is united in its aim 'to be the best', they know that to achieve this they must maintain their firm commitment to continuous improvement and as BEL grew, and learned more about its customers, its quality processes became more refined, and all staff became involved in the quality journey.

BEL's quality journey was given extra impetus by the introduction of the Benefits Agency Quality Framework in 1993. This is a Total Quality Management (TQM) programme designed for the Benefits Agency and based on the European Model for Total Quality Management. All Benefits Agency business revolves around four core quality values: customer service, caring for staff, bias for action and value for money. In the Benefits Agency Quality Framework these are expanded to the twelve criteria illustrated in Figure 7.2.

Business units within the Benefits Agency assess and score themselves against this model. They also provide evidence to support their scores and these are validated and confirmed by rigorous internal and external assessment. Those units which score high marks in all of the twelve areas are awarded the Benefits Agency Quality Award. BEL's Quality Focus Group meets on a monthly basis to consider quality issues within BEL and to ensure BEL's continuing improvement against this model. Such continuous quality improvement demonstrated by BEL resulted in their being one of the first areas within the Benefits Agency to achieve this award in March 1994.

The deployment of quality improvement throughout BEL

The BEL team also recognized that if their quality programme was to be successful it was vital that all of BEL's staff became fully involved – which they sought to achieve through good communication, through teamwork and through active support for staff.

Customer Service	Bias for Action
• Service Delivery • Customer Research • Handling Exceptions • Place in the Community	• Organisational Culture • Communication • Internal Customer Focus
Caring for Staff	Value for Money
• Staff Development • Equal Opportunities • Staff Services	• Managing Budgets • Process Efficiency

Figure 7.2 Benefits Agency Quality Framework

Communication

The BEL team firmly believes that the development of good communication is vital to the success of any quality programme. Good communications ensure the effective deployment of quality policies and strategies as well as creating a culture of openness and co-operation, so enhancing continuous improvement within an organization.

BEL's first written 'Communications Strategy' was developed using ideas raised at a staff team event. The strategy includes more than 20 avenues of communication within the BEL unit. As noted previously, all BEL staff are encouraged to become fully involved in a variety of discussion and consultative groups, which are outlined in Figure 7.3. All staff in the unit are involved in at least one of these groups each week, and in addition everyone at BEL is involved in contributing to the Quality Focus Group, because it is BEL's strong belief that the most informed decisions are made by the people who actually 'do the job'.

COMMUNICATIONS STRATEGY

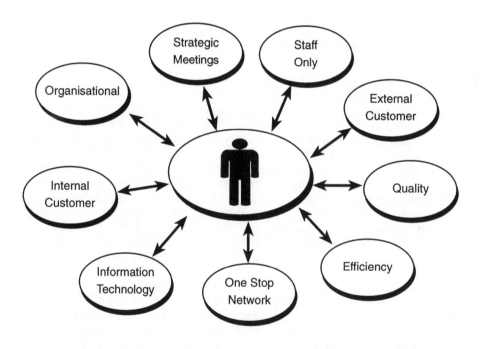

Figure 7.3 BEL's communication strategy

Teamwork

As Figure 7.1 illustrated, the overall BEL team is split into five smaller operational teams, each having its own manager. Each operational team is responsible for its own day to day management while also having responsibility to work with the other teams towards the common goal of delivering excellent service.

Support for staff

BEL also has a very open management culture: the managers support the staff in everything they do, and are very approachable and willing to accept new ideas. Staff are welcome to attend management team meetings – which they often do – and they are kept well informed of anything which might affect them or their work. Staff views are always invited and considered before decisions are made.

Two key innovations have enhanced this openness: firstly, at the staff's request, BEL's managers have relinquished their own separate offices to work at a desk in their own operational area. This has created an even more open management style, and staff have found this has resulted in the managers being even more approachable. Secondly, the Unit manager has weekly team talks with groups of cross-grade, cross-unit staff, and she regularly 'walks the job' to enable her to build up a rapport with the team and vice versa.

Empowerment and managing change

By the start of 1994 BEL had been in business for over two years. Although BEL had embarked on – and were strongly committed to – their quality journey, problems had begun to emerge. BEL had grown rapidly and was continuing to grow with the result that the team was beginning to experience some communication problems. Also, as junior managers, the advisers were beginning to feel frustrated by the relative isolation of their job. The BEL team was becoming increasingly concerned that if these problems were not quickly addressed the high quality customer service with which they had become associated would be compromised.

BEL looked towards empowerment as an effective means to address these issues and as a way to keep BEL moving forward. To personalize the concept of empowerment staff were consulted, and the phrase 'Shifting the Balance' was coined – in other words, the responsibility for doing a task should be 'shifted' to the best person for the job. BEL realized that if this type of programme was to be successful, it has to be maintained for a number of years to enable changes to become deeply rooted. However, by working together as a team, BEL has in a very short time created the appropriate atmosphere and environment for this to happen.

BEL's empowerment programme was implemented in several stages. Firstly, it was considered essential to obtain the total commitment of the management team to the programme. Empowerment can be a difficult area for some managers as it represents a change in role and a certain relinquishment of 'power'. BEL's managers were equal to the challenge and in giving their full support to the programme, they held a workshop to consider their changing roles and to define how they saw BEL's future. A 'Shifting the Balance' vision eventually emerged, and in the second stage of the programme individual teams within BEL were asked to discuss and personalize this vision to meet their own team's needs. After discussions, the original slogan was changed to 'everybody doing what needs to be done to ensure we successfully achieve our business objectives'.

As a result of these initial empowerment meetings, empowered behaviour began to emerge: staff began to accept greater responsibility, they began to question why things were done in a particular way and they started to challenge set procedures. However, despite these developments BEL felt the programme lacked cross-team initiatives – and they believed that if they could overcome this barrier they could achieve even more.

In stage three of the programme empowerment workshops were arranged for all staff, in cross-grade and cross-team groups, with the objective of these workshops being to build on the skills and knowledge BEL had already gained. These workshops ended the initial part of the change programme, and they were so successful that they are now included in the initial training for all new staff.

In the final stage of the empowerment programme a further workshop was arranged for BEL's management team. Prior to this taking place a '360 degree' feedback exercise was carried out, to focus on the managers' empowering behaviour. Questionnaires were completed by their peers, line managers, staff and themselves. It is intended that this exercise will be conducted annually to ensure that managers remain committed to maintaining an empowered culture.

Initial indications show that BEL's empowerment programme has been successful. Although staff numbers have increased, the management team has not, which has been possible because staff are more willing to accept greater responsibility. To take this development further, 'Self Directional Teams' were piloted, to create smaller, autonomous units within the larger teams. After much consultation though, the BEL team has decided not to implement Self Directional Teams at present, although some of the initiatives implemented in the pilot scheme have been adopted within individual teams. Communication barriers have also been overcome by encouraging problems to be discussed, and through such involvement and co-operation staff now have a greater understanding of each other's jobs.

BEL has also set up a fully integrated 'Quality Assurance System', with advisers' calls being randomly assessed to ensure quality is maintained. Originally, managers assessed the quality of advisers calls, but now peer quality assurance is accepted, and all advisers are given the opportunity to work in the Quality Assurance Team on a rota basis – a clear example of using the 'best person for the job'.

Although the full benefits of BEL's empowerment programme will only be felt in the long term, initial results are both positive and encouraging. Staff surveys show that in particular there has been a definite 'shift' towards empowerment within the team, and this has had a beneficial effect on the unit's organizational culture.

Quality education and training

'Training is the single most important factor in actually improving quality, once commitment to do so is present'. (Oakland)

The BEL team recognizes that training is an essential part of quality improvement. Every member of the team is particularly recruited for their commitment, their dedication and their communication skills, and every one of them has very high expectations of their own training and development.

At the launch of the BEL project, there was no formal provision for training and development: they did not have a training team, nor did they have training materials or formal methods of evaluation. This changed as the organization began to move along its road towards total quality. A Staff Development Officer was appointed to add structure to training, and following consultation with BEL team members a training programme evolved, and an in-house training team began to write and deliver training packages.

However, although this training programme was successful, there was a feeling within BEL that something was 'missing'. BEL had grown rapidly and the team felt that a more organized approach to training and development was needed and that BEL needed to plan its activities to meet its vision, to meet the needs of the business and to meet the needs of the individual. It was therefore important that each member of the team knew their own aims and objectives and how they would fit into the team. Consequently at the end of 1993 training and development became one of the major priorities for BEL in order to support their aim to become a total quality organization and, following more consultation with team members, BEL undertook several initiatives:

Staff profiles

When a new member of staff now joins BEL they are asked to complete a 'staff profile'. This gives them the opportunity to 'sell themselves', to tell about their experiences and skills and their work in other public or private sector organizations. This information is entered on to a database and is used to help fill vacancies for specialist jobs or projects: for example, staff with graphic design skills helped to produce a leaflet for people with learning difficulties, while staff with language skills are often in demand to translate for customers who are unable to speak English.

Personal development plans

To help staff plan their training and development and to focus on their strengths, weaknesses and aspirations, BEL introduced 'Personal Development Plans'. These plans are completed using a two-tiered approach: firstly, staff discuss their training and development with their line managers at annual appraisal meetings during which staff appraise themselves on their performance against key work objectives. Secondly, this interview is followed by a training needs analysis interview with the Staff Development Officer. All information is kept on a computer database to assist co-ordination of courses and budgets and all requests for training and development are also closely monitored to ensure they contribute to BEL's total quality development.

Secondments

BEL's management team is fully committed to the development of their staff, and one way in which they show this commitment is to support staff who apply for secondment. During 1995 BEL had four staff on secondment to disability-linked organizations and on their return to BEL such secondees pass on their experience and new knowledge to their colleagues to increase their understanding of BEL's customers. BEL believes that secondments help to increase the flexibility of team members, that they help to increase team motivation and that they also enhance BEL's reputation in the community.

Local school initiatives

BEL team members also take an active role in a range of initiatives involving local schools, including 'Industry Days', mentoring and 'Young Enterprise'. Being involved in such initiatives not only enables BEL's staff to develop new skills, but also enables links with the community to be strengthened.

In addition to these initiatives key elements of BEL's training programme were also developed, comprising:

Initial training course

A training team of three people delivers a comprehensive initial training course to all new BEL employees which lasts for eight weeks. The course includes training on over 30 Social Security Benefits, computer skills, disability awareness, telephone techniques, customer service, empowerment and quality.

All of the initial training courses and workshops are evaluated by both trainers and trainees and modified if necessary. Such an evaluation ensures that the training continues to meet both the needs of the business and the needs of the individual.

Workshops

All members of the BEL team are invited and encouraged to take part in additional technical and skills training and also in personal and career development activities. New ideas for training and development are warmly welcomed, and team members often suggest the topics for workshops. These workshops are considered very important to BEL in that they enable advisers to keep up to date with changes in benefit rules, and they also enable them to continue to provide a very high standard of service.

Quality training

Training in quality is regarded as one of the key ways of ensuring the success of BEL's quality programme. Every new employee has quality training as part of their initial course where a half-day workshop covers the concept of quality, BEL's approach to quality, and how the individual fits in.

External training and further and higher education

External training courses supplement those run by BEL's in-house team. Staff are able to nominate themselves for courses run by Benefits Agency Training, or where Benefits Agency Training cannot meet a particular need training can be obtained from other external sources. BEL also supports staff who wish to undertake further or higher education, offering both financial help and study leave – for example, during 1995 six members of BEL staff were working towards NVQ qualifications.

By late 1994 all of these new training and development ideas had been implemented. The last remaining initiative was a team event for all members of BEL staff.

Team event

The focus of this event was on teams, and to ensure value for money a group of BEL staff was trained in-house as event facilitators. The event comprised two exercises: firstly, there was a visioning exercise, where staff were encouraged to work in teams to discuss areas for improvement in current working practices and to consider new initiatives for BEL for the next five years. The second exercise looked at how BEL could publicize its services. Many new initiatives came from the day and have been included in BEL's 'Strategic Plan'. Feedback from the event showed that not only had staff taken a new interest in their work but that it also had helped morale, motivation and communication amongst the team.

Investors in People

BEL has made significant improvements in their training and development since they began and particularly since the beginning of 1994. In July of 1995 they received Investors in People accreditation in recognition of their achievements.

Setting standards and measuring performance

The importance of the customer

The importance of both the internal and external customers must not be forgotten in any Quality Improvement Programme. Consulting the customer leads to a better understanding of their needs and increases the likelihood of delivering a high-quality service.

Setting standards

To ensure that BEL's targets reflect customer priorities and are meaningful, they are set locally after consultation with staff and the 'External Customer Focus Group'. This customer group meets quarterly and includes people with disabilities, representatives from disability-linked groups, welfare rights groups, the National Association of Citizen's Advice Bureaux and of course members of the BEL team. In addition BEL is required to meet the Benefits Agency's national target of 85 per cent customer satisfaction, which is set by the Secretary of State.

Customer and staff research

Customer research enables BEL to tailor its services to customer's needs, with an annual in-depth survey which measures, amongst other things, customer satisfaction. Over the past three years this has risen, as can be seen from Figure 7.4, from 97 per cent to 99 per cent in 1994. Customer satisfaction is also tested daily to ensure that a high level of satisfaction is maintained throughout the year: one per cent of customers are contacted daily to ensure that they are satisfied with the service they have received and to ask for ideas for improvement.

Monitoring standards: BEL has a range of measurements to ensure that they make continuous improvement in all areas. The following chart shows the standards monitored, scope and responsibility.

Standard Monitored	Regularity	Scope	Responsibility
Customer Satisfaction (1)	Daily	1% of callers	Customer Services Team
(2)	Annually	Statistically valid proportion	Independent Research Co.
Call Attempt 1st/2nd try	Daily	Every 15th caller	Advisers
	Daily	1%	Customer Services Team
	Annually	Statistically valid proportion	Independent Research Co.
Call Answering	Weekly	Calls on ACD	Operations Manager
Complaint Handling	Weekly	100% of complaints	Customer Service Manager
Quality of Adviser Call Handling	Daily	75% of advisers	Quality Assurance Team

Recorded achievements

	BUSINESS RESULTS 92/93 TO 94/95: year on year comparisons						
Performance measured	Target 92/93 %	Result 92/93 %	Target 93/94 %	Result 93/94 %	Target 94/95%	Result 94/95 %	Improvement 92/3 to 94/5
1. Customer satisfaction Independent Survey – Advice Line	85	97	97	98	98	99	+2
2. Customer Satisfaction Independent Survey – Forms Completion	*	*	85	89	95	93	+0
3. Customer Services Daily 1% Survey	*	*					
– Advice Line			97	99.21	99	99.76	+.55
– Forms Completion			95	98.92	99	99.51	+.59
4. Quality of Adviser Call Handling	92	93	95	96.25	95	95	+3
5. Call Attempts 1st/2nd try	90	92	95	94	95	98	+8
6. Complaint Handling	† 72 hrs	100	48 hrs	100	48 hrs	100	Clearance
– Acknowledged	"	"	‡ in 24 hrs	100	in 24 hrs	100	times reduced
-- Written replies	"	"	‡ in 48 hrs	100	in 48 hrs	100	by 24 hr

Key: BA National Target
   * Measurement system not in place 92/93 year
   † BA National Target is 7 working days
   ‡ Measurement system enhanced April '93

Figure 7.4   BEL's achievements as recorded by the measurement system

If any customer is not satisfied then a manager contacts them to find out why and to put things right.

BEL conducts an annual service planning exercise in which it consults a wide range of internal and external customers about the services it provides and how they can be improved. Staff are also consulted in a SWOT (Strengths, Weaknesses, Opportunities and Threats) Analysis. The results of this exercise, plus customer feedback gathered during the year, are collated and analysed and used to formulate a strategic plan which BEL submits with its bid for resources from the central budget. When the resources are allocated BEL then formulates its operational business plan which is published and made available to customers.

Customer feedback is an additional method of ascertaining customer satisfaction. Despite a well-publicized complaints procedure BEL only receives approximately two complaint letters a month, yet they answer over 80,000 calls. In comparison, they receive many thank-you letters. All feedback is monitored and analysed to ascertain trends and to develop action plans for improvement. Moreover, all customer comments – whether positive or negative – are printed in a monthly newsletter and are also displayed on 'feedback notice boards' to keep staff informed of customer opinion.

Staff satisfaction is also considered important. Staff services is an area of the Benefits Agency Quality Framework and it is addressed through regular benchmarking against the rating scales of the framework. BEL's annual Staff Perception Survey also looks at staff satisfaction levels in all areas.

Measuring standards

BEL has a comprehensive system of measurement to ensure that its high-quality service is maintained and improved where possible according to customer needs.

All advisers have a quality standards guidance and procedures manual, written in consultation with staff, and have personal 'Quality Assurance' targets to meet. These standards are maintained by the Quality Assurance Team which tapes and checks a percentage of calls each day – BEL was awarded an OFTEL licence to allow them to carry out such quality checks. This system also informs training provision, in that areas of difficulty can be easily identified and quickly remedied.

BEL also keeps detailed statistics of calls received and lost, and how long it takes a customer to be connected. These are constantly monitored to observe patterns and trends which might affect service provision. Incoming call traffic is controlled by a British Telecom Call Plan and an Automated Call Distributor (ACD). The ACD is fully programmable and is managed on a reactive basis, thus allowing immediate implementation of pre-arranged contingency plans to respond to any unexpected increase in call traffic.

Benchmarking

As a further measurement of its standards BEL benchmarks its service in two ways : firstly by measuring its progress against the rating scales of the Benefits Agency Quality Framework and secondly by visiting other similar organizations both in the Benefits Agency and in the private sector and by comparing its service provision against theirs. For 1995 BEL is beginning a new, in-depth programme of benchmarking.

Management commitment

Demonstrating commitment

All BEL managers are very supportive of quality initiatives, always being open to suggestions for improvement and willing to give staff the time and resources to attend meetings and training courses. To underline this commitment, managers have a commitment to quality included in their 'Key Work Objectives', upon which their annual joint job appraisal reports are based. Managers work closely together and with their own teams towards the common goal of enabling BEL to give an excellent service to customers.

Developing a culture of teamworking

The BEL team as a whole, and the individual operational teams within it, have worked very hard at developing a culture of team working. The majority of staff are advisers, and because of this are somewhat isolated in their jobs. Managers can ensure that everyone is included in any consultation process and that everyone is able to attend a weekly team meeting. BEL also has potential problems in that the operational teams are divided between six floors of four separate buildings. Without inter-departmental co-operation this could become very divisive within the overall team.

Many of BEL's discussion groups and focus groups are intentionally cross-grade and cross-team to encourage teamworking and inter-departmental support. Each department also operates an 'open-door' policy and visitors from other areas are always welcome. Staff are able to spend some time working in other departments to gain a greater insight into the work of colleagues and as staff get to know each other, co-operation and mutual understanding grow to the benefit of all concerned.

REVIEW OF THE IMPLICATIONS OF THE PROGRAMME

The total quality programme has brought several benefits to BEL. For example, the quality initiative has focused on teamworking and staff have become more empowered and involved as a result. Processes have become more streamlined and efficient, thus representing better management of resources. Customers are regularly consulted and their views are used to help improve the service BEL offers. BEL also has developed a successful, effective and efficient complaints procedure. BEL's successes in achieving three quality awards has provided evidence of their achievements and all of this in turn has a beneficial effect on the standard of service given to the customer.

Embedding the programme

BEL's commitment to embedding the quality programme into its culture is demonstrated by their considerable investment in empowerment training for all staff, by the ethos of staff participation and involvement which is deeply rooted in BEL and in the successful operation of BEL's various discussion and focus groups. In addition, BEL is in the process of implementing a total quality system in their Information and Distribution Section, aiming to reach assessment standard in early 1996.

The latest development within BEL's quality programme is the European Model for Total Quality Management. They have been continuously improving towards this model since the end of 1994 and have already made significant steps in some areas.

A journey for life

BEL is aware that having embarked upon their quality programme they have begun a journey for life. Although they have been successful in the Benefits Agency Quality Award, and have achieved Charter Mark status and Investors in People accreditation, BEL are not complacent. They are constantly striving to build on their success and improve their services further by consulting customers, supporting staff, being proactive and managing budgets effectively. However, BEL acknowledges there is always room for improvement.

BEL's future

BEL's future within the Benefits Agency is both exciting and challenging. Its advisers are trained to provide a 'one-stop' advice and information service, and as the Benefits Agency moves towards its own 'one-stop' vision BEL advisers will clearly be at the forefront.

The Benefits Agency is also becoming increasingly quality-oriented. Again BEL is at the forefront of this drive by being one of a very small number of Benefits Agency units to hold three quality awards. They are, therefore, often asked to share their quality experience and expertise with other units – which they are very happy to do.

In the coming years BEL's commitment to providing an excellent service for people with disabilities will continue as their major priority. It is BEL's firm belief that the only route to true quality is through developing a united team: for them teamwork is the only road to success because they fundamentally believe in the maxim that *'together everyone achieves more'*.

REFERENCE

Oakland, J.S. (1989) *Total Quality Management*, Butterworth Heinemann, Oxford

EIGHT

BRITANNIA:

Quality improvement at Topsides Division

NICK JOHNS,
DEREK HARWOOD
AND
CHRIS GUYMER

EIGHT

Britannia:

Quality improvement at Topsides Division

INTRODUCTION

The Britannia gas and gas condensate field, located 130 miles north-east of Aberdeen, was discovered in the 1970s, but its potential was only confirmed by appraisal drilling in 1987. It is the biggest undeveloped North Sea gas reservoir, with estimated reserves calculated to last for up to 30 years. The field is owned by Chevron and Conoco (who are acting as a single operator) along with Union Texas, Santa Fe, Phillips and Texaco. In order to exploit the Britannia Field it is proposed to drill 18 (and eventually up to 45) development wells, served by a single steel platform and a single sub-sea centre. AMEC Process and Engineering Ltd holds the engineering and management contract for developing the field facilities, which includes the production platform, sub-sea production centre and associated flow-lines. Chevron and Conoco are 50 per cent shareholders in a single company, Britannia Operator Ltd (BOL). BOL is an innovative arrangement which provides a single identity for the development project. It owns no assets and does not make a profit. It exists only to develop and operate the Britannia field. It permits clear decision making, as well as many economies of scale and coherency. BOL employs no staff of its own. It has an integrated management structure, rather than parallel Chevron/Conoco organizations, and draws upon expertise from the partners freely as required. BOL and AMEC make up the basic Britannia Topsides team, which has been further expanded by adding contractors in topsides fabrication and hook-up and commissioning (HU&C). Together they form the Topsides Division of Britannia Operator Ltd.

Like its parent organization, Topsides Division is an integrated structure, with personnel drawn from both operating partners, from AMEC and from other major

Table 8.1 Breakdown of staff functions, Topsides Division

Function	Percentage of workforce
Engineering	50
Planning, cost control and procurement	20
Training and personnel	5
IT support	5
General management	5
Clerical, secretarial and house management	15

contractors. It is responsible for the design, fabrication and installation as well as the hook-up and commissioning of the topside facilities.

During its first year, Topsides Division concluded the preliminary phase of the project: selecting the basic form of development, procuring materials and beginning detailed engineering work. Project execution plans, training and communication strategies were also drawn up during this time. The Division grew rapidly through the year, increasing (in round figures) from 70 to 150 associated staff. By the end of 1994, personnel functions were approximately as shown in Table 8.1.

TOPSIDES' QUALITY JOURNEY

Topsides' strategy is ultimately driven by the key factors which influence the UK oil and gas industry as a whole. The UK continental shelf is now regarded as a mature field, where the easy pickings - large, easily-developed reservoirs under shallow waters, have already been exploited. Oil prices are comparatively low and future fields are likely to be small, while capital and operating costs have continued to rise rapidly. Topsides' priority is to reverse these rising costs, which otherwise put the future of oil and gas development in UK offshore waters in serious jeopardy.

An industry-wide initiative known as Cost Reduction In the New Era (CRINE) has been established since 1992 to address problems of rising costs and marginality. CRINE aims to achieve a transformation in the way the oil and gas industry works, aiming at reduced capital and operating costs. This can only be reached through equal and parallel efforts by oil companies, suppliers, manufacturers, contractors and providers of major services. At the heart of the initiative was the formal adoption by all sectors of the industry of the CRINE philosophy of standardization, simplification and open communication.

The Britannia project recognized from its inception that it would have to adopt all of the CRINE principles, but this was difficult during its early stages of evolution. Little material was available from CRINE, and as a result Britannia had to adapt many of the principles into an appropriate form. Communication and training were identified as a central thread in the CRINE philosophy. The challenge was to learn from past experience and to train personnel quickly enough to produce a significant benefit within the limited lifetime of the project. It was fundamental as a first step to change the organizational culture, so that every person on the project was oriented towards cutting costs and towards a general process of change.

Topsides produced its Division Execution Plan (DEP) during the first year of operation. This described in broad terms the scope of the work and detailed the management structure, style, culture and the use of procedures. The DEP specifically aimed to create a 'learning organization' to bring about the desired cultural change and hence achieve the cost reduction goals. All interested parties were consulted during preparation of the DEP, which was structured in a hierarchical way so that users could enter the system at the appropriate level. This avoided duplicating documents and allowed individual execution plans to remain small and user-friendly. The hierarchical structure also allowed the development plan to be cascaded down to all personnel in such a way that sections could maintain ownership of it. For example different sections were free to draw up their own mission statement within that of the Division.

A new non-adversarial mode of contract management, called Alliancing, optimizes the learning process. Alliancing focuses individual capabilities, by rewarding partners according to the final out-turn cost of the whole Division, not just their basic share. The Topsides Alliance consists of the operator (BOL), AMEC, the fabricators and the HU&C contractor. Alliancing maximizes cost reduction, operability, quality and safety by eliminating layers of management. Experts from each company interface directly and training is provided to help team members to work together. AMEC's management team was expanded to include a senior representative from each of the Alliance participants to maintain the project objectives (safety, environmental, schedule, quality and cost).

Inclusion of operations personnel ensured that the operator's requirements were incorporated into the design from the start. During the first year, multi-disciplinary value engineering teams also examined alternative design options and identified opportunities for cost savings. The 'zero-based engineering' concept was adopted, which aims to achieve each process function with a single equipment item (a special case must be made if one item is not considered adequate). Besides helping to control capital costs, the zero-based approach reduces inventories, addresses issues of redundant equipment and promotes safety.

Topsides' working ethos embraces the principle of empowerment, devolving a considerable amount of management control downwards to the people closest to the work. This gives clearer definition of accountability and responsibility. Lead engineers are budget holders for their discipline, increasing both their accountability and their insight into the project as a whole. A consultative approach to planning has allowed work groups to relate to the Division's external customers, to better understand internal customers and to adjust their outputs to meet customers' needs.

Topsides Division has held a number of specific reviews and technology transfer sessions, where engineers from partner companies have examined and discussed progress. Engineers from AMEC's other oil and gas project have also been invited to make suggestions. In parallel with this there have been peer reviews, in which specialist teams from the other corporate organizations have probed and challenged the Topsides Division's work. A project 'think tank' within the Division itself contains personnel from a variety of backgrounds who examine and promote new opportunities. A steering committee reviews the think tank's ideas and considers how to incorporate them into the project work.

At the beginning of the project, a communications team examined the flow of information throughout the organization, recommending that a variety of communication media and processes be used. The Division responded by setting up a system of bulletin boards, newsletters and group communication meetings, targeted at various organizational levels.

QUALITY IMPROVEMENT IN PRACTICE

A Division-wide system re-engineering exercise took place during 1994 to eliminate non-value-adding activities. This process was relatively new to the oil and gas industry and time had to be allocated in accustoming staff to it and in explaining its function. Each work group produced a process map showing its traditional activities on a sheet of brown paper, in what became known as the 'brown paper exercise'. The groups then examined how the current chart reflected current customer needs and whether advances in information technology or other facilities made it possible to do things more efficiently. They paid particular attention to their output and to the specific requirements of their internal and external customers. As a result of this exercise, each group produced a new 'brown paper', containing the basis for an improved work process. These proposals were examined by peer groups, who made further suggestions for improvement. The finalized process maps were used to update execution plans, schedules and scope of work definitions. The exercise brought substantial cost savings through a 30 per cent reduction in engineering man-hours and avoided customer/supplier misunderstandings. It also gave rise to activity control packs (ACPs), which defined the detailed scope of engineering work. In addition everyone in the organization learned what everyone else did, and this further increased team bonding and focused staff awareness on customer satisfaction. Britannia Topsides also uses the innovative RACI tool (standing for Responsible, Accountable, Consult and Inform) to review a work sequence and identify each party's role.

Despite all efforts, Topsides' first proposal for the Britannia design configuration was rejected by BOL and their co-venturers on economic grounds. Rather than abandon the project, the Division was able within only three months (the time period set by the operator) to develop a new design concept at a still lower cost. This enormous feat was achieved as a result of the previous successful culture change and the development of a learning organization. Team spirit within Topsides was greatly enhanced by this achievement, which also pinpointed the key factors for success:

- Clearly identified, concentrated focus
- Use of personnel from all disciplines, to exploit individual strengths
- Use of quality management techniques such as brainstorming
- Effective communication at every level, through a variety of media.

Following this success Topsides Division had the further challenge of ensuring that the project would be accepted by the Government and the co-venturers. During the following four months, the Government was assured that the new field would be drained effectively and safely. Topsides Division also demonstrated to the co-venturers that the proposals were robust and accurate, and that the final out-turn cost would be achieved with at least a 35 per cent probability (the industry norm at this stage of a project).

Another aspect of Topsides quality improvement was the development of special teams for problem solving and system improvement. This complemented the Alliance initiative, which was aimed at contractors and service-providers. Specialist teams included:

- Maintenance team who reviewed equipment activities, including enquiries, purchase orders, maintenance and material requirements and operational expenditure.
- Certifying authority, with responsibility for design safety, located in the project offices. (Often they are remote from the project.)
- Control system supplier. (A contractor with a full-time in-house representative.)
- Operational representatives, permanently located in the project office to provide input about the operators' problems and perspectives of the work.

QUALITY EDUCATION AND TRAINING

Initiatives such as the Alliance concept represent considerable innovations in the industry. Education and training have been essential for changing the organizational culture of Topsides and for developing new approaches. Topsides Division believes that improvements will only begin to happen when all personnel understand the need for them in their working practices. Education and training are seen as the means to achieve these ends. They are addressed in three main areas: induction, team-building, and the development of individual skills.

Rapid growth in personnel numbers within Topsides Division means that induction sessions must be held weekly for new starters to the project. Induction helps new personnel to understand project issues and get a good overview of the project. There are also one-day follow-up sessions about a month after induction, where individuals talk about the mission, values and objectives of the project.

Team-building is mainly achieved through the TWINE (Team Work In the New Era) workshops, which aim to:

- improve understanding of the project goals;
- underline the importance of skills and tools to achieve goals;
- strengthen teamwork;
- develop action plans for practical project issues.

About a dozen individuals attend each workshop, drawn from a cross-section of discipline groups within the Division. The day is structured around project goals' individual needs. A member of the management team attends throughout the day, and others usually join a working lunch, where employees can put questions to them. At the close of the sessions, individuals present action plans, so that there is continuity between the workshop and the workplace.

Besides the TWINE workshops, tailor-made workshops are set up as required, for example to address specific internal issues. Sometimes two groups train together, to improve the working interface. Such workshops have been run for the Topsides management team (that is, the Topsides manager and five senior Section Managers) on styles of working, avoiding adversarial attitudes and improving goal focus.

Individuals can address their personal training needs using the project open learning resources centre. Training materials in a variety of media (for example, interactive video, computer-based learning, VHS video and written packages) are available through a catalogue on the computer network. Topics include business management and managing change, international industry issues, project management and personal effectiveness. Internal and external personnel with particular skills may also run training courses as required.

Information technology has dramatically affected Topsides Division's operations, and it was recognized at an early stage that its staff would have to be computer-literate. An Information technology Competence Programme (ICP) provides ongoing training in the applications available on the project network. The ICP administrator is a dedicated post responsible for running the programme. Each new trainee is also assigned a local facilitator, a computer-competent individual who can help with problems and questions as they arise. The principles of the ICP are threefold:

- Shared commitment between Topsides and its personnel: the Division provides resources and support, while individual personnel are expected to participate in their own time.
- There are six basic programme modules, dealing with aspects such as word processing, spreadsheets and graphics. They are run on a self-study basis, though occasionally classroom sessions may be made available to support learning.
- The programme uses learning materials specifically designed to Topsides' needs.

New personnel are introduced to the ICP during induction sessions. They then register for programmes, which they study by working through the interactive module booklets, referring to the learning materials as necessary. At the end they complete a short competence test which is marked by the ICP administrator. A senior manager then awards the certificate if they achieve the required standard. Progress (numbers trained, modules used and individual achievements) is recorded by the training department and posted on the notice boards. The ICP evolves constantly to keep up to date with the needs of the Division. A recent innovation has been the nomination of 'champions' who liaise with their work group colleagues, identifying needs and encouraging them to participate in training. Besides the in-house ICP, staff occasionally attend outside courses to learn new techniques such as AutoCAD. When they return they pass on this knowledge to colleagues on a cascading basis. For instance, a new CAD room has been set up in the project office, in which all new CAD operators receive at least one day's training. This may be followed by specific additional training as required.

Topsides' personnel development is also achieved through the innovative SPACE (Sharing Performance and Career Expectations) initiative. The work performance of all individuals is considered against the agreed tasks which make up their job. Reviews take place every six months, with an extra review at the close of each project assignment. SPACE offers a structured way to inventory specific strengths and to identify weaknesses for corrective action. Reviews are in two parts: performance reviews consider current project assignments, while development reviews deal with longer-term career progression. They are conducted by supervisors and result in agreed targets which conform to 'SMART' criteria (that is, they must be Specific, Measurable, Achievable, Realistic and Timely).

MEASURING QUALITY PERFORMANCE

Each oil and gas installation is a one-off design and build operation, each project having its own unique characteristics and problems. Topsides' work is therefore basically a once-through process, rather than a work cycle. This affects the quality improvement approach, since classical Continuous Performance Improvement (CPI) work cycle techniques are not generally appropriate. However, comparison to previous projects is possible after normalization, since AMEC have provided data from all their previous work. Topsides is firmly committed to CPI principles. It is not possible to apply one or two overall measurements, due to the size and diversity of the work. Therefore a wide range of measurement techniques are used to monitor and regulate performance. These cover softer, less accessible aspects such as quality of design, customer satisfaction, employee motivation and team integration, as well as the traditional elements of cost, time, materials and progress.

Britannia uses metrics and benchmarking techniques widely to gauge itself against previous projects,. and ensure that its performance is 'best in class'. In addition, measurements make it possible to:

- feedback progress to all working on the project;
- set tough targets;
- stimulate further cost reduction;
- provide both high- and low-level monitoring tools to supplement other project controls;
- provide comparative metrics for future projects.

The project has put considerable effort into identifying the most appropriate metrics for monitoring performance. The most important metrics are those most closely linked to the critical cost/quality drivers. As well as the 'high-level' metrics which were selected to measure the performance of the Division as a whole, each discipline has identified the best 'low-level' metrics to monitor its progress and ensure that its performance is stretched. Some examples of metrics used at Topsides are shown in Table 8.2.

Topsides Division constantly examines new areas for measurement. One proposed focus is the number of supplier documents, which currently cost the project around 5 per cent of the total equipment cost (that is, £6 million). Trials have shown that it is possible to achieve a 50 per cent reduction in the numbers of documents needed for purchasing and packaging equipment. The number of individuals who need to see these documents has also been reduced, bringing further resource savings. The time taken between issuing an initial enquiry to placing the order is another metric used. Analysis of past projects indicates a typical procurement cycle of 16 weeks, with the best in class 14 weeks. Topsides aims to reduce this to 12 weeks overall for the Britannia project.

Audits monitor the quality of Topsides' work at regular intervals, ensuring that the design conforms to technical and statutory requirements and follows sound engineering practices. Audits also examine alternative designs and advise on possible improvements to the design process. All major documents with a multi- disciplinary input are subject to specific safety reviews by specially convened review teams. There are also regular AMEC corporate safety audits which aim to:

Table 8.2 Summary of high-level metrics at Topsides Division

	Measurement objective	High-level metric
1	Overall capital efficiency in producing reserves	Topsides Capital expenditure/Barrels per day of oil equivalent (BOE) recoverable
2	Efficiency of capital costs in providing a specific oil output capacity	Topsides Capital expenditure/BOE design capacity
3	Topsides dry weight as a contributor to designed oil output capacity.	Tonnes/BOE design capacity
4	Topsides capital efficiency per tonne of structure	Topsides Capital expenditure/Tonne (i.e. metric no. 1 divided by metric no.3)
5	Fabrication cost efficiency as a contributor to total capital cost	Percentage fabrication cost of total Topsides Capital expenditure (factors out effects of fluctuations on market conditions)

- obtain positive evidence that company safety policies are being implemented;
- discuss and agree actions to be taken to resolve any outstanding safety issues;
- provide a forum in which lead engineers can express any concerns about the safety of the project.

Schedule milestones are very important at Topsides. Three-dimensional computer models showing current progress are common in the industry, but Topsides Division has developed a program which rates the maturity (that is, the up-to-date accuracy) of all data items shown on the model on a 1–5 scale. Customers can then decide whether to start an activity in a particular area, or wait for more mature data.

Personnel are encouraged to be innovative. Anyone can add a new idea to the 'good ideas' database on the Britannia computer network. The Division can thus draw upon the creativity of all its personnel and capture good ideas as they arise, and new ideas statistics are published regularly. Previous projects have also been reviewed in order to learn from past mistakes. One of the design disciplines has used questionnaires to identify problems noted by its members from past projects. Their findings have been added to the good ideas database, presented to other teams and incorporated into project procedures and guidance notes.

No task can be reported as 100 per cent complete and closed out unless the customer's acceptance has been recorded. This is done through ACPs (the activity control packs introduced as a result of the 'brown paper' process mapping exercises). Each ACP identifies the customer of the activity and specifies the format of the output. The group which produces this output is only awarded 80 per cent completion (even though the task may be 100% complete) until the recipient agrees that the product has been delivered as specified. A database reports how quickly the different groups' output is accepted. Another example of close customer relationships is the electronic transfer of data from the process group to the piping group. This gives the stress engineer a much better overview of the maturity of the process and of any changes. An interactive line list allows the piping group to control further process design after stress calculations have begun so that further changes can only be introduced with their agreement.

The satisfaction of all Britannia personnel is surveyed and measured both quantitatively and qualitatively. Results of this survey were used (for example) to formulate the Division's CPI plan. A questionnaire survey within Topsides Division has shown general acceptance of the need for change. Topsides management also regularly invite personnel to air their concerns on issues affecting the project and its management. These issues are addressed at regular communications sessions at which all personnel are welcome. The Topsides Division manager also meets regularly with the design team during normal work time to discuss issues raised by the engineers.

QUALITY ACHIEVEMENTS

In terms of high-level metrics, Topsides Division has achieved considerable performance improvements over previous projects. These can be seen from Figures 8.1 and 8.2.

Low-level statistics such as the ratio of structural design man-hours per tonne of integrated deck show a comparable achievement. The Division has an effective cost control system in place, based upon the principle of empowerment. There are also 600 cost-saving ideas in the data bank, many of which have been acted upon, and all of which demonstrate the teamwork ethos of Topsides personnel. There has been a saving of around £10 million since the inception of the good ideas programme. Other initiatives include the engagement of specialist consultants to facilitate programmes in benchmarking, in procurement and Alliancing.

Weight control has made it possible to monitor the viability of the design precisely in terms of dry, lift and operating weights. Measurements showed an initial decrease in operating weight, to an acceptable plateau some 500 tonnes below the maximum acceptable weight. Near the end of the first year of design, this began to increase slowly to just below the maximum. At the time of writing Topsides is actively investigating this potential threat to the project. Weight control has also made it possible to hold the integrated deck lift weight within viable parameters.

ICP attendance and completion figures reveal the tremendous impact of this initiative upon staff IT competence. Questionnaires (completed by all attendees) have provided valuable feedback about the training programmes and the way they are managed. Customer satisfaction data relating to engineering output is measured in a number of ways. In addition to ensuring that deliverables are issued on time, the ACP database has a number of pre-loaded reports available for monitoring quality and customer acceptance of the work. These include for example:

- *'ACP outputs completed but not accepted or rejected'* gives working groups constant visibility of the outputs which have been received but not acknowledged as accepted or rejected.
- *'ACP outputs completed but rejected'* enables working groups to identify and correct quality problems.
- *'ACP outputs not received'* provides a tool for listing work deliverables which have been issued but not acknowledged as received by customers.

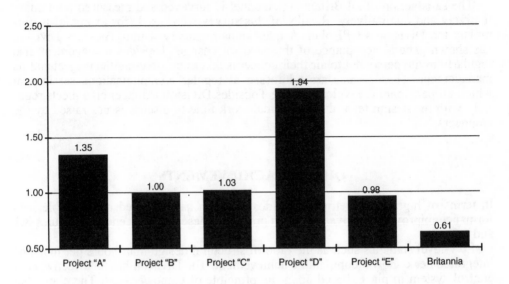

Figure 8.1 Capital cost/BOE recoverable, comparison with other projects

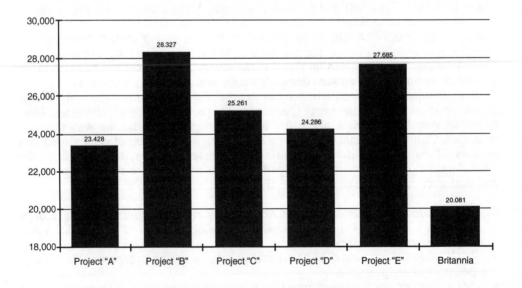

Figure 8.2 Capital cost/dry weight, comparison with other projects

Surveys show that Topsides Division personnel are committed to changing their working practices and believe that positive attitudes towards change are valuable and will increase in the future. Also the end customer, BOL Operations, expresses satisfaction at all levels with the product as it takes shape.

MANAGEMENT COMMITMENT AND RECOGNITION

The management team's (TMT's) commitment to Topsides' quality process is clear from the variety of quality initiatives already discussed. Their open, consultative management style is quite different from the 'command and control' approach traditional in the industry. In order to achieve it the TMT have undergone extensive training and team building themselves in order to shape the way they work. They are also demonstrably committed to training, education and communication, through their input on induction and feedback sessions. Topsides management have underwritten considerable resources to support training initiatives such as TWINE and ICP. The TMT demonstrates its commitment to the Alliance by inviting the participation of representatives from all Alliance participants.

During 1994 three separate incentive schemes for personnel were examined and tested by Topsides. However, the potential divisiveness of schemes which involved extra payments or shares in the company raised concerns, and none was implemented in full. In the system that was eventually adopted, a candidate (small group or individual) can be nominated by supervisors, peers or subordinates. Awards are made by a committee and consist of recognition through a bulletin report, a tangible memento such as a tie pin and entry to an annual draw.

FUTURE DEVELOPMENTS

The next phase faced by Topsides Division during 1995 is the establishment of the full Topsides Alliance, by bringing in the remaining fabrication and offshore hook-up contractors to the team. By this time virtually all key purchase orders will have been issued. Manufacture of necessary equipment and the fabrication of platform modules will have begun. The total workforce will increase in round figures from 150 to 2000, including those at Alliance member companies. The current, predominantly professional white-collar workforce will give way to a high proportion of blue-collar workers and the geographical base will widen to include three fabrication sites in the UK and supplier companies located worldwide. Britannia's present quality improvement thrust will continue on its present basis of cultural and procedural change.

Cultural change

Induction and feedback sessions involving senior management will be maintained. TWINE workshops will also be maintained, but with their format revised to allow for the changing workforce. Teamworking sessions will be conducted at all sites, as well as with teams drawn from different locations. The latter will establish a link between personnel at different sites. A specialist consulting group will be engaged to develop the team-building process within the Alliance. TWINE and other team-building sessions will be substantially increased, and there will be greater emphasis on the visibility of targets and achievements at all locations.

Procedural change

Two areas, procurement and the Alliance, have been identified for major cost-saving initiatives. Tools and procedures are being created to develop these ideas and training sessions are planned. In the area of procurement, the supplier quality initiative will improve communication and minimize unnecessary data flow. In addition, 'win–win' relationships will be developed, in which contracts are adjusted to produce cost benefits for both the project and its suppliers.

Alliancing initiatives will aim at integrated work programmes between designers and fabricators, which recognize critical factors, yet leave scope for adjustment to suit local work conditions. There will also be efforts to minimize growth and change, which have led to poorer quality and higher costs on other projects.

The Britannia Supplier Quality Initiative (BSQI) will also gather momentum. Senior management will visit suppliers and fabrication sites to inform the workforce about the Topsides project and its quality ethos. Structured process mapping along 'brown paper' lines will be extended to all work sites and built into all working practices. A specific resource group will develop some of the improvement initiatives outlined earlier. They will get the change message and the Topside goals across to all locations and all new entrants. They will also train key members of the existing project supervisory group to conduct further team-building exercises at all organizational levels. Team-building has been found to be more effective when conducted by known team members, rather than by external consultants. Quality assurance ethos and procedures will be extended to all fabrication contractors using new relevant performance indicators, which will provide accessible feedback for all personnel.

The Division continues to review performance recognition schemes in order to find an optimum balance between maximum individual motivation and minimum team disruption. The Division is also considering ways in which it can improve its social awareness goals, which include donations to charities, away-days and parties. In this way it hopes to continue on the quality road for this project and for many projects to come.

NINE

RHP Bearings Ltd Ferrybridge:

Rolling out a programme of culture change through structured involvement

ANDREW LOCKWOOD
AND
MARK THOMPSON

NINE

RHP BEARINGS LTD FERRYBRIDGE:

Rolling out a programme of culture change through structured involvement

INTRODUCTION

This case example provides a picture of a traditional precision engineering-based manufacturing company, supplying a range of bearings and other products to other companies for inclusion in their own products. Although somewhat protected from the demands of the end customer, the company is nonetheless striving to improve the levels of quality throughout the manufacturing process and has recognized that will be achieved best through the direct involvement of all members of the workforce. Based in the heart of a traditional industrial area, it was recognized that to achieve this aim would require a two-stage process. First, putting into place the necessary structures to allow and encourage involvement in all parts of the operation and second, changing the culture to make this participation second nature.

RHP Bearings Ltd Ferrybridge is one of the seven manufacturing sites making up the RHP group which employs a total of over 2500 people. Formed in 1969 by the amalgamation of Ransom, Hoffmann and Pollard, the company was acquired in 1990 by one of the world's leading bearing companies, NSK. The Ferrybridge site was founded in 1946 and now employs around 620 people, making it one of RHP's largest sites. Ferrybridge has four main product lines: Self Lube Inserts and Units, Integral Shaft Bearings and Radial and Clutch Ball Bearings. Manufacturing these products involves the co-ordination of five major processes: the supply of raw materials, turning, heat treatment, grinding and assembly.

The RHP group launched its Total Quality programme in 1992 with the objective of achieving business excellence. The commitment of top management was demonstrated with the formation of a Total Quality Steering Committee and by communicating the company's aims through the introduction of business reviews, missions and policy statements. It was obvious, however, by the start of 1994, that these initiatives alone had not developed the desired team-based approach at the Ferry-bridge site for the reasons highlighted in Figure 9.1.

Before 1994, there was really only a handful of teams in regular operation and they tended to be working on problems that had been set for them by management. The reasons for this were many but included the fact that although the teams were receiving problem-solving training there was little ongoing support and little attempt to assess the effectiveness of the training they had received. In addition, there were no formal reviews in place to allow the teams to present their progress and discuss the problems they were trying to overcome. The recognition for participation in the teams was also very limited and was not even consistent across the Ferrybridge site. Even if the teams had been working efficiently, their achievements would have been limited by the fact that, in general, people did not have any vision of the future of the factory. They did not know where the factory should be heading or what objectives needed to be achieved to reach those targets. If the teams had this information they might still not have recognized how their team could have contributed to making it happen. From the management perspective, improvement initiatives were largely reactive – once a problem had arisen, a team was directed to look into it – and there was little attempt to plan for proactive continuous improvement.

It was recognized that to develop teamworking throughout the site there would have to be a change in the culture of the organization and the way in which the teams were involved in the day-to-day operation of the site. The vehicle chosen to drive this change was the Total Manufacturing Concept illustrated in Figure 9.2.

Changing the culture of any organization is a difficult and long-term project. The Total Manufacturing Concept (TMC) provides a structure to the policy deployment process which ensures that all parts of the organization are informed of the company's vision for the future and the targets they are involved in reaching. It then allows them to become involved in finding the best way to meet those targets. As confidence in the system grows and as the culture adapts to the team approach, teams at all levels take a more active involvement in deciding future strategies. Until this culture is strongly in place the TMC structure provides the support to make sure that targets will be achieved and so reinforce the teams' feelings of success.

Figure 9.2 shows that the RHP mission is set at Board level and is translated into the group policy. This overall group policy becomes the focus for the Ferrybridge Factory Policy. This policy, expressed as a series of strategies and targets, is passed down to individual process departments. These departments, incorporating the three-year product manufacturing plans, develop their own annual targets. These in turn are passed on to individual teams for their contribution to be identified. Once the manufacturing departments have agreed their plans, these are passed on to the support departments who develop their own policy at departmental and at team level. In this way, annual plans and targets are translated into individual site plans, which in turn become departmental and task team targets.

THE QUALITY JOURNEY

RHP Bearings have, therefore, developed a clear strategy on how they can evolve into a total involvement operation. Initially this started at group level where a Total Quality Steering Group was established. This group, made up of the main Board of Directors and the group Total Quality Manager, has developed the Mission Statement shown below which shows the company's long-term objectives.

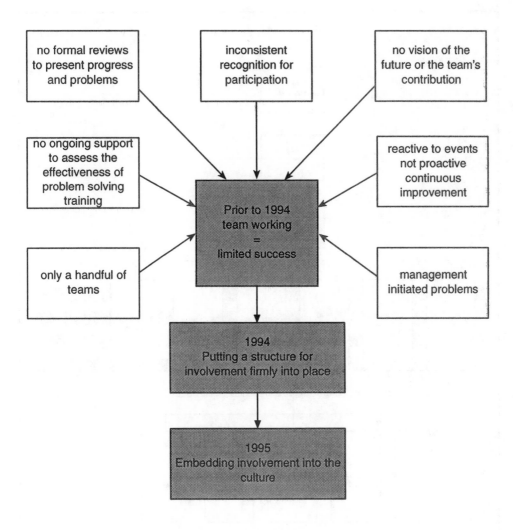

Figure 9.1 Moving quality forward at Ferrybridge

MISSION

- To be the leading manufacturer and supplier of high-quality bearings to our key markets throughout the world
- Through a policy of continuous improvement and attention to our customer needs, our mission is to achieve world-class standards in all areas of manufacturing and services, at all times recognizing our duty towards the environment.
- To ensure that our employees are properly trained and are recognized as a major resource in pursuit of excellence.

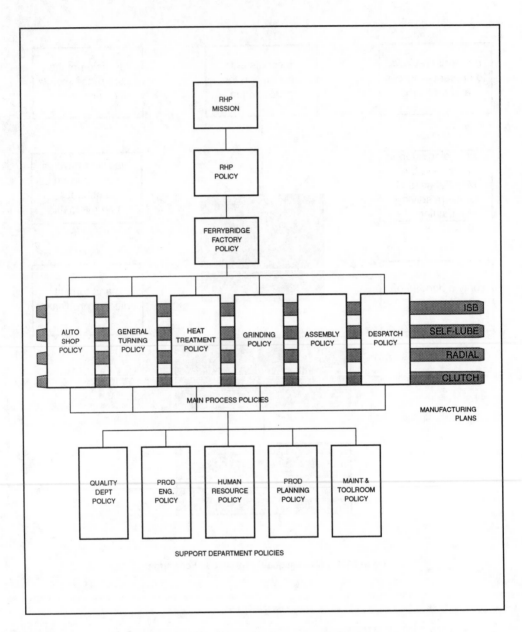

Figure 9.2   The Total Manufacturing Concept

With this mission firmly in mind, annually the TQ Steering Group develops an RHP Bearings policy statement that gives a clear focus for the next year. All the factories and divisions are involved in this process to gain commitment and acceptance at the factory and divisional levels. The RHP policy for 1994 is shown below.

RHP POLICY 1994

- To play its part in NSK's group strategy, RHP will be expected to supply core products worldwide.
- Therefore we must continuously improve Quality, Cost and Delivery to the world-class standard of NSK.
- We will achieve this by pursuing Total Quality with
  - thorough communication
  - and strong teamwork

By achieving these objectives we shall enhance the RHP brand and contribute positively to our community.

Once the group policy for 1994 was agreed, the Ferrybridge management team developed their own factory policy together with the factory strategies and targets for 1994 shown below.

FERRYBRIDGE POLICY 1994

Continuously improve Quality, Cost and Delivery through capable processes, standardized training and teamwork. Champion safety, encourage involvement.

The strategies and targets are identified against the key areas of quality (Q), cost (C), delivery (D), safety (S) and people (P).

FERRYBRIDGE STRATEGIES FOR 1994

QCDSP   **Housekeeping**
Achieve pride at Ferrybridge through further improvements in housekeeping.

QCD   **Core Products**
Achieve world-class manufacturing standards.
(a) Enhance QCD levels to competitively supply worldwide.
(b) Implement Superfinishing, new seal designs and grease specification.
(c) Expand capacity through increased productivity and flexibility.
(d) Fulfil NSK requirements and orders.

D   **Delivery**
To reduce product arrears by 25%.

QCDP   **People**
Enhance job satisfaction and motivation through involvement site-wide.
Teamwork within and across departments.
Standardized training.
Improved communication.

CD   **Scrap**
            FScrap 94 down 30%.
CSP   **Environment and Safety**
            Reduce industrial disposal.
            Promote recycling.
            Save energy.
            Establish a safe working environment.

	1994 Target	
Assembly output £K/Day	UP	50%
Despatch output £K/Day	UP	70%
Scrap %	DOWN	30%
Output value/attendance hour	UP	25%
Product arrears	DOWN	25%
Standard hours/working day	UP	50%

The factory policy and strategies are deployed through all the manufacturing departments where policies and plans are written and agreed involving employees at all levels. Also considered are the long-term manufacturing plans for the factory products, shown as Integral Shaft Bearings (ISB), Self Lube, Clutch and Radial bearings. Once all the manufacturing departments have completed their policies and plans, the support departments write their policies and plans specifically to link into and support all the manufacturing operations.

This clear structure for policy deployment could not be relied on to achieve the desired results without a similarly clear process of review. There are systematic review schedules for all parts of the policy deployment process, with time-scales varying from daily to annual. These can be seen in Figure 9.3.

In order of time-scale these reviews include:

1. Output Review. These daily meetings take place between the internal customers' and suppliers' heads of department to review the production output requirements and identify any appropriate countermeasures as they are required.
2. Factory Indicator Reviews. Bi-weekly, departmental heads meet to review factory performance against targets and to agree any necessary countermeasures to ensure that targets can be met.
3. Departmental Review. Departmental meetings also take place monthly, to review departmental performance against the agreed indicators.
4. Review of Performance. Each month, the Group Chief Executive, Financial Director and Operations Director, with the Ferrybridge Management Team, meet to review the factory performance against its indicators and to identify any areas where assistance may be required.
5. Quarterly Review. At Ferrybridge, the Factory Policy, Aims, Strategies and performance indicators are reviewed each quarter and are amended as necessary to ensure that they continue to meet the factory's requirements at the strategic level. The same procedure is then followed at departmental level to ensure their strategies still reflect the factory strategies.
6. Annual Review. At the end of each year all departmental performances are reviewed alongside the factory performance, identifying strengths, weaknesses and

therefore, opportunities for the coming year. At the same time, the factory goes through a self-assessment process to the European Quality Model (EQM) as defined by the European Foundation for Quality Management. Any actions highlighted from this review then form key elements to be included in the plans for the following year.

To a large extent, the overall effectiveness of the strategies and plans is dependent upon the effectiveness of this dissemination process. Therefore, all employees are kept fully aware of the company's, site's and department's progress during the year. Ferrybridge had established team briefings several years ago and this mechanism was used to keep all employees informed on progress. A major presentation was made to all employees in March 1994, outlining the plans for the future. In addition, all the group, factory and local department policies, strategies and targets, updated monthly, are displayed on local notice boards, so that all employees are aware of them.

With this structure in place, several other moves were made to start to move the culture of the factory towards the desired team-based approach.

1. Early in 1994, as an initiative to overcome barriers, all site work-wear was made the same. All managers, team leaders and shop floor colleagues wear the same general style and colour of work-wear. Within the factory, there is little doubt that this has broken down barriers.
2. Team rooms have been established all around the site. These have been built to allow for team meetings to take place and at the same time have provided better mess facilities.
3. Greater degrees of flexibility have been introduced so that any employee should be capable of and prepared to work anywhere in the factory to increase production. This initiative has also included managers spending time working on the production lines.
4. Team leaders now act as tour guides for any site visitors, and they usually involve their team colleagues to explain issues on their line.
5. Visual display boards have been set up throughout the factory, maintained by team leaders, showing task team work. They show the nature of the problems the team is currently tackling, the team members involved, the stages of the PDCA problem-solving process and all achievements to date.

With these initiatives in place, the move from a highly traditional 'us' and 'them' culture towards self-directed teams and shop floor empowerment within the clear structure of the Total Manufacturing Concept has been started. Thus has generated several key examples that have involved people in teamwork activities. These are described in the next section.

THE DEPLOYMENT OF QUALITY IMPROVEMENT THROUGHOUT THE ORGANIZATION

The following examples provide an indication of the involvement of all areas of the factory in teamwork initiatives, and also show the extent of the participation and the ways in which any difficulties encountered were overcome.

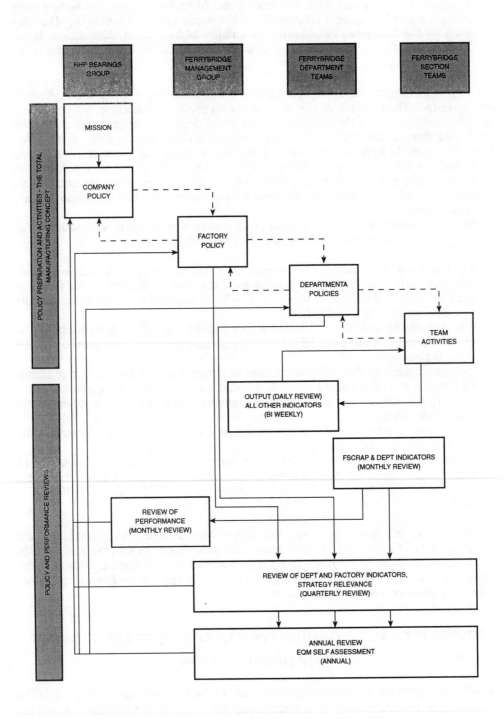

Figure 9.3   The policy and review process

Example 1: FScrap 1994

With the reduction of factory scrap (FScrap) identified as one of the key targets for 1994, the company set up a steering committee to develop a clear strategy and to plan to reduce rejects by 30 per cent during 1994. Indeed, 'FSCRAP DOWN 30%' became a factory-wide slogan, and the objective was communicated from top to bottom and across the organization.

The comprehensive data already available from the Quality Assurance department was put to immediate good use. Analysis enabled the teams to understand the current situation regarding scrap and reject levels throughout the factory. A network grid of trend graphs and Pareto items was produced, and this information was communicated to all areas, with the belief that if it was being measured, it could be managed and improved. Each department identified its own areas for improvement based on the Pareto data available.

The already established improvement teams were using problem-solving tools and techniques, but with limited success, and so it was decided that there was a need for some retraining in problem-solving techniques if the focus on FSCRAP DOWN 30% was to be a success. The teams, which were all made up of volunteers, took part in comprehensive training as a team in specific quality problem-solving methods, including Plan, Do, Check, Act (PDCA), Brainstorming, Cause and Effect analysis and Pareto analysis.

Some of the previous year's team initiatives had run out of steam. One of the major causes of this was identified as the perceived lack of attention given to these teams. The strategy to overcome this was to develop a formal review schedule, where each improvement team would give a short presentation monthly to the FScrap Steering Committee, consisting of experienced managers and engineers. The purpose was for the teams to update the committee on progress and the committee to provide continual support and guidance to each team so their targets could be met. The support could be given in many forms, for example ensuring that the relevant resources, such as skilled labour, funding and time to perform tasks, were made available. The reviews also identified teams that were making excellent progress and others who needed further training or additional help in extra team members. The emphasis was clearly on levelling up the teams to achieve best practice across the board.

Communication from these reviews also became a platform for good news and progress, resulting in improved morale and friendly internal competition. Teams made comprehensive use of the new notice boards, showing planned actions and trends that were visible to anyone walking into the area.

FScrap achieved many things: rejects were down 18 per cent, scrap was down 30 per cent, there were fifteen teams involved with over 90 people directly involved. Because of the success achieved from FScrap 94 Down 30%, FSCRAP 95 was targeted to reduce scrap by 50 per cent. The programme has been reviewed and improved so that it is the top four Pareto items that are being addressed with real force. These four items potentially affect more than one area, and so the teams for 1995 are mainly cross-functional.

Example 2: Integral Shaft Bearing (ISB)

ISBs are used on water pump bearings, and have been made by RHP Ferrybridge for 35 years. They are supplied to the automotive industry, to customers such as Ford, Volvo and Peugeot, and are an important component in the engine coolant system as part of the water coolant pump. The bearing is manufactured to a strict specification, and competition across Europe to produce a high quality product at a minimum cost is particularly intense.

A cross-functional task team was established to develop an action plan to improve the product quality, cost and delivery to meet the needs of the automotive industry for the future. The team, led by Production Engineering, comprised people from many aspects of the business, including Sales, Marketing, Manufacturing, Quality, and Production Planning. There was a core team of ten, but in total over 70 people became involved in the project, with many sub-teams addressing the key problems identified.

These problems included a large percentage of rejects after the seals had been assembled, final durability tests were proving only just successful, grease leakage results were poor, and noisy bearings were being identified by customers.

A range of standard problem-solving tools and techniques was used by the teams, including Design of Experiments (Taguchi), to identify what could be done to reduce grease leakage and increase durability. Most of the resulting actions, which required product and process design improvements, have now been scheduled into the three-year ISB manufacturing plans on a priority basis.

The product improvement results to date are extremely encouraging, but just as important are the barriers that have been broken down, not only at the Ferrybridge site, but also between Manufacturing and Design, Sales and Marketing, which are at a different site.

Example 3: Open Day

An Open Day Committee was established involving some fourteen employees. The Open and Fun Day in September 1994, open to current and retired employees and their families, where everything from charity stalls to factory tours was available, was the first to be held. The obvious purpose was to increase morale and motivation, but there were also clear benefits to the company with people working together from all departments breaking down internal barriers. The day was such a success that the Open Day will become an annual event.

Example 4: Line approach

A major change in the way the grinding shop operates was introduced in 1994. This involved the establishment of flow lines for the core products and the movement of some 90 machines during the summer shutdown period. This was achieved through two task teams involving people from all levels of the factory. The first team's objective was to select the best machines to go onto the lines and to decide how these should be laid out. The second team looked at the people and health and safety issues. The result of these teams, which involved some twenty people, was that the moves were finished on schedule and they have since led to a 30 per cent improvement in productivity.

These examples alone, not to mention the teams working on vending facilities and terms and conditions of employment, show how quickly the team approach has led to significant benefits for factory and company objectives and for employee satisfaction and morale. These examples provide an excellent platform for the continued development of the team-based approach.

QUALITY EDUCATION AND TRAINING

RHP Ferrybridge has had an official training policy for many years. The current company policy is:

> The Company is committed to achieving world-class standards in all areas of manufacturing and services, through the implementation of Total Quality Management and associated training. It is the aim of the Company to provide advice, opportunities, facilities and financial support to enable its employees to acquire the skills, knowledge and related qualifications needed to perform effectively the duties and tasks for which they are employed, and to develop their potential to meet the future manpower and business needs of the organization.
>
> The Company shall establish and maintain procedures for identifying the training needs of its personnel; and provide training for all persons performing activities affecting quality. Appropriate records of training shall be maintained. Training standards shall reflect the requirements of ISO 9001-1.
>
> The Company intends to achieve the Investors in People award in December 1995.

To support this quality commitment to training, the budgets have steadily increased from 0.98 per cent of wage cost in 1993 to 1.11 per cent for 1994 and 1.45 per cent in 1995. Perhaps more significantly, the number of days' training has almost doubled with 2595 in 1994 (4.63 on average per employee) and 5140 (8.65 per employee) in 1994. Each year the management team draws up its training plan designed to meet the needs of the business, as agreed through the site objectives and TMC.

The key aims for 1994 were to increase shop floor competence and to further develop quality awareness. Shop floor competence has been developed through the adoption of Standard Operating Procedures (SOPs) across the site. The SOPs provide a format to describe all tasks and processes. They incorporate a guaranteed means of meeting quality standards and ensure that the task can be completed using minimal effort, power, tools and materials. They can be easily understood by the operator, given the appropriate education and training. It is seen as the best method currently available for getting the task done and gives a firm foundation for review and improvement.

Standard Operating Procedures are written by the task teams who work on a particular section,. They are seen as the best people to write them as they will be the ones to work with them and should also have the best understanding of the job. Once written, the procedures are regularly reviewed by the team and amended to reflect improvements in best practice.

These procedures have many uses including the obvious use as a training document – providing a concise and comprehensive guide for the qualified operator, instructor and the trainee – use as a monitoring document, use as an audit document, and perhaps most importantly as a basis for improvement. The benefits of the standard operation procedure have been shown to be in improving quality, safer working practices, reduced costs, improved efficiency and more effective training.

On the shop floor, radar charts now exist as shown in Figure 9.4.

The axes of the chart refer to specific SOPs (EG09, IT55) while the numbers relate to five grades of competence (new starter to highly experienced worker). Using the tests of competency built into the SOPs, it is possible to establish current performance levels and establish targets. In the example shown, the dense line shows the current competence level while the dotted line shows the planned level that was to be achieved by 30 June 1995. As the procedures are improved there can be little doubt that there will be substantial improvements across the site.

A new site induction procedure for all new starters to the company was also introduced in 1994. The purpose was to ensure that all employees were fully aware of the site's objectives and of the formal structure. Particular emphasis has been placed upon quality training and formal modules have been set up for Quality and Product Awareness, Statistical Process Control, Defect Procedures and PDCA training.

In 1994, the Company also purchased an interactive video. This has been used extensively by existing employees. The principle behind the purchase was to increase awareness, but also to create personal ownership of training and to move towards developing a learning culture. There are currently six video discs: Time Management, SPC, FMEA, Machine Capability, Process Capability, and Measurement for Engineers, but further videos for employee use are planned. In 1995 the intention was to set up a self-development room, to incorporate interactive video, TV and video, cassettes, books and other learning packages. It was hoped this would extend further the learning culture on the site to bring about greater willingness for individuals to be developed in their jobs.

The key quality training conducted in 1994 included PDCA training to Team Leader level (the Plan, Do, Check, Act approach to problem solving), Kaizen Awareness, Quality Concerns, Team Working, Product Knowledge and Quality Awareness. In addition, three individuals were trained to become assessors in the European Quality Model as a fundamental part of the quality review process.

In July 1994 the Company declared its intention to achieve the Investors in People award, with December 1995 targeted as the date for assessment. The major benefits to the Company were perceived as greater levels of job satisfaction, striving to make work more enjoyable and happier, greater personal recognition and development, better quality products and service, greater customer satisfaction and greater job security.

It is always difficult to adequately evaluate the contribution that training makes to any organization. However, for RHP Ferrybridge, this continued and developing commitment to training has resulted in several tangible examples. These have included: a 30 per cent reduction in Self Lube Assembly etching rejects following a review of operating methods and the introduction of SOPs; a 100 per cent increase in ISB Assembly output per day, although mostly attributed to the introduction of new equipment and methods, would have been impossible without SOPs, operator training and quality awareness; rejects as a percentage of standard cost of input have reduced significantly in two areas of the grinding shop since the introduction of SOPs, namely face grinding rejects down 86 per cent and outer diameter rejects down 47.7 per cent.

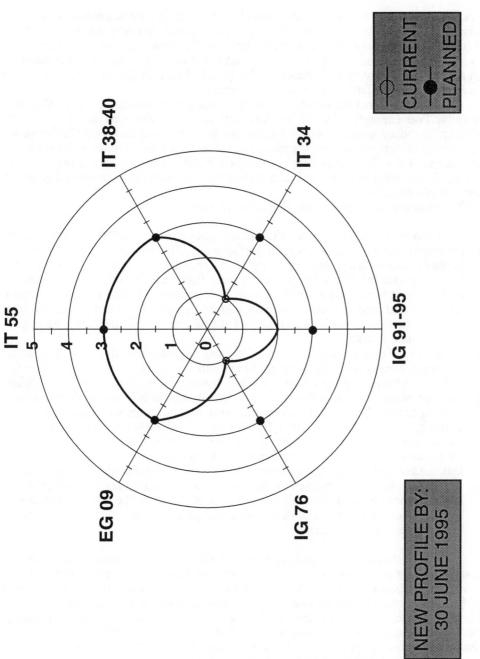

Figure 9.4   A sample training radar chart

MAKING MEASUREMENT COUNT

The Total Manufacturing Concept provides an extensive measurement and monitoring system. The system is displayed on notice boards in every department of the factory, which are kept regularly up to date. All the measurements are liked to the overall company and factory objectives and these are linked to the main goals of Quality, Cost, Delivery and People, with people being further broken down into three categories: Safety, Morale and Environment.

All these measures are closely linked and sometimes impinge on more than one activity. Foe example, one of the key activities in 1994 was scrap reduction. Clearly, to reduce scrap improves Quality as there is less chance of defective product getting to customers. Cost is reduced as there is no need to make a second batch to make up for scrap and Delivery is assured. Furthermore, Morale is improved as people do not need to do rework and finally the Environment is improved as better use is made of resources.

The measurement system can be used in two main ways:

1. As a monitor. Measures from the factory policy are cascaded down to all departments and are used to monitor performance. The volume of output from the factory is one measure of the factory's performance. At Ferrybridge, this is broken down into the four main product groups that make up output. The output of each product type is monitored through each department. The assembly outputs are then combined to give the overall factory outputs. The team in each section monitors their own performance so that if problems occur they can take appropriate countermeasures.
2. As an improvement tool. Setting challenging targets forces the need for continual improvement and may help find new and better ways of working. The approach used on scrap reduction is a good example. The scrap figure was broken down in many ways monthly and used extensively as a focus for improvement team initiatives. First, the scrap figures were broken down by department: Auto Turning, General Turning, Heat Treatment, etc. This allows departments to focus in on the main processes or other causes of scrap and develop action plans for improvement. Next, the figures were broken down by product: Self Lube, ISB, Radial and Clutch. This shows which products are the main causes of scrap so that efforts can be directed to the root causes. Finally, they are broken down and monitored by fault type. By using Pareto techniques, the major scrap causes are identified independent of department and product type. These are then tackled by cross-functional teams.

As with all improvement programmes, initially major achievements are made as people 'cherry pick'. However, as time goes by this becomes more difficult. As processes are brought more under control, ever more sophisticated quality tools and techniques for data gathering and for use in team problem solving are necessary. At Ferrybridge, these have included Statistical Process Control, Taguchi – enabling vast improvements in Heat Treatment – Failure Mode and Effects Analysis and Quality Function Deployment. The use of these tools, with the existing measurement systems, has helped in many of the site's achievements.

The measurement system as seen above is comprehensive. It covers all aspects of the business and is the basis for monitoring improvements. There are of course many other measures used within the group to show business performance, such as profitability and value-added productivity. They are, however, of less use in running a single factory. They are either complicated and not easy to understand, or of little value to Ferrybridge due to aspects such as transfer pricing, etc. The assumption must be that if the targets set in the policy are achieved, then the other business measures will come automatically. Looking at RHP Ferrybridge's performance against the 1994 factory targets should certainly mean that profitability and productivity will follow.

Based on 1993 figures	Target	1994				1995
		Q1 (%)	Q2 (%)	Q3 (%)	Q4 (%)	
Assembly output	+50	+0.6	+10.4	+9.8	+31.7	+46.5
Despatch output	+70	+36.3	+50.8	+73.2	+77.3	+107.1
Scrap	−30	−38	−18	−20	−44	−54
Output value/attendance	+25	−1	+11	+17	+16	+30
Product arrears value	−25	−0	−0.5	+14	−14	−29
Standard hours/working day	+50	+5.5	+17.6	+14.4	+25.9	+39.5

The figures in the table above show a very creditable performance. Although only two out of six targets are achieved by the end of 1994, all the targets bar one are achieved or exceeded by the end of the first quarter of 1995. Similarly, with only an odd exception – notably the blip in product arrears on quarter three due to the introduction of a new scheduling system – the changes are consistently in the right direction. This is a noteworthy achievement because, as pointed out earlier, it is much easier to make dramatic changes at the start of a quality campaign, when the possibility to 'cherry pick' is greatest, than to sustain continued improvement from one period to the next.

MANAGEMENT COMMITMENT AND THE RECOGNITION PROCESS

With the appointment of a full-time Total Quality Facilitator in 1994, the Senior Management Team recognized that continuous improvement in all areas of operation was essential to the long-term survival of the business. If a business is to make this commitment to continuous improvement, the approach has to be proactive and systematic to ensure that the factory policy and goals are communicated effectively, and so that they are recognized and worked towards at all levels throughout the factory.

In line with the commitment to continuous improvement, significant changes were made to the management structure. Before 1994, all manufacturing operations were managed by processes; that is, a manufacturing manager would be accountable for all product groups' output from a particular manufacturing department, which could be one link in the chain of manufacturing a bearing. This department would then be supported by the relevant service departments. In 1994, this structure changed so that manufacturing was managed and supported by product group. This has created an environment of product ownership, developing even closer internal customer/supplier working relationships. Managers and shop floor personnel from different departments are now members of the same improvement teams, working together to solve problems.

There is also increasing recognition of the customers' voice – both external and internal – throughout the factory. Indeed the same quality concern procedures are in use for both internal and external customer complaints, linked through a common approach to classification of the complaint.

Internal concerns are raised, usually at shop floor level, through team leaders who through discussion with Quality Engineering raise a quality concern. This is categorized by degree of severity from X – for alert only – through Y and Z up to Z+ for extreme cases. External complaints are logged through Quality Engineering and investigated by the department where the complaint originated, advised by Quality Assurance. Once identified, all concerns, either internal or external, are addressed by the appropriate teams using accepted PDCA problem-solving techniques to decide the appropriate corrective action.

The development of such task team working is recognized as the key to the success of continuous improvement. However, some people were very reluctant to participate in improvement activities for fear of working themselves out of a job, particularly if improvements were related to productivity. The company had to find a way around this barrier if it was serious about developing the levels of improvement it was hoped to achieve. Therefore, in 1994 the Board of Directors announced a two-year job security commitment. This meant that productivity improvements in one particular area would just mean that people resources would be transferred to an alternative area. More people now feel they have the freedom to contribute and positively express themselves without fear of recrimination. There are also many other initiatives, some complete, some ongoing, but all addressing the issue of breaking down barriers, developing a culture where everyone feels free to contribute to continuous improvement and most of all want to contribute. These include:

- the introduction of common protective clothing as mentioned earlier;
- the change in task team working from being specific to a particular department toward numerous cross-functional teams, with supplier and customer representatives from the relevant support departments and the involvement of managers in most teams, either as leaders of coaches;
- encouraging all members of a department to get involved in team meetings now taking place in their own team rooms on the shop floor;
- the use of monthly team briefings and visual displays in all departments with actual factory performance against target on key indicators being displayed at vantage points all across the site;
- the introduction of a factory newsletter produced every two months and circulated to all employees with everyone encouraged to submit articles to the editor for publication.

Although great strides have been made, it is still felt that there is significant room for improvement. As a result a team made up of a cross-section of people has recently been established to decide the format and content for future communications across the site.

It is one thing getting people involved in continuous improvement, it is another keeping them involved. Recognition is an essential part of this process. At the moment there are no direct financial rewards given as a form of recognition. Instead there are celebration evenings where teams are invited to celebrate a particular success. There are also annual team competitions on site, where the winners go forward to represent the site in the RHP Bearings competition against representatives from the rest of the RHP group. The competition is judged by members of the Board of Directors, including the Chief Executive, and a representative from an external teaching body. There are certificates, photographs, videos, an informal dinner and coverage in the company newsletter for all participants. The winners get a shield that they keep for twelve months together with gift tokens. Ferrybridge was fortunate to become joint winners in the 1994 competition,.

Teams are also encouraged to take time out from their job, so they can visit other sites and develop relationships where problems and solutions can be shared between sites. In the future it could be that task teams may be not just cross-functional but even cross-site.

FUTURE CONTINUOUS IMPROVEMENT PLANS

There were two main actions in 1994 that helped Ferrybridge to enhance its future continuous improvement plans. These were:

1. The development of manufacturing plans for core products. Previously capital investment at Ferrybridge was apportioned to areas of greatest need on a purely reactive basis. Little thought was given to the long-term implications, often resulting in a poor decision-making process. Generally, the process lacked focus in achieving the strategic business goals.

   The manufacturing plans have been introduced to provide the focus for manufacturing and engineering to achieve the factory objectives, the emphasis being placed on working proactively to continuously improve product quality, cost and delivery. Sales forecasts are received on a six-monthly basis. The three-year manufacturing plan is then created against this forecast, outlining production routings for new and existing business. Consideration is given to all machine histories and standard operating times. The plan should then automatically highlight any areas of concern – bottleneck processes, inefficient processes, requirements for new equipment for new products and so on. Capital investment can then be targeted at these areas on a rigorous cost/benefit basis.
2. The adoption of the EQM. The European Quality Model was adopted in 1994, and now allows self-assessment against the model's key criteria. The self-assessment process allows the management team to identify the factory's strengths and weaknesses. Areas for improvement can then be identified and prioritized to maximize benefits from the available resources.

The co-ordinated planning cycle is shown in Figure 9.5.

All the actions for forthcoming years are identified from a combination of all the issues identified by the task teams' efforts in the previous year, the three-year product manufacturing plans, and the EQM self-assessment. They are then deployed through the factory TMC process – the driving force behind both the short- and long-term improvement plans – where the plans are cascaded down throughout the site to all sections.

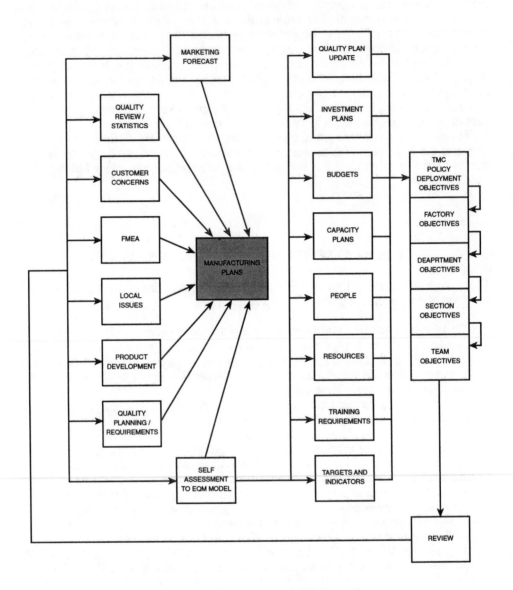

Figure 9.5   The co-ordinated planning cycle

As with any working document, there has been a continual search for ways to develop its effectiveness in all areas, and these is evidence to prove that the success achieved in 1994 was significantly greater than in 1993. For 1995, the ongoing development is geared towards changing the culture, so that the process progressively becomes accepted as a natural part of the day-to-day activities.

The emphasis must be on people involvement, where ultimately everyone should be involved in developing the relevant strategies and targets for their section. In

1995 there was indeed greater involvement at all levels of the TMC deployment stage, with many team sessions at each stage. This helped to develop greater levels of ownership and commitment to achieving targets. The levels of success can be seen to be directly related to the levels of ownership and commitment achieved. For those who were not directly involved in developing the strategies, it is essential that there is an understanding of the strategies and how they contribute to the factory's aims. This understanding should allow everyone to make the necessary commitment to achieve the targets.

During the annual review of 1994's factory TMC and the development of 1995's, it became apparent that there was a need to change the format of the process. There was a mission statement that outlined long-term aims and a policy statement as a one-year focus. However, it was felt that if Quality, Cost, Delivery, Safety, Morale and Environment improvements were to be achieved, there was a need to focus people's minds on what the factory should be aiming to achieve in each of these areas, which would then indirectly achieve the Policy and Mission statement. New factory aims and strategies were developed that used the above categories as the focus of attention.

Factories' Aims	
Quality	Zero defective product. Zero complaints.
Cost	Continually reduce cost of manufacturing bearings.
Delivery	On time in full delivery. Reduction in lead times.
Safety	Zero accidents. Safe working environment.
Morale	Enjoy work. Highly motivated people. Wanting to contribute. People feel free to contribute.
Environment	Minimize impact of our manufacturing processes on people and local environment.
Review	Assess effectiveness of strategies. Generate countermeasures when necessary.

If people have a vision of where the factory is going, then it becomes easier to develop strategies for the following year, which should improve the areas of weaknesses identified from either the manufacturing plans or the EQM and thus take the factory some way towards the aims. The strategies for 1995 are identified below.

Factories' Strategies 1995	
Quality	Cross-functional teams on top four defects, supported by local department initiatives.
Cost	Improve productivity through local initiatives and investment.
Delivery	Schedule adherence.
Safety	Behavioural Approach to Accident Prevention (BAAP).
Morale	Individual development training plans. Establish fair terms and conditions framework. Develop involvement system, include recognition. Improve communication.
Environment	Increase awareness – education and training. Nominating responsibility. Focused investment. Enhancing external partnerships.
Review	Plan/schedule.

The strategies are then regularly reviewed to assess their effectiveness against the targets that have been set, developing suitable countermeasures as and when required.

Factory Targets 1995		
Customer returns	down	50%
Factory rejects	down	50%
Productivity	up	30%
Product arrears	down	100%
Factory output	up	40%
Accidents	down	25%
Environment	up	100%

As more people become involved in the development of the TMC document or at least understand why the document has been developed in that way, greater levels of commitment to achieving target can be achieved.

There was evidence to prove that the results achieved in 1994 were better than those in 1993, and there is now evidence to prove that this trend has continued into the first quarter if 1995. The results shown below indicate that the company was already well on its way to achieving its 1995 targets.

Results of First Quarter 1995		
Customer returns	down	10%
Factory rejects	down	57%
Productivity	up	24%
Product arrears	down	8%
Factory output	up	36%
Accidents	down	10%
Environment	up	20%

REVIEW

Looking back at the progress that Ferrybridge has made since the beginning of 1994 and the undoubted improvements in performance achieved since that time, a number of key features can be seen to emerge.

- The introduction of a clear structure to cascade the mission, plans, strategies and targets of the company through all departments and to encourage their involvement in deciding how those targets could be met.
- The use of regular reviews to identify where things were going according to plan and where action needed to be taken to put things back on course.
- The development of several key projects, such as the FScrap project, to tackle a single serious factory problem cutting across departmental barriers and providing reward and encouragement to continued involvement through concrete success.
- The recognition that culture can only be built slowly and on solid foundations. The decision that all staff, supervisors and managers should wear the same colour and style of protective clothing was a tangible signal of a change in culture. However, the success of task groups in tackling and solving identified problems and watching performance targets being met and exceeded has probably achieved more in developing the team culture than the more tangible signals have.
- The use of an annual review of the quality process based on the EQM model. It is all too easy to develop procedures that are seen to work and then to sit back and expect everything to continue to improve. RHP Ferrybridge has, however, invested time and resources in developing in-house capability for annual self-assessment review against the EQM model. This has already led to improvements in the way that the TMC has been carried out and this can only add to the success of the process as a whole.

Overall, RHP Ferrybridge demonstrates the importance of a clear structure that will allow team involvement and continual improvement to snowball with small successes building into greater successes and the whole factory rolling forward together in the right direction.

TEN

ROYAL INSURANCE:

Brainwaves + Processes = Progress

BRENDA MCDONNELL
AND
DAVE RUSK

TEN

ROYAL INSURANCE:

Brainwaves + Processes = Progress

INTRODUCTION

Royal Insurance Life and Pensions (the Royal) is part of the worldwide Royal Insurance Group which was founded in 1985 and now trades in over 60 countries. The group employs over 23,000 people through some 900 offices, making it one of the biggest providers of general and life insurance products in the world. The Royal provides a complete range of pension, investment, protection and mortgage-related products through three distribution channels – Direct Sales, Tied Agents and Independent Financial Advisers. During 1994, the period of this case, the divisions employed 2089 people, with the following mix:

Staff type	Number
Managerial	297
Sales	137
Supervisors/Technical	561
Operators	487
Administration	607

The business the Royal operates is extremely complex, made more so by the company's decision to continue to sell a wide range of diversified products through three delivery channels – one of the few life offices to do so.

In 1991, the company recognized that they faced an extremely competitive market, an increasing cost base and an increasingly complex legislative environment. This, combined with increasing evidence of a general public suspicion that insurance companies were not behaving honourably towards them, forced them to radically rethink their strategic direction. A major strategic review was undertaken which led to many new developments including the implementation of a Total

Quality Management (TQM) programme to enable the company to regain its former successes. The TQM programme began in Autumn 1992 and major areas of focus were:

- improved management
- improved morale
- more efficient and effective processes
- more satisfied customers with higher retention rates
- improved market place reputation
- improved change environment
- cost savings

THE TRADING ENVIRONMENT

It is useful to consider the trading environment that the Royal faced around this time in more detail. Trying to gain competitive advantage is a difficult task at any time, but consideration of the battery of regulatory and market changes facing the Royal gives an insight into the pressure generating the change imperative.

Throughout the 1980s several well-publicized irregularities in the financial markets of which life insurance is a part had caused the public to become very suspicious of business motives in this sector. In addition, the economy was in a period of recession. Due to structural changes in the middle-management job market this recession was having an exceptionally large impact on the housing market with house prices falling in many areas and unprecedented low levels of house moves. This had direct knock-on effects for the Royal who sell the endowment policies which often accompany a new mortgage. At the same time, the Royal's customers were becoming more sophisticated and educated in their demands, requiring a very customer-focused response.

In order to restore public confidence and to prevent further irregularities, the industry significantly tightened its regulatory procedures. The environment became one with an emphasis on audit and control. Every insurance provider has had to install systems for monitoring and ensuring compliance with some fairly onerous requirements. This in turn added a cost burden at a time when sales were falling. The requirement to increase the quality of advice to customers at point of sale has become paramount and resulted in an extensive and ongoing programme of training for sales staff. This too clearly has an associated cost.

The challenge for the Royal, then, was to manage down this increasing cost base, while improving customer service.

Consequently, the board undertook a major strategic review in mid-1991. The specific issues subject to the review were:

- distribution and products
- organization and structure
- costs and productivity
- future IT direction.

The output from the review was a Business Improvement Programme, designed to deliver benefits across the wide range of activities subject to the review. The one theme running through all the proposed improvements, however, was that of quality. The review showed that quality delivery was fundamental to success: quality of service, quality of products, quality of distribution, quality of sales and quality of advice to customers.

This commitment to quality is demonstrated by the mission statement, issued in 1992. This is described as the very *raison d'être* of the Royal. The Royal mission is to:

'satisfy the protection and savings needs of all our customers, profitably'

This is to be achieved by providing good products and service, that is:

'We shall do this through:

our TEAM of well-trained, highly motivated staff and sales associates, providing:

* courteous, efficient and effective SERVICE to all our CUSTOMERS, with
* attractive products offering value for money and
* superior PERFORMANCE for our shareholders and policyholders

In short, through the delivery of QUALITY'

The Board decision to adopt the TQM philosophy was made in the autumn of 1992 and since then the company has worked thoroughly and systematically towards achieving its mission. They recognized that the highly regulated environment in which the company now operates makes the concept of self-managed teams and empowerment all the more challenging though none the less relevant. To reflect this, the theme of the implementation has been recognition that practical changes and cultural or behavioural changes need to go hand in hand. It is recognized that achieving one without achieving the other would not maximize benefits to customers. This case concentrates on the 1994 quality effort, but this should be viewed as one leg of a continuing journey. The next section goes on to describe the systematic and comprehensive implementation strategy adopted.

MANAGING THE CHANGE

The first stage of the development process for the Royal was to set up a formal Strategic Planning mechanism. This systematic methodology facilitates the setting of strategic priorities which, once agreed, are then used to drive the operation planning process. As an active, founder member of the British Quality Foundation (BQF), the Royal is keen to enact the criteria for business excellence as laid down in the BQF model and the 1994 strategic priorities fully reflect these. Strategic priorities will be reviewed each year although it is not envisaged that these will change frequently. The strategic planning process is well documented and will be subject to continuous review. In addition, all of the Royal's general management level received training on the models during the year.

The enhanced strategic planning function had considerable impact on the 1994 operational planning process which was documented in a systematic way for the first time, in 1993. All major changes to the operational plan are being carried out via formal project management disciplines and methodologies. In order to further support this development, a Project Manager was appointed in 1994, with the brief to co-ordinate and report on the progress of these major projects against the operational plan. The main thrust of the role is to oversee improvements in a structured and disciplined manner. All initiatives are subject to formal Project Management Methodology and a further level of improvement will be sought and secured through a Post Implementation Review. This is a formal exercise, generally taking place some months after the project has been completed.

As a result of the initiatives described below, the operational planning process at the Royal has become a more participative process. Ideas and input come through a 'bottom-up' process rather than solely through managers at senior levels. As a result of this additional input the Royal recognized the need for a vehicle for project prioritization and resourcing, hence, in 1994, the Project Assessment Working Group (PAWG) was set up. The brief of the Group is to review all possible projects against the agreed operational plan and make recommendations to the board. From this process, Vital Few Projects are identified. These are the projects which best match the organization's short-term plan, at least cost. The procedure for consideration by the PAWG is submission of an initial document with a cost–benefit analysis included. These two documents act to give ownership to the proposer, while giving decision-making authority to the board (via the PAWG) and can be seen as a direct form of communication between them. The operational plan at the Royal is subjected to quarterly review by the General Management team where performance is compared to plan and either improvement initiatives are agreed or plans are forecasted. The plan is then issued to all members of the Royal staff.

MAKING IT HAPPEN

From its inception, the TQM initiative has sought to engage the workforce in the process of change and development, by involving staff in improvement initiatives and harnessing the creative and innovative capabilities of staff to spawn yet more initiatives. The programme to promote staff participation in improvement activities is known as 'Brainwaves'. Although launched in September 1993 Brainwaves became fully operational in 1994, bringing a co-ordinated, holistic approach to the three distinct strands of the programme:

- Company initiatives
- Local initiatives
- Suggestion scheme

In addition, Critical Business Processes (CBP) were identified, which operate on a cross-functional basis. Steering groups were set up to ensure that continuous improvement was the focus of the change effort in these processes.

Critical business processes

These have been set up to identify and prioritize improvement opportunities within each cross-functional process. Where improvement opportunities have been identified, the CBP then sponsors a Continuous Improvement Team (CIT) to investigate and recommend actions. The team then goes on to implement the recommended process changes and hold post-implementation reviews. By using the tools and techniques of systematic improvement the CITs pass on the skills acquired in the Quality Department to the business areas. CBPs are led by a Single Point Owner (SPO) but staff at all levels are involved in the process through representation on the steering group or CIT. The SPO is the manager whose function is most affected by CBP improvements, but benefits from the CBP are cross-functional, with benefits coming at various stages of process delivery. In this way, the CBP development can be seen as a temporary step in advance of the full restructure towards process-based organization design. CBPs considered in 1994 include:

- Servicing Individual Business
- Product Development and Launch
- Recruitment and Retention of Staff
- Business Planning and Control

The Royal recognized that to be successful, the quality programme had to engage every member of the workforce so the Brainwaves message is continually transmitted through formal and informal channels, reaching each individual.

Company initiative

The company initiative is the first layer of quality development; it is a company-wide idea, aimed at improving quality. These are primarily behavioural developments to be adopted by everyone in the Royal and compliance is mandatory. They are designed to focus staff effort on a particular quality theme and enable them to improve performance together as a company. In order to achieve conformance to a company standard, a formal and systematic system of constructive criticism and guidance is offered to those failing to conform in the short term. Four company initiatives were launched in 1994 which sought to bring about performance improvements in the ways in which:

- telephones are answered
- effective meetings are held
- internal memos are used
- staff take responsibility for the accuracy of the documents they issue.

Following these initiatives, monitoring showed that, for example, 92 per cent of telephone calls were answered to standard, and internal memos demonstrated 94 per cent compliance. Each department strives to continuously improve and progress is tracked by ongoing monitoring.

Local initiative

The main aim of this approach is to make continuous improvement a way of life, bringing teamworking and a systematic approach to problem solving to be recognized as best practice at a local level. Local initiatives therefore relate to continuous improvement ideas generated at a local level and implemented immediately. These changes were classified as 'quick hits' as little further investigation was required. They ranged from form redesign to relocation of office equipment. One hundred and sixty-two CITs were formed to tackle deep-rooted issues, either customer, service or cost related, or all three.

Suggestion scheme

The suggestion scheme supports the Local Initiatives strand, by giving staff the opportunity to suggest improvements outside of their own work area. Obviously, staff can make most suggestions about the areas with which they are familiar, so this scheme does not attract the same volume of ideas as the Local Initiatives; however, the management team are satisfied with the steady flow of 30 to 40 suggestions which came in each month in 1994.

All of the company initiatives, local initiatives and suggestions were considered in the operational planning process, with bigger initiatives becoming a Vital Project.

This development is seen as a way of moving towards the process-based organizational structure ultimately preferred by the company.

This multi-stranded approach to quality implementation means that even though they may not be co-opted onto a Continuous Improvement team the enthusiasm and expertise of all staff is still harnessed through some or all of the Brainwaves initiatives. In the way the Royal believe they are capturing the commitment of as many staff as possible.

SPREADING THE WORD

In order to ensure that staff focus on company priorities the Royal has adopted a structured approach to keeping staff fully advised and involved. In particular, 1994 saw an emphasis on encouraging and reinforcing Quality attitudes and behaviour while reporting progress against Quality objectives. Various communications media are in use, the three main formal ones being:

- *Fanfare*, a weekly in-house newsletter
- *Team briefings*, held monthly
- *Directors' Roadshows*, held annually.

Their effectiveness is regularly tested by the annual Attitude Survey. The survey covers a broad range of issues including a test of staff's understanding of company policy and strategy.

Fanfare

A frequent, regular communication to all staff. Presented in an upbeat, lively format, focusing on key issues, often presented by senior members of the organization. In addition, regular features by members of staff at all levels and 'bumper editions' dedicated to reports on specific subjects of importance, such as the results of the

Attitude Survey. The frequency of this publication is seen as vital in the bid to continuously reinforce the Quality message.

Team briefings

The main feature of these meetings is that they facilitate and encourage two-way communication.

Directors' roadshows

The Royal directors first embarked on a programme of roadshows in 1994; during the roadshows they were able to meet all staff and communicate future plans to them at a general level but always with an emphasis on Quality.

FUNDAMENTAL CHANGE

The Royal board realized early on in the drive for quality that the then current organizational structure was a serious hindrance to full implementation of the TQM philosophy and what was needed was a process-based structure. The company had been organized along functional lines (see Figure 10.1). This bringing together of specialists into functional departments had suited the Royal management in the past, but was now identified as being incompatible with a Quality approach. The board recognized that what was needed was a structure which brought together staff from several different functions who worked on the same process. Thus 'process' must become the focal point of staff effort (see Figure 10.2).

The restructure programme commenced in 1994. It was on an ambitious company-wide scale and recognized the need to focus on customers, giving the end-to-end process of service delivery a team of committed individuals, dedicated to its delivery. Typically, a team consists of individuals representing the different functions which make up the process, bringing together a variety of disciplines in one focused group. The restructure also recognized that the support function, or 'backroom' services, were just as important in the organization so the idea of the 'internal customer' was developed to harness the effort of these teams. A beneficial spin-off from the restructure is that it will also help the Royal maximize the benefits from IT developments and new IT systems will be installed to support the processes even further. Although the change programme will span several years, some early benefits were delivered in 1994 and the year saw much development and formalizing of the programme.

Another important feature of the restructure is the deployment of specialists from corporate units into the new operational processes. For example, specialists from the Quality Department have been deployed into the customer-facing operations to facilitate and promote the adoption of quality techniques in those units. The Royal sees this as an opportunity to enjoy 'the best of both worlds' by integrating quality professionals into the business units while at the same time maintaining the control links back to the Quality Department in respect of professional standards and disciplines.

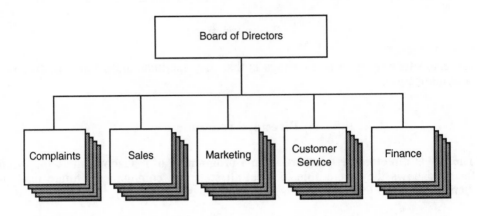

Figure 10.1 An extract from the old organization chart at RILP. Each specialist area contains a hierarchy of line management within the specialism

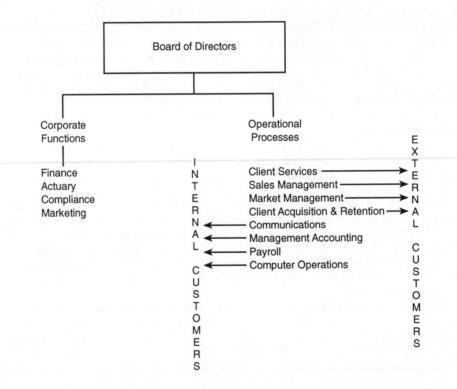

Figure 10.2 The new RILP structure, focusing on end-to-end processes, wherever provided

QUALITY EDUCATION

The Royal recognizes that the ambitious change programme outlined above can only be achieved through a comprehensive and practical approach to education and training. A major strength of the Royal programme has been the clear and explicit linkage between the human resources plan and the operational plan. This link ensures that training and education effort is deployed to assist achievement of operational goals, particularly in relation to continuous improvement and delivery of improved service to customers. The importance placed on this link is clearly demonstrated by the fact that Human Resources and Quality Issues are both the responsibility of one member of the General Management Team.

To ensure that quality education is seen as relevant to the workplace, classroom-based courses and training have been avoided wherever possible. Instead, a practical approach has been adopted; training has been mainly through the quality management vehicles described above (CBPs, CITs) and is, therefore, 'on the job' rather than 'classroom' centred. Training has included tuition in quality tools and techniques, facilitation and meetings behaviour, and continuous improvement methodology.

In order to identify further training needs of individuals, Royal introduced a new style of personal appraisal which reflects the behaviours required by an organization which has truly embraced TQM philosophies and methods. It included a specific training and development plan for all members of staff, each plan seeking to examine TQM knowledge and competency with action plans and training needs being specified and agreed as a result. Now, individuals see their own participation in the quality exercise as an important contribution to the overall plan. Following the success of the 1993 staff survey the Royal decided to make this an annual event. They commissioned an independent company to survey staff on a range of issues. The survey consisted of a postal questionnaire. The wide-ranging survey included identification of areas where training and development needs exist, as well as monitoring TQM behaviours, attitudes and practices. This proved a very effective means of ensuring that the TQM message was reaching its target.

In addition to the 'on the job' training described above, several other courses and developments also happened in 1994. In order to gain maximum benefit from the TQM tools available, over 100 managers attended a series of courses throughout the year, including a one-day course on Statistical Process Control (SPC). This training was developed during the year and reached an advanced stage. The day dedicated to understanding the technicalities and management implications of SPC proved particularly worthwhile because now an increasing amount of management negotiations can be produced in control chart format. Other courses which ran during the year included the training of an additional 26 facilitators and further training was provided for 50 staff involved in Continuous Improvement activities. In addition some of the staff involved in the CBPs recognized the need to re-engineer these processes and so were given appropriate training.

In terms of senior management involvement in training, there have been several developments. For the first time, a series of workshops were held for all managers to ensure that those behaviours which move the Royal towards a participative management culture will be encouraged and rewarded. A typical workshop included topics such as:

- managing relations with other functions
- managing and developing teams and individuals within them
- conducting oneself as a role model
- managing across and between functions.

Each workshop led to action plans being developed at team and individual level. Since these personal training needs were identified they have become part of the overall training and development plan and feed back into the appraisal system.

Firstly, the Royal board were given a comprehensive introduction to corporate self-assessment using the BQF model of business excellence. In addition the Board have taken on the task of trainer, or role model, by carrying out a series of road-shows. These enable directors to talk directly to staff and stress, face to face, the importance of continuous improvement activities. During the year the board gave visible and sincere commitment to the Company Initiatives. Key communications were signed personally by the Managing Director, and all directors work at meeting the prescribed standards themselves, reinforcing the message that to be effective, the TQM message has to apply to everyone in the organization. At the roadshows, the directors stressed the importance of Continuous Improvement activities and recognized the need to further develop the TQM training and education. Following the roadshows, the Board examined and redefined team roles following clarification of the implications of the process-based restructure currently under way.

This comprehensive training programme, combining practical education and learning by example with the application of increasingly sophisticated tools taught in the classroom, is enabling the Royal to turn its mission into reality.

MEASURING THE OUTCOMES

Prior to the TQM programme in the Royal the performance measurement system was mostly very traditional. It was a system focused on financial figures, it concentrated on results, not actions and it was very detailed. The detailed information was prepared for top-level management and consequently local management had no sense of ownership of the results. The information being produced had no link back to performance improvements.

However, it became apparent within the Royal that to assess the effect of the TQM programme new measures must be incorporated into the regular reporting system and must be directed at the right people. So during 1994 the Royal started to introduce new types of measure. These new measures are directed more at the performance of the processes which give rise to the financial results rather than the results themselves, and are more customer focused. An important feature of the new measurement system is that it is 'owned' by the Continuous Improvement group members, rather than top management. One of the major accomplishments of 1994 was the development of the new measurement system. This involved devising a Balanced Scorecard for the organization. The Balanced Scorecard consists of a range of measures designed to represent the interests of various stakeholders. Hence, the measurement system reports on performance of interest to customers, staff and shareholders. However, due to the nature of this project, benefits only started to come through in 1995. As well as devising more appropriate measures for the new quality-focused organization the new system also presented information differently, making extensive use of statistical process control (after managers had been appropriately trained).

The system now incorporates the traditional measures alongside new measures, called, in the Royal, key performance indicators (KPIs). The traditional measures are there to honour DTI obligations as well as monitoring performance against budget. They are expressed as monetary values or ratios. The KPIs monitor and support the work of the CBPs. They represent the most important aspects of process performance and are used by the CBP steering group to manage the process of continuous improvement. Areas such as employee perceptions, customer satisfaction and the volume of improvement activity are measured.

The employee data comes from the Annual Staff Survey and in future this will be broken down by process. To gather customer opinion, questionnaires are sent to a random sample of customers shortly after their purchase has been completed. Results of this survey are analysed over time and by sales channel. The level of activity in the CBPs is monitored by a tracking system, which also records expected and actual cost savings and other data. In addition, activities such as adherence to company initiatives are monitored via surveys, and reported regularly.

Using measurement as a tool for improvement was a new concept for the Royal in 1994, but really took hold very quickly, as the payback materialized. Here are some examples:

- Lead times were established by the Servicing of Individual Business CBP group and were monitored using SPC. As process improvements fed through, it has been possible to redefine the limits.
- The rate of compliance with Company Initiatives is monitored. Any failure to maintain target standards will lead to a campaign to re-invigorate the initiatives.
- The Staff Attitude Survey is carried out each year. In 1994 it revealed a particular group within the company whose satisfaction was significantly lower than that of their colleagues. Action was taken by senior management to identify and redress the cause of this dissatisfaction.

As the type of performance measure used in the Royal has changed during 1994, so have the attitudes towards the performance measurement system as a whole. Managers and employees have seen the measurement system as a positive development, providing useful information which contributes to achieving quality targets. Overall, the KPIs are far more widely communicated than the old traditional measures ever were; for example, a special edition of *Fanfare* was produced which celebrated the improvement in customer service recognized by the Royal being honoured by an award from the National Federation of Independent Financial Advisers (NFIFA).

ACHIEVEMENTS SO FAR

In 1994 the Royal was still relatively early in its journey towards total quality but they feel that throughout the year they made major strides down the route. Everyone is justifiably proud of the progress made during the year to become a company which fully embraces the principles and practices of Continuous Improvement. In addition, the scope of measures used to track this progress was greatly extended and made more meaningful and relevant. However, in view of the relative immaturity of many of the quality programmes and initiatives, the benefit yield from all this work cannot as yet be fully discerned.

One area where clear improvements have been recognized already is that of customer loyalty. This high-level measure is estimated by the rate at which new customers cancel their policies within two years of inception. Across all distribution channels, the overall defection rate reduced by several percentage points during 1994. This measure is considered to be a direct indicator of product competitiveness and the quality of service delivery.

Recognition of the Royal's improvements also came from outside the organization. The fund management skills of the company were recognized in the prestigious *Sunday Times* and *Sunday Telegraph* Unit Trust Awards. Also, the company secured four awards in the *Micropal* Unit Trust Survey (*Micropal* is the recognized authority within the financial services sector on fund performance). Yet it was the NFIFA award mentioned above which was particularly pleasing to the Royal management. The award of an upgrading from a 1 Star rating to a 2 Star rating was secured following the launch of an improvement programme dedicated to meeting this objective; over 500 staff were involved in workshops to generate improvement ideas and the award was evidence that their effort had been worthwhile. Another source of feedback to the Royal came from the customer survey, with 78 per cent of respondents answering that they would be likely to recommend the Royal to a friend following their experience with the company.

All of these successes were communicated to staff, generally through the internal newsletter. The regular communication of quality successes is seen as a vital part of the quality programme, and ensures staff commitment to future initiatives.

The rate of response to the Staff Attitude Survey in itself was considered to be evidence of the staff's belief that their views will be acknowledged and actioned. The 64 per cent response rate was the fourth highest ever recorded by the independent company which undertook the survey. Comparing the responses with the 1993 survey, major improvement had been made in areas such as:

- receiving the *right kind* of training for the job
- receiving training and development for the job
- *encouragement* to take advantage of training and development opportunities
- knowing how to *find out about* training and development opportunities
- *confidence* that the Royal will treat staff fairly.

These results were communicated back to staff and used by management to develop and adapt future training plans.

MOVING ON

The Royal made great progress during 1994 in obtaining and understanding information on what customers (both consumers and intermediaries) think of their products and services. They progressed too, in ensuring that those products and services were of an appropriate quality. The company is now consolidating successes and achievements while identifying and realizing opportunities to promote continuous improvement in a systematic and structured way. To help the company's progress towards its stated goal of 'achieving quality in all we do', 1995 will see the development of KPIs which will focus on quality delivery, with the deployment of measures both vertically and horizontally throughout the company. The company considers that using external criteria is useful in the measurement process. They intend to self-assess against the BQF model of business excellence in the year. Their longer-term aims are to receive Investors in People accreditation by 1997 and to be a major contender for the UK Quality Award by 1999.

On the ground, the restructure will continue around a set of key customer-facing processes, reframing corporate units whose experts will be deployed into the operational processes where appropriate. During 1995 the largest operational process, Client Services, will come into being. This process embraces activities which are currently carried out across several functional areas. In total 800 staff – a third of the company – are involved and successful migration to the new structure will be followed by the creation of the remaining key processes as corporate units which will embrace all staff. It is believed that the implementation of these plans will make the Royal truly a customer-focused organization. In addition the restructure will facilitate the deployment of trained quality professionals into the operational business and therefore hasten the acceptance, promotion and implementation of continuous improvement throughout the organization.

In order to focus attention on areas most in need of it, and to fully understand the quality/cost trade-off, the Royal will, in 1995, develop its performance measurement system further to produce a Balanced Scorecard for the organization. The measures are by and large already in place and the IT is being developed accordingly.

One of the lasting rewards to come from the TQM programme has been the development in the organizational culture of an outward-looking perspective. Gone is the introspection, a former characteristic of the Royal, and in its place, a team of people gaining in confidence who feel able to help others and start promoting Total Quality outside the company. For example:

- The Royal is Founder Member of the British Quality Foundation.
- Two Royal managers acted as assessors for the 1995 UK Quality Award and more have asked for training to enable them to assess for the 1996 Award.
- The Royal is a major sponsor of the North West Quality Award and two of its managers acted as lead assessors for the 1995 Award.
- The Royal hosted a seminar in 1995 to give guidance to local businessmen contemplating self-assessment against a model of business excellence.
- The Royal acted as quality mentors for small local organizations; this included advice on submitting an award entry to a company who eventually won one of the North West Quality Awards.
- Seven Royal managers were assessors for the Wales Quality Award and the Royal received special thanks from the organizers for the extent of this contribution.

This external dimension complements, rather than detracts from, the progress which Royal knows it still has to make, particularly as most of the above work, such as mentoring and assessing, is done in each manager's own time, highlighting a strong personal commitment to Total Quality.

ELEVEN

THE SLAG REDUCTION COMPANY:

Weaving the rope of quality

PETER STANNACK
AND
JAMES HORSBURGH

ELEVEN

The Slag Reduction Company:

Weaving the rope of quality

INTRODUCTION

Systems thinkers and writers such as von Bertallanffy (1968) show us that the world which we, as social scientists, attempt to understand and, as practitioners, manage is made up of interlocking systems and subsystems. Within this system of systems we can identify hierarchies like Venn Diagrams in which a subsystem in one configuration can be a suprasystem in another.

When we consider the issues which surround quality and particularly the implementation of quality management (QM) and quality improvement (QI) programmes, it seems that systems thinking can be of great use. Often the implementation of QM and QI programmes is underpinned by a range of metaphors which suggest that QM can be achieved through a 'path' or 'road map' to quality (Juran, 1985; Crosby, 1979). This road can be 'built' using a range of 'tools' such as Quality Function Deployment (QFD) or Statistical Process Control (SPC).

This chapter will consider this 'civil engineering' approach to quality, because of the obvious benefits which such an approach can bring. It offers, for instance, a clear vision which can bring a coherent approach to the implementation programme. It also offers clear 'milestones' against which progress can be measured. Furthermore, it gives a clear focus for leadership in the oldest sense. As Borland and Deal (1993) have noted, the word 'leader' stems from the Anglo Saxon 'Laedere' whose original purpose was to guide on a journey.

It will also, however, consider the nature of thinking as it applies to quality. We do not question the need for quality road maps and the tools to build and maintain a road. We do, however, consider the implementation of quality programmes as a negotiated, less linear process. This may be likened to the weaving of a rope or cable. We will also argue that this rope-making process requires skills which incorporate the different existing 'strands' of quality, rather than civil engineering skills which may lead to the creation of a super highway using bulldozers and graders to cut across all terrain regardless of its value. This rope provided, we feel, the link between action and effect – successful effect – needed to implement a quality programme effectively.

SETTING THE SCENE

The genesis of many QM initiatives can be seen in the field of high volume manufacturing environments. Indeed, in the United States winners of the Malcolm Baldrige Award have included companies such as General Motors, Cadillac Division, IBM Rochester, Motorola Inc., Westinghouse and Xerox (Schmidt and Finnegan, 1992).

The stimulus for the introduction of QI and QM programmes is often a shift in market conditions as new offerings are launched in existing markets and existing players in these markets find themselves facing a retracting market share. In the case of Slag Reduction Company, however, the stimulus was internal.

During the 1980s British Steel had invested heavily in both its iron-making and steel-making facilities and had also worked to develop the skills and motivation of its employees. Extensive training programmes were undertaken as one major component of a strategy which was designed to ensure that British Steel maintained its position as a major force in world steel-making.

Under the labour practices in place at the time, employees at the Redcar Ore Terminal had not been involved in these activities. This was largely due to limitations imposed by the National Dock Labour Scheme which regulated their employment. The repeal of the Scheme in 1989 presented an opportunity to examine the future operation of the Terminal and the management of both systems and human resources. The National Dock Labour Scheme had imposed a heavy cost burden upon the operation of the terminal. This was managed by entering into a partnership subcontracting relationship with The Slag Reduction Company Limited. The Slag Reduction Company is a subdivision of Faber Prest plc.

British Steel's Teesside Works is one of the Company's three integrated steel-making sites with an annual liquid steel production of 3.75 million tonnes accounting for about 30 per cent of the Company's output. To produce this quantity of steel requires the importation of up to 11 million tonnes of raw materials, principally ores and coals from every continent in the world. The materials are received at the Redcar Ore Terminal which has an overall berth length of 320 metes and a dredged depth at low spring tide of 17 metres. The berth can accommodate vessels up to 150,000 tonnes. There are three unloaders, two of which are rated at 2000 tonnes per hour and the third at 3000 tonnes per hour. Materials are carried to stock piles by conveyor systems and prepared for further processing.

The programme described in this chapter was developed in partnership between British Steel plc and The Slag Reduction Company. This joint strategy for the future involved a re-assessment of manpower needs and job roles within the terminal, The employees based at the Redcar Ore Terminal prior to deregulation were offered these new posts which included the redefinition of the role of existing dockers as terminal operators and training to meet the demands of the deregulated climate.

This resulted in efficiency savings and the recruitment of a number of new employees.

The human resource climate which this exercise left within the terminal had both positive and negative effects. Positive effects included the fact that workers within the terminal felt that they had a 'clean sheet' to manage the new processes. Also the fact that staff had 'self-selected' meant that the sense of commitment to new processes was high. This commitment was the first stage in negotiating the implementation of the quality management programme. Potentially negative effects were that the shifts within the terminal would possibly lead to uncertainty amongst staff.

KEY OBJECTIVES OF THE STRATEGY

Because of the need to maximize the positive effects of changes, the response to this potential uncertainty was to develop a clear strategy and to develop an effective and efficient communication strategy in order to share the strategy with the staff. The key objectives of this strategy were:

1. To produce a highly skilled, flexible workforce capable of performing all the tasks required for world-class efficiency and quality. This meant that there were key elements of attitudinal shift and training and development to be taken into account.
2. To improve employee utilization from previous standards and protect the employment of the Wharf team. This was an essential element of the strategy as it was felt necessary to communicate reasons for the strategy which were aligned to employee interests.
3. To improve the utilization of the Wharf and the terminal for new activities including the export of semi-finished and finished products as well as the import of raw materials.
4. To change the attitude and culture from one in which the staff saw the 'job' as hardly being part of their responsibilities to one of active interest in safety, efficiency and quality together with a willingness to accept and contribute to innovative working practices.

The management of any process requires that it be controlled. Otley and Berry (1985) have noted the need for effective measurement in control systems. In order to achieve these objectives, the following measurement systems were selected:

- Increases in team utilization and team management methods.
- Increased tonnes per day discharged.
- Reduced demurrage costs.
- Creation of available berth time at the Ore Terminal to enable business developments, e.g. export capability.
- Reduction in lost time through injuries which would act as a measure of attitude change.

As well as a measurement system, the implementation process required a training management system, in order to ensure that staff were not only motivated to take up new practices and new ways of working but also that they were capable of doing so. The next sections of this chapter will consider in more detail how each of these systems was designed and implemented.

IMPLEMENTING THE MANAGEMENT STRATEGY

Once objectives have been set, measurement systems selected and training policies developed, the next stage of the QM process is implementation. As noted above, this can be seen as a control process (Otley and Berry, *op. cit.*) the purpose of which is to identify those mechanisms which can be used to correct any variance from objective (see Figure 11.1). This involved the development of a management structure.

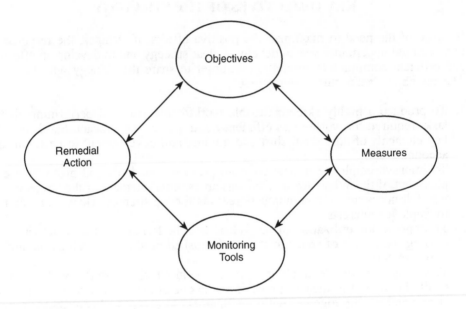

Figure 11.1   The elements of a control cycle

A steering team was selected comprising of representatives from British Steel and Slag Reduction Management, including experts on terminal operations and, perhaps most importantly, representatives of the operators. This was seen as the second stage in the negotiation process in implementing the quality road map. The involvement of operators at this early stage improved information gathering and facilitated the establishment of innovative solutions to implementation. It was made clear to the team that the continued success of Teesside Works as a world leader in Steel rested upon the successful implementation of the changes needed. This could then be communicated by the operators' representatives to other staff.

Once the management systems had been designed, the next step was to split the programme into phases. This was designed to ensure that the implementation process could be clearly visible. Phase One of the programme was planned to involve a 'fast track' approach, the purpose of which was twofold: first, to ensure a high degree of labour mobility within the terminal by employing multi-skilling and multitasking programmes; second, to offer the employees clear, immediate rewards which would build on existing commitment. The later phases were to develop in a more evolutionary way.

Due, however, to the enthusiasm and involvement of the team members the second phase of the programme was planned during Phase One and implemented immediately after the completion of the initial phase.

DEVELOPING MANAGEMENT COMMITMENT

One of the classic components of quality systems is to ensure 'top-down commitment' from senior managers. Traditionally, a lack of commitment in this area can be seen as fatal to the process of QI. The development of management commitment is not, in itself, enough. Such commitment also needs to be communicated effectively to employees.

We were particularly fortunate in that the project was carried out in partnership between British Steel and The Slag Reduction Company Limited. Particularly during the work of the action teams, borders between British Steel Departments and Slag Reduction Company staff became so blurred as to be invisible. Although this was a particular project, it was not developed in isolation but as part of Teesside British Steel's continuous drive for Total Quality Performance. All levels of Slag Reduction and British Steel's management have been totally committed to the policy. This required a clear role for senior managers. Senior management's role is to facilitate, guide and control TQP policy. The translation of this role was demonstrated by increasing current major spend aimed at raising plant to best world standards and therefore matching the commitment of the workforce.

As well as strategic commitment, it is also possible to identify what might be termed 'tactical' commitment. Here, middle managers and supervisors were the 'engine' of the project. Some of the consequences of implementation at this level were unexpected but still welcome. Implementation has resulted in an increased workload and as a result managers and supervisors had to allow the workforce new levels of involvement and empowerment. This is not to say that there has not been a willingness on the part of managers to modify fixed attitudes and views and employ a new flexibility of approach.

As noted above, in order to be effective, commitment requires communication. This was carried out through two strategies. The first of these was the management of group targets or milestones. Targets were set incrementally in order to facilitate process visibility. Some of the milestones were:

1990/91	Rapid improvement in throughput with development of new methods and skills.
1992	Achievement of BS5750 (ISO9002).
1993	Wharf team wins Teesside Directors Quality Award.
1884	Teesside Award for Education and Training. National Training Award.
1995	Wharf Operatives presented a paper to 1st World TQM Congress, Sheffield

The second stage was that of recognition of achievement. Management has always shown commitment by recognizing achievement and publicizing success. This recognition has taken various forms including:

- Social events
- Publicity in works bulletins and local papers
- Visits to other European facilities
- Presentation of gifts recognizing particular achievements.

Overall the commitment of senior managers has been demonstrated through placing trust in the labour force, and convincing them that their skills, experience and commitment are valued. In this way, progress is shown to benefit not only the companies involved, but each individual.

As can be seen, commitment from senior and other managers is a process which needs to be clearly communicated to workers in a variety of forms throughout the overall lifetime of the project. In this sense, senior management commitment is one strand in the rope or cable of quality. The next strand in the programme is that of measurement.

DEVELOPING MEASUREMENT SYSTEMS

As we have seen, any quality improvement or quality management system requires a system of measurement in order to ensure that it is effectively controlled. The choice of measurement systems is an essential element in the overall implementation programme. Any measurement system must contain at least three components. The first of these is the data which is to be collected. The second is the way in which data is collected. The third is the way in which data is interpreted or presented.

All systems of measurement were chosen as appropriate to the task to be controlled. In addition, further criteria are that data for measurement should be simple to understand, simple to gather and comparable both nationally and internationally. The final criterion for such systems was that the measurement system should be closely linked with the activity being controlled, in order to ensure that employees could identify clear cause and effect linkages between activities and results.

The measures

Overall it was decided to use the international measure of Bulk discharge performance of Ore Equivalent (OE) tonnes discharged per day. This has been the prime measure for Redcar Wharf since 1971. It had the advantage of being clearly understood by all employees.

While the work of the action teams directly affected the OE measure, many of the teams needed measures more closely linked with their task,. This enabled workers to perceive the result of their actions as effective or otherwise and this, in turn, facilitated process improvement. Examples of measures chosen included:

- Rate of loading steel slabs per hour.
- Cost of loading steel per tonne.
- Average damage caused per vessel.
- Life of unloader ropes in tonnes discharged.

All of these measures demonstrate progress to both the customer and the workforce.

Data collection and interpretation

Once the data indicator has been chosen, the next stage of the process is to decide how the data will be collected and measured. The philosophy behind the programme was that external controls and measures would be replaced wherever possible by internal controls and measures. This meant that the data was collected by the employees themselves where appropriate and by the various customers as well.

Once the data was collected, the final step in the process was to make the data useful. This was done by the employment of statistical process control charts of different types. These included cumulative sum charts where appropriate. The charting of measurements by operatives gave an excellent control tool through which progress can be monitored and problems identified.

Occasionally the measurement method was beyond in-house resources, but where external measuring methods were employed, the presentation of results was made simple and understandable. It was decided, for example, that the best measure of progress for Wharf Unloader 3 action team was an unloading and reloading cycle time. In order to eliminate variables these complex timings required continuous measurement over long periods. These were produced by British Steel's Work Study and Operational Research Department, interpreted by them and presented to the supplier, customer and workforce in clear graphical form. The purpose of these measures was made very clear to the workforce in order to ensure that they were involved in the corrective action process.

The next strand of the quality implementation process is the development and management of training for quality performance.

TRAINING FOR PERFORMANCE

The third strand of the implementation involved the actual introduction of the quality programme. This involved further training for attitudinal and culture change which would release the pool of expertise and knowledge available in the personnel. The vehicle chosen to release this knowledge was multi-disciplinary action teams involving Wharf operatives. Each team was targeted by the Steering Committee at particular objectives. Although these objectives had been chosen by the Steering Committee, the operative representatives were a part of the ongoing discussions and negotiation throughout the selection process. This fostered problem ownership amongst the teams. As problems were solved and permanent fixes achieved, new targets were set.

We can identify a number of components which were essential to the effective introduction of the programme. These include:

- Education and training programmes which were relevant to the needs of the staff as well as the needs of the organization
- Teamworking with consensus on clear targets, roles and responsibilities throughout the organization
- Effective communication in order to manage the attitudinal and cultural shifts needed
- The development of measurement systems and future objectives.

These are set out in more detail below.

QUALITY EDUCATION AND TRAINING

We can identify a number of elements which are essential to the design of any training programme. These are:

- A clear set of objectives for the training
- A range of delivery methods tailored to the requirements of the employees to be trained
- An effective evaluation programme in order to modify and improve the training programme
- Links, where possible, to national accreditation to 'prove' that the training has wider applicability and is thus transferable to other situations.

Management demonstrated that they were committed to training as a means of ensuring that the requirements of the business are met through applications and entries for awards. This 'public' statement also had a number of benefits as staff felt that there were 'larger' targets to work for. During 1994 the efforts of management and workforce were recognized locally and nationally by the award of the Teesside Business Award for Education and Training, and a National Training Award.

Training policy and objectives are based upon a divisional training manual. This is designed to meet requirements of legislation, the needs of the customer and also to add value and skills to the individual contribution of the team. Needs are identified through ongoing training needs analysis (TNA) and through appraisal. This TNA also will involve feedback from customer groups within British Steel and also among the suppliers who may be seen as 'customers' during the unloading process.

This policy is also linked directly to teamworking We were aware that individual learning can be augmented and supported by learning in groups (Knowles, 1976). Furthermore the teams' involvement was developed through feedback to modify and develop the training policy. The results produced by teams are routed into safe working procedure documents and the team's final task is to ensure those concerned are trained in them. The Steering Committee ensured in 1990 that all efforts would be directed in this way.

VOCATIONAL TRAINING AND DEVELOPMENT

It was possible to identify two sets of objectives within the training programme. The first of these were *vocational* training objectives. These included the elements necessary to ensure the safe and efficient operation of the terminal. The final set of vocational objectives within the programme comprised the following elements:

- Training of the newly recruited operators in unloader driving to become fully skilled team members.
- Training for the introduction of changed working methods and new types of mobile tools.
- Revised discharge procedure developed by team members.
- Training in use of the new mobile ship cleaner.
- Development and implementation of safety and safety-related issues within an annual plan, e.g.
  - kinetic handling
  - immobilisation.
- Contact training – training in four topics per annum – Isolation, Access to Ships, Disaster Plan, Enclosed Shipladders.
- Development of trainer training to keep abreast of the above initiatives and to eliminate the need for professional mobile tool trainers. Two trainers attended a Quarry Products training course on mobile tools.

These objectives were formalized through the development of a description and training matrix for each duty. Evaluation of the training took place through the continuous appraisal and competency testing of all terminal operators.

In addition to vocational training programmes, the Steering Group also identified a clear need for training and development in attitude and culture.

DEVELOPMENT FOR ATTITUDE AND CULTURE SHIFT

The vehicle chosen to develop the change in attitude needed by both management and operators was British Steel's Total Quality Programme, itself renowned nationally and internationally for its effectiveness. Every member of the terminal management team and every operator attended a training course delivered by trained and experienced British Steel facilitators/trainers. Training embraced a number of core elements. These included the principles and philosophy of Total Quality. They also included problem-solving tools and techniques such as Ishikawa diagrams and Pareto Analysis. Communication and team-building skills were also developed in order to facilitate the transfer of information within the teams and to lend the immediate focus required by the programme.

The effect of the attitudinal shift was effectively to transform the team into a self-managed quality improvement team which continued to embrace training and development. The team ensures monthly shift briefing, communications and feedback, and the operational team participates in improvement teams where *all* their newly gained skills can be utilized to maximum effect. A total of 44 terminal operators and nine managers received 1064 days of training costing £95,000.

The benefits gained from the attitudinal and cultural shift programme can be identified at both the individual and organizational level.

BENEFITS TO THE INDIVIDUAL

The Wharf operatives and supervisors took to TQM principles and problem solving by action teams like 'ducks to water'. There were a number of reasons for this. The nature of the unloading task does not particularly lend itself to standard 'job enrichment' approaches such as those promulgated by Herzberg and Hacker *et al*. Instead we can see that training in problem-solving techniques can become a job enrichment programme in itself.

Positive benefits were identified in that the team members became aware that they were capable of a much wider range of skills which, with a positive approach, could be used constructively to achieve success through change. A further benefit is the effect upon the working environment. The individual approach no longer exists. Everyone is a member of a flexible, multi-talented and highly focused team. They remain keen to develop their skills into the future through a process of continuous improvement.

The application of the Total Quality approach has given a new dimension with individuals personally contributing to the development of new tools, new procedures and, very importantly, new business opportunities for the Terminal. They have been empowered to contribute to all aspects of Terminal operations and their ideas have become crucial to the development and success of these operations. This pride is typified by a recent statement from a team member: 'We can achieve anything by working together with management to develop and implement the approach.'

BENEFITS TO THE ORGANIZATION

The benefits gained from this training programme have been spectacular and beyond the best estimates considered possible in 1989. Over the five-year development period the Ore Terminal at British Steel, Teesside is seen as comparable with the world's best as witnessed by the visit of study groups from five different countries during the first quarter of 1994. Specific benefits relating to the original business needs include:

- All working methods have been designed for efficiency regardless of task and all restrictive practices have been eliminated.
- Employee utilization has increased from 50 per cent to 88 per cent (verified by British Steel's Work Study and Operational Research Department).
- Increase in tonnes discharged from 36,000 tonnes per day to 52,000 tonnes per day.
- Demurrage costs have been reduced from £3,000,000 to £214,000 per annum.

The management of the training programme was the third strand in the successful implementation of the strategy. The results of our 'rope making' have shown the way forward for a number of other projects. The next section of this chapter will demonstrate the effects of the 'rope' on the productivity, quality, and quality of working life within the company (see Figure 11.2).

EFFECTIVE COMMUNICATION
CLEAR, SHARED GOALS AND OBJECTIVES
TRAINING AND DEVELOPMENT
EFFECTIVE MEASUREMENT AND MANAGEMENT

Figure 11.2 The 'rope' of quality

THE RESULTS OF THE PROGRAMME

This section deals with the work of the action teams throughout 1994 and particularly with a new action team which started work in that year.

The work of the teams in 1994 fell into a familiar pattern. The philosophy of the implementation was, as noted above, one which emphasizes involvement in change and pride in achievement. It is important to stress the excitement and enjoyment which has been gained from the increased levels of ownership and the strong linkages between action and success within the project. Success reinforces commitment. Suppliers and customers are often included within the teams, on a part-time or full-time basis, and the enthusiasm is shared within the team. This enables the team to draw upon resources to which it would not normally have access and also improves communication links with the teams' environment.

The total labour force is 44 men, of whom 26 have been directly involved in action team work. In addition, all five supervisors have led or participated in action teams. The remainder of the labour force are involved by monthly toolbox meetings during which progress is reviewed and suggestions canvassed.

A typical example of the system in operation was a new task completed in 1994, the loading of steel blooms into a vessel. The steel loading action had produced a method of loading and the job was completed very successfully. On completion, 106 ideas for improvement were presented by the workforce, this total being derived from 170 separate suggestions, some of which were duplicated.

Our success in using action teams for problem solving has given the management of Slag Reduction and British Steel greater confidence in the techniques and it is now a routine method used within the Redcar Terminal site. While we have noted above that senior management commitment was communicated through capital investment, it should be pointed out that improvements made from 1990–3 were all achieved without any significant capital spend. It was these improvements which gave management within British Steel the confidence to plan and execute a major capital spend of some £5 million to update the Wharf unloaders. We can see here that TQ implementation can be interpreted as a 'customer centred' marketing exercise (Kotler, 1985) where the process of implementation requires tailoring to the needs of the internal and external customers and where the results of the implementation can be employed as a 'product' to 'sell' in exchange for further improvements.

This is not to say that the implementation of TQ led to the disappearance of all problems. Instead the implementation led to the discovery of new problems, but also to the discovery of new solutions. For example, the first phase of the work on Unloader 3 was completed in August 1994 and a major problem was encountered. The cycle time of the refurbished unloader had changed form 59 seconds to 78 seconds. The contractor responsible for the work and British Steel Engineering were unable to solve the problem and the response was to institute an action team of experienced drivers, British Steel Engineering Department and the contractor. The cycle time of Unloader 3, which relates directly to throughput, was improved by 30 per cent. The benefits of this are being seen in the rate of throughput for the plant; the actual cost saving in terms of loss avoidance has not yet been calculated.

Other results included the following:

- Dramatic reductions in demurrage costs which are simply the rental paid on vessels held at the port during discharge. This results in a change achieved of £2.5 million year on year.
- Improvements in free berth time. As throughput improved, berth occupancy fell from 75 per cent in 1990 to 57 per cent during 1993–4. This free time was filled by developing the business into new areas.
- Reductions in ship damage. An unloader grab full of ore weighs 63 tonnes and some damage to vessels' internal steelwork during discharge was thought to be unavoidable. This team broke the accepted mould and trained the workforce to complete the task with much reduced cost effect. Prior to the action team's work, damage costs averaged £2,573 per vessel. Latest levels are running at £502 per vessel.

The final section of this chapter relates to plans for the future. British Steel plc and the Slag Reduction Company are aware of the dangers of complacency in TQ, where initial gains can be lost because staff and managers 'let go' of the process after success.

FUTURE CONTINUOUS IMPROVEMENT PLANS

In some ways 1994 was a watershed in the undertaking. The refurbishment of the plant which will be completed by mid-1995 gave pause for thought. A number of the major action team projects came to successful conclusions and efforts had to be redirected.

The Steering Committee made plans to maintain current efforts and to direct the project in new directions. The work from 1990–4 has been seen simply as a start, getting the basics right, developing the mindset and culture of all involved.

The future holds golden opportunities to develop and advance. Plans are laid for new action teams which, while not expected to produce the startling gains of the first four years, will allow us to refine and steadily improve the service. PLC control of the major plant gives new opportunities to measure and understand the system. Improvements to equipment are expected to create further free berth time and an action team with five task forces is well advanced with plans to take advantage of this.

Projects are well advanced for a commitment to IIP and to achieve NVQ rating for the unloader training programme.

A deliberate policy decision has been taken to involve the remainder of the workforce, not yet part of an action team, in the new plans, thus giving fresh ideas and personalities to the project. The view of the customer is paramount. We attempt to emphasize the key questions. How does the customer want the service to develop? Has he or she problems we may be able to solve? Can the successes achieved and the lessons learned be of value in other areas of customer business?

Particular stress has again been placed on safety. A 30 per cent reduction in accidents was achieved during the first four years, but this was unsatisfactory. Development of personnel training, writing of new safe working procedures, the training and placement of Safe Working Party Leaders and the development of the role of Safety Representatives are all in hand and will produce the required improvement.

Continuity is the key note. Refresher training of TQM principles is planned to help maintain the impetus. The TQM project is no longer a project, it is fast becoming a way of life. As Collins and Porras have shown (1995), companies which are 'built to last' have something approaching cult status for their employees. This is the exciting challenge for the future. It has been suggested by a number of writers that the journey rather than the destination is the reward in Total Quality as well as to other areas. At The Slag Reduction Company, we have certainly found it so.

BIBLIOGRAPHY

von Bertallanffy, L. (1968) *General Systems Theory*, Penguin, Harmondsworth
Bolman, L. and Deal, T. (1993) *Reframing Organisations*, Jossey Bass
Collins, J. and Porras, J. (1995) *Built to Last*, Century Books
Juran, J. (1987) *Quality Control Handbook*, McGraw-Hill
Finnegan and Schmidt (1992) *The Race Without a Finish Line*, Jossey Bass

TWELVE

WELLMAN INTERNATIONAL:

Shaping and sustaining a vision of quality

HADYN INGRAM

AND

FRANK GLEESON

TWELVE

Wellman International:
Shaping and sustaining a vision of quality

The key to business success in the 1990s will (also) revolve around how well business uses and involves its workers. This means that a new style of leadership and management will be needed that places more focus on developing workers' skills and requiring management to trust employees more. Successful organizations are those with greater awareness that employee loyalty, commitment and concern for quality depend on effective management–employee communication. (R. Zeffane (1992) 'Organisational structures: design in the nineties', *International Journal of Hospitality Management*, Vol. 13, No. 6, pp. 18–23.

INTRODUCTION

An organizational quality improvement strategy is born of clear management vision, but it can only grow and gain strength if that vision is fully espoused by employees. Wellman International sought to build on the achievement of ISO 9002 accreditation in 1990 and develop a fully integrated Total Quality Management programme. This chapter chronicles Wellman's approach to overcoming potential obstacles and transforming culture in order to embed their vision as an enduring reality.

WELLMAN INC.

Wellman Inc. is a large manufacturing organization producing a range of polyester and nylon products from its operations in the USA, Holland and Ireland. The company is also the world's largest recycler of post-consumer soft drinks bottles made from a plastic substance called PET. Wellman Inc. had its origins in the 1950s as a family-run manufacturing firm in the USA which, up to the 1980s grew by business development and subsequently expanded as a public corporation by acquisition. In 1995 it further strengthened its position in the post-consumer soft drinks bottles market by acquiring Akso, a PET resin facility in Holland.

WELLMAN INTERNATIONAL

The European operation centres on the plant in Ireland, trading as Wellman International Ltd. The primary product is a fibrous polyester material, similar in appearance to raw cotton or wool that is converted either into yarn for carpet or rope manufacture or into a matrix structure for non-woven products. The non-woven material may be used as an insulation medium in quilts and pillows or in sports clothing. It may also be used as a filling in domestic furniture, as filtering material or for medical purposes. Alternatively this non-woven product may be needle-punched or stitch-bonded for the production of carpeting, geotextiles, abrasives or roofing felt. Wellman International supplies these raw materials to manufacturing organizations to be further converted or prepared as a finished product. Its second main manufacturing activity is as the European market leader in the recycling of post-consumer soft drinks bottles made from long-chain polyester molecules called Polyethylene Terephthalate or PET. Every year, three hundred million such bottles are processed initially in the plant in Holland prior to being transferred to Ireland for integration into the normal polyester raw material stream.

In 1973, the parent organization established a plant in Ireland which supplies polyester and nylon products to the Irish, UK and European textile industry. The plant is located at Mullagh which is 40 miles to the north-west of Dublin in the Republic of Ireland and is set in the fertile farmland of County Meath. In all, 469 people are employed in the following capacities:

Managerial	12
Sales	10
Administrative	57
Production	27
Technical	15
Supervisors	50
Operators	243
Craftsmen	55

Organization

The European operation reports to the main board in the USA which recognizes differences in local markets and product specifications, and permits Wellman International a high degree of autonomy. The Wellman International plant in Ireland is headed by a Chief Executive, Managing Director and Plant Director and arranged in five functions:

- Commercial affairs Exports, sales and shipping
- Raw materials   Purchase of raw materials for the manufacturing processes
- Operations   Manufacturing, quality and technical concerns
- Personnel   Employment and training
- Finance   Financial and management accounts and information technology

The full organization chart is shown in Figure 12.1.

Development of quality improvement at Wellman International

In 1989, Wellman International embarked upon a programme of accreditation to ISO 9002, which was achieved in 1990 after 15 months of preparation. In order to build on this success and to focus upon quality involvement by all members of the

Organisation Chart

Wellman International Ltd.
Figure 12.1

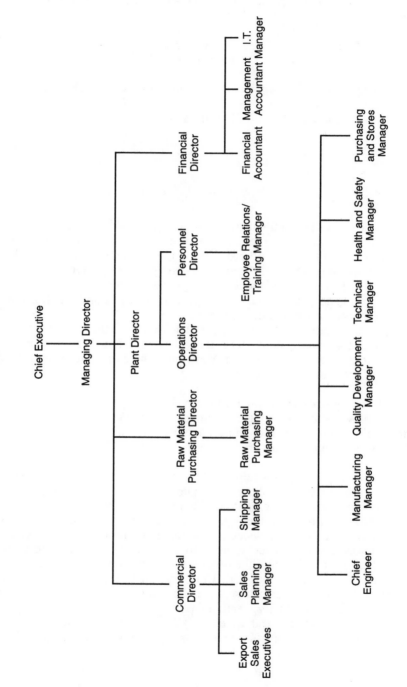

Figure 12.1 Organization chart

organization, a second management initiative was developed which was called 'Total Customer Satisfaction' (TCS). The significance of this term was explained as follows:

T   TOTAL   Involving everyone
                               Everything we do

C   CUSTOMER   Without him/her we wouldn't be there

S   SATISFACTION   Meeting all our customer needs

Stage 1   Vision

The objective of the Total Customer Satisfaction process was to involve every employee in the company in meeting customer expectations, reducing process imperfections and quality costs and providing opportunities to improve work methods by real participation. As a first step in realising this objective, consultants were retained to carry out an independent diagnostic survey of the views of a range of stakeholders. They included 62 employees at all levels and functions, nineteen major customers and seven major suppliers.

In order to direct and co-ordinate the efforts of the TCS process, a Steering Group was appointed which was composed of directors and senior managers across all functions and chaired by the Managing Director. The responsibilities of the Steering Group are as follows:

- Selecting processes or themes for development
- Examining and improving communication methods
- Developing a formal recognition policy
- Approving expenditure on resources as required.

The Steering Group developed a four-stage strategy for quality improvement at Wellman International as shown in Figure 12.2. The initial stage was to articulate aims through a vision statement and then to specify how quality improvement was to be deployed throughout the organization. Stage 3 identified the quality education and training that would be necessary in preparation for the final stage of measuring and monitoring performance against pre-set targets. The Steering Group took the initial step towards focusing the organization's efforts on the TCS strategy by compiling a vision statement entitled 'Commitment to the Future', which is shown in Figure 12.3. The statement affirms the Company's quality focus and its intention to develop a series of mutually beneficial partnerships.

In order to make the strategy explicit, a Forward Plan covering 1993/4 was devised specifying dates for training and communication events in the period.

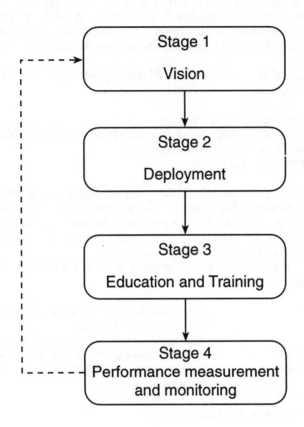

Figure 12.2   Wellman International's Quality Improvement strategy

Commitment to the Future

Wellman will be the leader in our chosen business of fibre production and PET recycling, achieving excellence and innovation through the dedicated involvement of all employees.

We will fully meet our customers' expectations by making products fit for purpose, cost effective and available as required.

We will build strong partnerships with our customers, employees and suppliers, with full regard to health, safety, environment and community.

Figure 12.3   Wellman International's 'Commitment to the Future' vision statement

Stage 2   Deployment

The Diagnostic Report and vision statement were communicated to directors and senior managers through a three-day 'Commitment Workshop' conducted by the Consultants. This workshop focused upon the identification of potential barriers and the initiation of both short-term and ongoing actions through teamwork, as shown in Figure 12.4.

The objectives of the Commitment Workshop were to develop a clear understanding of the following:

- Total Customer Satisfaction strategy
- Relationships between Total Customer Satisfaction and ISO 9002
- Implementing Total Customer Satisfaction
- Barriers that might occur.

Discussions during the workshop identified a number of barriers that might hinder the implementation of the strategy. These barriers included fear and suspicion on the part of employees and a lack of commitment from the management. In addition, it was felt that if the strategy was not visible to all or was poorly communicated, it was unlikely to be effectively implemented.

Accordingly, both short-term and ongoing actions were taken to address these potential problems. Short-term actions included:

- Involvement   Discussions with employees, organized plant tours for employees' families
- Training   New training centre, training schemes
- Communication   Monthly newsletters, information boards
- Customer awareness   Showroom to educate employees, customer profile features.

Ongoing objectives for action were:

- Active listening to people's points of view
- Greater interaction between departments and individuals
- More open and effective communication methods
- Financial briefings on company performance
- Introduction of a profit sharing plan.

Project teams

In order to encourage wider involvement and ownership of problems and solutions, a series of project teams was formed in the period from October 1993 to December 1994. The project teams are composed of between four and eight members who meet according to their needs; typically every three or four weeks. Teams use a systematic and disciplined problem solving approach comprising the following six steps:

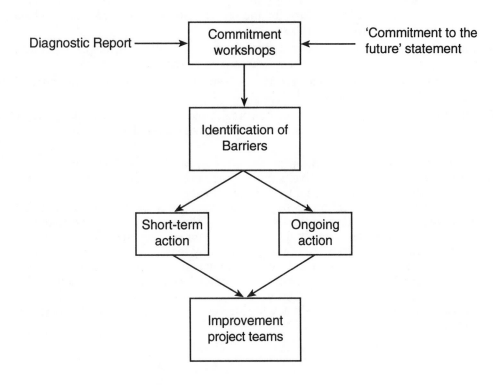

Figure 12.4 Deployment of Quality Improvement at Wellman International

1. Define the task to be addressed clearly.
2. Identify root causes by measurement and prioritization.
3. Generate possible solutions through consensus.
4. Plan and implement solutions.
5. Measure and monitor progress.
6. Modify procedures based upon successful solutions.

In all, 23 project teams were formed involving 143 people across all departments and addressing subjects as diverse as delivery performance, family plant visits and expansion programmes. Teams were required to complete their projects before being formally recognized by the Steering Group.

Project team recognition

Each project team member adopted one of four roles:

Problem owner	Usually a senior manager who initiates and takes ultimate responsibility for the project but does not necessarily attend team meetings
Team leader	Organizes and directs team activities. Arranges meetings, minutes and co-ordinates subsequent action plans
Team members	Active participants in team activities who form the core of the team
Facilitator	Keeps the team 'on track' and encourages team progress by ensuring that the problem solving approach is followed

This team role approach was based on the work of Meredith Belbin who suggests that teams function most effectively if they incorporate a balance of roles based upon members' skills and personalities (Belbin, 1981).

The project team recognition policy was designed with the aim of ensuring that contribution to improvement activity within the Wellman plant should be acknowledged in an appropriate, clear and consistent manner. The Steering Group was given responsibility for listening to presentations by teams, for conferring recognition awards to successful teams and for communicating this success throughout the com-pany. Upon completion of a project, an explanatory presentation is made to the Steering Group, with formal recognition given to each team member. Details of the work done and the achievements made are subsequently communicated throughout the company.

Problem-solving techniques

The method used to analyse problems and to generate solutions is the CEDAC system, which in an acronym for Cause and Effect Diagram with the Addition of Cards. This works by considering, in a team environment, firstly the possible causes of a problem and secondly potential actions that may be taken to improve the situation. Problems are recorded on yellow fact cards and ideas for improvement on blue cards and they are all displayed on the CEDAC board. Prominent exposure of this kind enables the team to review their progress regularly and to record this progress on the cards for all to see using the following codes:

*			Under consideration by the team
*	*		In preparation for trial
*	*	*	On trial
*	*	*	**It works! Now standard practice**

The CEDAC board is regularly reviewed by the team to progress improvement cards and to add any new cards to the board. Contributions from everyone concerning problems and ideas for improvement are welcomed, all of which are regularly monitored.

Case Study 1
Project team task: To improve telephone and fax response time

This project was launched in October 1993 as a result of feedback from the TCS diagnostic survey.

An audit of the existing situation through a survey of external and internal users revealed no problems with the fax system but some delay in responding to incoming telephone calls. The response time was established at 10 seconds and a target of 5 seconds was set.

This objective was addressed in the following ways:

- Training for all telephone users
- Replacement of obsolete equipment
- Increased awareness of direct-dial access to telephone extensions
- Purchase of bleepers for people who were 'hard to contact'
- Installation of call distribution system for each department

The results of these measures were to reduce telephone response time by 24 per cent while increasing the number of incoming calls by 17 per cent. Training was successful in increasing awareness of all users of the telephone facilities and increasing usage of the direct-dial facility. More effective internal communications were achieved by adding new telephone extensions, improving bell and tannoy systems and by the use of bleepers. The success of this new system is monitored by means of a 'telephone problem log' in which actual problems are recorded and remedied.

In summary, this project enabled the company to enhance customer service by improving both telephone response time and internal communications.

Stage 3   Education and training

Having defined the management vision and deployed the project teams, the next stage was to introduce the concept and principles of Total Customer Satisfaction across the organization through training and education. This process of training and education is shown in Figure 12.5. The 'Commitment Workshops' in April 1993 had clarified top management's perceptions of TCS and this new understanding was passed on to all managers, supervisors and some administrative staff through a series of one-day workshops. The objectives of these workshops were to determine the following:

- Implications of TCS to the plant as perceived by the group
- Group contribution to the company vision
- Barriers to achieving TCS and ways of overcoming them
- Suitable problem areas for project team contributions

Tool and Technique training

The first step in communicating the TCS strategy was through 'Tool and Technique' training for managers and supervisors that was scheduled from September 1993 to January 1994. The aims of the training were as follows:

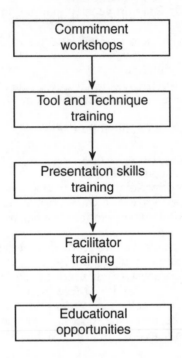

Figure 12.5   Wellman's quality training and education

- Outline the role of management and supervision as group leaders
- Permit the expression of fears and inadequacies in a supportive atmosphere
- Prepare for the broader delivery of the training programme between February and July 1994
- Emphasize the need for a culture of continuous improvement

The Tool and Technique training took place over three days and included theory and practical elements in a team environment with sessions designed to illustrate the power of teamworking. The first section addressed the main focus of quality: the external customer. Secondly, the role of the manager was explored in enabling people to deliver quality and providing relevant training. The final section detailed an approach to quality based upon sustained obsession with continuous improvement. In an attempt to improve understanding of business processes, attendees examined potential conflicts inherent in both process and results' orientations as well as practical issues such as measurement and variability.

Presentation Skills training

Tool and Technique training enabled managers and supervisors to develop their understanding of the key issues so that they could progress to the next stage of training to communicate the TCS message effectively. Accordingly, a Presentation Skills training programme was delivered to groups of 6–8 managers and supervisors over three days. The objectives of the training were as follows:

- Develop presentational skills
- Introduce the TCS Awareness Training package
- Evolve the training package based upon contributions from participants
- Enable participants to communicate TCS effectively to others
- Prepare for roles in supporting the delivery of the TCS Awareness Training package

The Presentation Skills training was conducted in a manner that reinforced the spirit of TCS and its focus upon ownership, participation and teamwork.

Awareness Training programme

Subsequently, an Awareness Training programme was devised to cover the remaining 380 employees who would be trained by their immediate departmental supervisor. The first session explained the vision of TCS and suggested areas for improvement opportunities. Session two addressed the practical questions of problem solving within a team environment and the use of techniques such as brainstorming to reveal creative options. The full diagnostic results and 'Commitment to the Future' vision statement were reviewed and discussed with each group of employees.

Following the Awareness Training programme, groups were encouraged to select problem areas through the formation of project teams.

Facilitator training

In order to support the project teams, a core of eight facilitators was selected from a wide representation of employees and underwent a three-day training programme. The objectives of the facilitator were to develop understanding and knowledge of the following:

- TCS strategy and the tools and techniques
- How teams function and can be facilitated
- Skills necessary for effective facilitation

In the near future, a leadership programme is planned to enhance the skills of team leaders and their understanding of such issues as: team dynamics, personal skills, effective team working, team structures, team-building and meetings' skills.

In addition to training on-site employees, European sales personnel and agents were given an awareness programme in order to ensure the consistency of the TCS message and its customer focus.

Educational opportunities

The process of Total Customer Satisfaction generated other ideas and opportunities that enabled teams to become more independent and autonomous. Some examples of these ideas were:

- Seek external advice and visit national customers and other organizations
- Organize family visits to the plant
- Involve plant personnel in expansion plans
- Identify and address training needs by the team
- Provide specific training for computers and new technology

In summary, the training at Wellman International was carried out in a systemic fashion. Its primary objectives were to ensure that the TCS ethos was fully discussed and understood by managerial and supervisory staff before being communicated to the remaining personnel. The team approach enabled new ideas to be generated which would further build upon the ethos of continuous learning supported by all employees.

Case Study 2
Project team task: Family plant visits

In 1993, some employees had expressed an interest in bringing their families to a guided tour of the plant. This project team decided to determine the level of interest in such a scheme by circulating a questionnaire to all employees. There was a huge positive response, so the project team planned the visiting schedule in the mutually suitable period of June to September. As a result, invitations were sent to the families and the visits were scheduled at the rate of one, two or three families a day, depending on family size. The visits were conducted by guides with experience of their particular departments and refreshments were provided by canteen staff. Schedules were checked and progress monitored during weekly team meetings.

Feedback from the meeting was very positive. Every employee in the plant was offered the opportunity to take up the visit offer and during the summer a total of 583 visitors was welcomed to the plant. Following this success, the project team recommended that the family visits should become a regular attraction, co-ordinated by the Personnel Department. The core of 60 trained guides expressed a willingness to continue this useful and enjoyable activity.

Stage 4   Measurement

The final stage in Wellman's quality journey was to ensure that progress was being effectively measured. Figure 12.6 shows the path that was followed from ISO 9002 through visioning and planning for Quality Improvement. Wellman's experiences in obtaining accreditation to ISO 9002 involved the formal documentation of a comprehensive Quality Assurance system that included the following elements:

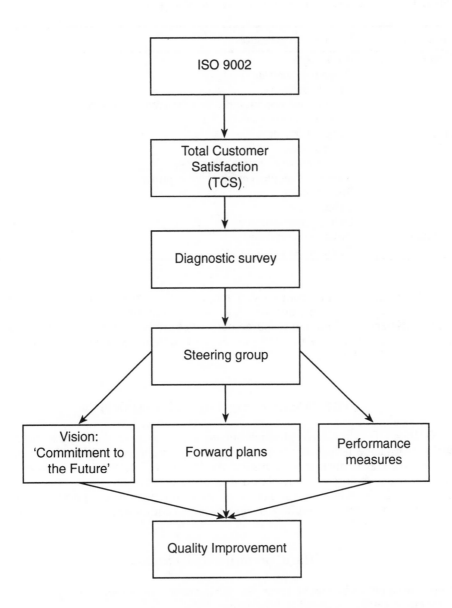

Figure 12.6   Wellman International's path to Quality Improvement

The Steering Group felt that additional measures were needed which focused upon performance in the five critical areas of production, quality, employees, sales and customers against predetermined targets. Table 12.1 shows the performance measures that were established for each of those five critical areas of focus.

Table 12.1   **Performance measures in five critical areas**

Critical area	Performance measures
Production	Plant output
	Downtime analysis
Quality	Actual quality
	Quality cost opportunities as measured by departures from standards, waste and credit notes
Employees	Accident free days
	Absenteeism
	Employee participation measures
	Number of employees involved in projects
Sales	Product sales
	Debtors days
	Delivery performance
Customers	Customer complaints
	Customer satisfaction surveys

Wellman International combined a range of performance indicators, most of which are easily quantifiable and which assist in monitoring the extent to which the quality, efficiency and human resource objectives are being met. There are plans to repeat the diagnostic study in 1995 in order to obtain an external view of the progress of the TCS initiative.

ACHIEVEMENTS OF THE TCS INITIATIVE

The Wellman TCS initiative produced positive results assessed by both 'hard' and 'soft' performance indicators. Improvements were recorded in those 'hard' quantifiable performance measures identified by Wellman International themselves as critical success factors as shown in Table 12.1. In addition, 'soft' anecdotal evidence is available, which is less easy to quantify but equally as important, suggesting that there is a new atmosphere of openness and commitment.

'Hard' performance indicators

Using the same five critical areas for performance measurement, many tangible improvements were recorded at Wellman in 1994.

Production
- Productivity rose by 17 per cent over 1993
- Pack failure (which halts production) reduced to 3 per cent from 12 per cent

Quality
- Cost of non-conformance was reduced by 26 per cent
- Sub-standard output reduced by 27 per cent

Employees
- Employees in projects increased from 14 to 143 in 1994; 30 per cent of the total workforce
- Improvement projects increased from 3 to 24 in 1994
- Training man days increased by 187 per cent
- Absenteeism reduced by 17 per cent

Sales
- Delivery performance improved by 31 per cent
- Debtor days reduced by 7.3 per cent

Customers
- More frequent customer visits
- Telephone answering delay reduced from 10 seconds to 4 seconds

'Soft' performance indicators

Some writers argue that 'hard' performance indicators offer a 'snapshot' of events that present a record of the past but which do not assist managers in predicting the future success of their current strategy. Kaplan and Norton (1993) suggest that a 'balanced scorecard' of performance indicators bridges the gap between output- and input-oriented approaches. Outputs include production, sales and profits while inputs are, for example, cultural changes in more open management processes or improvements in working 'atmosphere'. These 'soft' indicators may be difficult to measure, but may have crucial effects upon the success of Continuous Improvement initiatives.

At Wellman, there is anecdotal evidence of improvement on the part of both management and employees. Management is displaying a more 'open' management style in which delegation is becoming easier and a greater commitment to the workforce. Employees are responding to this increased freedom by their involvement in problem solving in team situations. All of these improvements have been assisted by more effective communication and training in a team environment. This change of culture came about from a change of management attitudes which, through training and communication, has led to a change in employee attitudes.

Management attitudes

Managers at Wellman International recognized that an autocratic style of management acts as a barrier to the TCS vision. As a result, management has espoused a more open style in which the focus is changed from a traditional 'blame culture' towards one in which honest discussion and debate is actively encouraged. An example of this new approach is the way in which all employees now dine together in the same canteen facility where there is no differentiation by status. Another is the personal commitment 'actions' by directors and managers which demonstrate their changes in attitude and in problem solving. Management senses that a degree of suspicion still exists, particularly in the area of hidden agendas, but recognizes that the challenge of changing the culture depends upon management behaviour and commitment.

Project teams

The work of project teams is encouraged by the attendance at project presentations by directors and senior management, followed by a social gathering with refreshments. The achievements of teams are publicly acknowledged through the awarding of personalized gifts at project presentations.

Training

Training at Wellman has been given greater priority. Employees are trained during working hours with no loss of wages in a new, custom-built Training Centre. Specialist training programmes have been introduced to address such topics as safety and fire fighting as well as computer and presentation skills.

Communication

An integral component of the TCS initiative has been the recognition that a plant-wide awareness of the vision is necessary to attain the quality objectives. Inspired by management's more open approach, communication has been increased using such methods as newsletters, information sessions and notice boards. In this way, all personnel at the plant can share in the quality journey and monitor its progress.

Employees

This change of approach by management together with the greater emphasis upon training have had beneficial effects upon the workforce. There is a growing perception of involvement in the operation of the plant that is demonstrated by increased interdepartmental co-operation. Employees are now able to monitor evolving trends and to personally benefit from improved performance through a newly introduced profit sharing plan.

In summary, the TCS initiative has proved successful as measured both by quantitative and anecdotal indicators. Improvements have been recorded in terms of 'hard' measures of productivity and quality, as well as the culture of the company. Management's clarity of vision has been matched by its clear-sighted view of those factors that may prevent its effective implementation. Accordingly, a more open approach by managers together with greater commitment to training and communication have yielded positive effects. There is now at Wellman a more positive working atmosphere characterized by a consensus approach to problem solving. The central strategy has involved the creation of conditions that permit the power of teamwork to bring people together in order to solve problems mutually and effectively.

FUTURE CONTINUOUS IMPROVEMENT PLANS

In order to build upon the success of the TCS initiative, Wellman have elaborated a system for cascading objectives down the organization through departments to individual employees as shown in Figure 12.7. The identification of critical success factors enables departments and individual employees to develop their objectives and action plans. Performance against these objectives may then be assessed and supported by appropriate training and development.

In addition, changes are proposed in the areas of teamwork, customer focus, planning and benchmarking.

Teamwork

Wellman International has plans to place greater emphasis upon teamwork as a vehicle for continuous improvement. Project teams will be encouraged to address both cross-functional and local problems so that all employees are able to contribute to ongoing continuous improvement. New training programmes are planned to improve the skills of team leaders and facilitators as well as generally to develop the technical and personal skills of every employee.

Customer focus

Wellman International plan to re-emphasize their commitment towards the customer by developing a process by which customer satisfaction can be monitored more effectively. Relationships with customers are seen as partnerships in which both parties drive progress. This concept of the 'customer' is to be developed internally as well as externally to include functional departments and other work teams. Internal administrative systems will be adapted to better capture, monitor and evaluate improvement proposals.

Planning

It is proposed to encourage wider involvement and ownership of the planning process by modifying the structure of the Steering Group to include representatives from a cross-section of the workforce. An update of the Diagnostic Study will lead towards a more integrated Forward Plan that will be supported by improvement plans by department and by project teams. In this way, the Forward Plan will truly reflect efforts of all employees towards the quality goals.

Benchmarking

The company would like to develop their capacity of learning and external awareness by benchmarking the improvement methodologies of other 'excellent' organizations throughout the world. Good practice, like quality, must be continuously

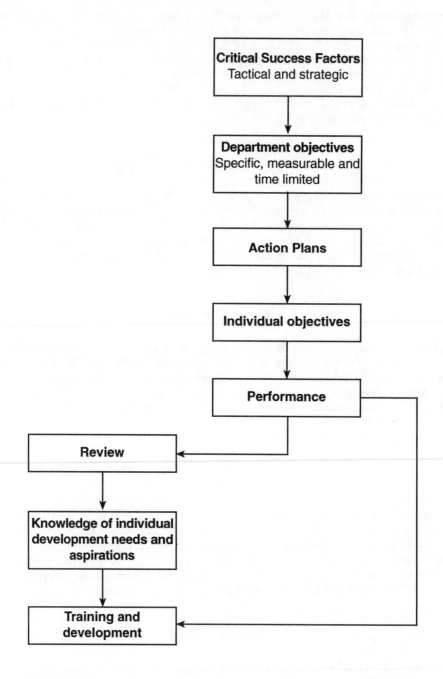

Figure 12.7   Future Continuous Improvement plans at Wellman International

monitored and modified so that it meets the needs of the customer. Quality awards, such as the Perkins Award, have been identified as potential benchmarking opportunities.

SUMMARY

The Total Customer Satisfaction initiative was built upon the solid foundation of successful accreditation to ISO 9002 at the Wellman International plant in Ireland in 1990. Since then, the management has been systematic and thorough in elaborating a plan for continuous improvement that took account of the factors likely to frustrate their efforts to achieve success. They realized at an early stage that the adoption of an open management style could encourage involvement and commitment among employees. Dialogue was achieved by encouraging open debate and critical analysis. In short, teamwork forms the key strategy through which the company is able to formulate a vision, elaborate objectives and solve problems by involving all its people.

GLOSSARY OF ABBREVIATIONS AND TERMS

CEDAC   Cause and Effect Diagram with the Addition of Cards.
ISO 9002   An international Quality Assurance system standard used in most manufacturing industries. Controls are specified in critical areas with the aim of getting things right first time.
PET   Polyethylene Terephthalate; a long-chain polyester molecular polymer used for the manufacture of plastic soft drinks bottles
TCS   The Total Customer Satisfaction initiative formulated by Wellman International

REFERENCES

Belbin, M. (1981) *Management Teams: Why they Succeed or Fail*, Butterworth Heinemann, Oxford
Kaplan, R.S. and Norton, D.P. (1993) 'Putting the balanced scorecard to work', *Harvard Business Review*, Vol. 70 No. 5.
R. Zeffane (1992) 'Organisational structures: design in the nineties', *International Journal of Hospitality Management,* Vol. 13, No. 6, pp. 18–23.

PART 3

CORPORATE QUALITY PERSPECTIVES FROM NORTH AMERICAN SERVICE LEADERSHIP FIRMS

THIRTEEN

CORNING INCORPORATED:

Living the value of total quality

CAROLE CONGRAM
AND
MARTIN R. MARINER

THIRTEEN

Corning Incorporated:

Living the value of total quality

A diversified products and services company, Corning Incorporated has a strong tradition of technological innovation, with research and development expenditures representing 5–6 per cent of sales. Management is leveraging this strength in three rapidly evolving markets: communications, life sciences and environmental products. In communications, Corning is the global leader in manufacturing optical fibre. In life sciences, Corning Clinical Laboratories is the health-care industry's largest blood-testing organization. In environmental products, Corning's gasoline-engine emission-control substrate is the world's best-selling product of its type. Corning also dominates a fourth market as the world's leading manufacturer of speciality glass and glass-ceramics products. Pyrex, Corning Ware, Corelle dinnerware, Steuben crystal and Serengeti sunglasses are among the Corning brands that are popular with consumers.

Corning's 43,000 employees produce over 60,000 products in 41 plants and perform over 2000 different types of tests in 60 laboratories. Virtually all manufacturing workers are unionized. In addition, Corning owns up to 50 per cent of 20 affiliated companies in eleven countries. Among the largest of these equity ventures are Pittsburgh Corning Corp., which produces architectural glass, and Samsung-Corning Company Ltd, the South Korea-based maker of panels and funnels for colour television picture tubes.

Developing a quality process – and making it take root in such a large and diverse organization – is a formidable challenge, yet Corning is experiencing success after success as its people around the world advance toward a common goal: to make quality integral to their daily lives. In this chapter, we will describe Corning's quality journey, including the philosophical underpinnings of the company's quality process and the quality management and support systems for continuous improvement. We will also give readers some indications of the results Corning employees have achieved. First, let's look at the reasons why Corning's management embarked on the quality journey.

QUALITY ... WHY?

Like many American companies in the 1970s and 1980s, Corning found itself in a rapidly changing environment. First, Corning employees had to scramble to meet new standards in the marketplace. For example, when Congress passed pollution legislation, a Corning plant was already positioned to capture the automotive substrate market. However, a Japanese competitor quickly met and improved upon Corning's standards and won new customers at Corning's expense. After other experiences like this one occurred, Corning's management quickly recognized the strategic importance of quality in competitive positioning.

In the early 1980s, Corning also had profitability and operating margins of three per cent, the lowest they had ever been. Management recognized that the systems in place planned for shrinkage; people expected to throw away a percentage of what was made. Some approach to reducing costs – without disrupting the economy of the small town of Corning, New York – had to be identified, and raising quality appeared to be an attractive alternative because of its emphasis on eliminating waste.

A third factor influencing Corning's management was the poor morale of employees. Corning's unionized hourly workers had expertise and wanted to contribute, but the management policies and systems in place invited them to 'check your brains at the door'. Again, quality seemed promising because a quality process involves commitment and participation by every employee, resulting in a contributing and satisfied workforce.

In summary, Corning began its quality quest in 1983 for three reasons:

- to improve its competitive positioning,
- to increase profits, and
- to increase employee satisfaction.

In the next section, we will summarize Corning's journey thus far.

CORNING'S QUALITY JOURNEY: FOUR PHASES

Since its inception in 1983, Corning's quality process has evolved in four phases. Each phase has milestones that provide insight into the process of developing and nurturing a quality process in such a complex organization.

Phase I: Start-up – 1983–85

The objective of the initial phase was to build quality awareness and to make error-free work the prime value. James R. Houghton, Corning's chairman and chief executive officer, stepped forward to champion the initiative and to lead management in formulating the philosophical foundation for cultural change.

In awareness training programmes, employees focused on identifying their own customers and suppliers. The Quality Institute was created to deliver a standard message to 28,000 people in a 24-month period. This massive effort – state-of-the-art at that time – involved a train-the-trainer system, with line employees participating in a two-week course so that they could teach the quality awareness course in local units.

By the end of 1985, 80 per cent of all employees had completed quality awareness training.

With Houghton as its champion, this phase was internally focused, with emphasis on the formation of quality improvement teams and the development of systems for recognition, team building, communication and corrective action. Results were largely anecdotal. Teams shared their success stories at the First Quality Milestone in 1984.

Phase II: Break-out – 1986–89

In the second phase, leadership of the quality process shifted to the units as the focus moved to the external customer. The introduction of Corning's Customer Action Planning System (CAPS) gave Corning employees feedback from customers about their perceptions of Corning's level of service quality. This feedback resulted in the formation of partnerships with customers and suppliers to find more effective and efficient ways of doing business. Customer satisfaction measurement was initiated during this phase.

Employees forged internal partnerships as they redesigned work processes. In 1988, 40 per cent of employees served on 2,244 quality teams, and corrective action suggestions numbered 16,366. As teams proliferated, training courses were developed for such specific quality skills as group dynamics, interpersonal skills, problem-solving skills and statistics (covering data collection, graphs, basic statistics, sampling, and statistical process control). The results of this phase were mixed.

A significant push forward came from the Partnership in the Workplace agreement formulated during union contract negotiations in 1989. Union leadership asked management to move faster in implementing the quality initiative, which was being blocked by middle managers who were fearful that they would lose their jobs. As part of the agreement, the bonus system was changed so that management, administrative and production employees all participate in the same system. (Previously, it had been possible for a shift supervisor or a technician to receive a bonus while the production employees received nothing.)

The new system, GoalSharing, awards bonuses based on how well employees and their unit did in relation to the unit's objectives, which are set by a joint committee of management and union leaders and reviewed by a higher-level joint committee for fairness and difficulty. A typical unit has four unit-specific objectives that relate to such critical areas as customer satisfaction or waste. An additional objective relates to corporate earnings. Each unit sets its own strategy and plans for achieving its objectives. Everyone in the unit from the plant manager to a new hourly employee receives the same bonus, which can range from 0–10 per cent of pay.

The effect of GoalSharing was, and continues to be, powerful: Everyone in a unit is working towards the same long-term business objectives. Continuous feedback is provided so that everyone in a unit knows how it is progressing, and employees ask such questions as, 'How can I impact (a particular objective)?' Clearly the spirit of GoalSharing is consistent with the spirit of Total Quality.

Phase III: World-class quality – 1990–92

Assessment is a defining characteristic of this phase, which began with the introduction of the Quality Corning Cycle:

1. Collect data.
2. Assess.
3. Benchmark.
4. Decide strategy.
5. Decide measures; set goals.
6. Plan and deploy.
7. Implement.
8. Repeat and improve.

The operating units began using the Baldrige criteria as the basis for evaluating their quality processes and for developing improvement plans. Benchmarking was introduced, and the search for best practices began. On more than one occasion, the search surprisingly wound up at another Corning unit. New tools were introduced during this phase, including ISO 9000, IMPACT (a process improvement technique) and Solutions (a decision-making tool).

Key Result Indicators (KRIs) – such as measures of agreed-upon customer deliverables, process efficiency and customer and employee satisfaction – were established and reported to senior management. Customer delight became a clear objective, as people recognized and internalized that quality is integral to the business process.

To recognize superior performance by a unit in the pursuit of world-class quality, the Houghton Quality Award was established in 1990 and was first awarded that year to the Telecommunications Products Division. The current criterion is the Corning self-assessment tool, a combination of the Baldrige and ISO 9000 criteria. The award is made to units that achieve a self-assessed level of 600 points or greater on the Baldrige criteria and that are ISO-registered, if appropriate. A second award, the Houghton Quality Challenger, was created for units with self-assessment scores between 500 and 599 on the Baldrige criteria.

Phase IV: Integration – 1993 …

Full integration of the quality process with daily business practice is the goal of the fourth and current phase. The units have responsibility for deciding what strategies, approaches, tools and measures are required and following through on their plans. Support systems for Total Quality are in place. The involvement of corporate staff is shifting to one of supporting expressed unit needs and overseeing the KRI-reporting process, rather than offering hands-on support. Similarly, the role of quality leaders in the units is shifting from support to strategy.

There are risks associated with these changes. The first is the possibility that the quality momentum will diminish, or at least hiccup as the transition to unit ownership takes place. A second potential problem is that some unit leaders may not give Total Quality a high enough priority. Third, some people may conclude that top management, in passing responsibility to the units, was not really serious about Total Quality. To gauge the extent to which management has built a foundation for the achievement of integration, consider first the philosophical underpinnings of Total Quality.

CORNING'S QUALITY PHILOSOPHY AND STRATEGIES

Corning's management communicates its quality philosophy consistently in several significant ways, beginning with a statement of the company's purpose, its values and its Total Quality policy.

Corning's purpose, values, and quality policy

Corning's purpose is 'to deliver superior, long-range economic benefits to our customers, our employees, our shareholders, and the communities in which we operate'. The key to achieving this goal is a set of eight 'values (that) guide our choices, defining for us the right courses of action, the clearest directions, the preferred responses. Consistent with these values we set our objectives, formulate our strategies, and judge our results.'

As the first value among equals,

> Total Quality is the guiding principle of Corning's business life. It requires each of us, individually and in teams, to understand, anticipate, and surpass the expectations of our customers. Total Quality demands continuous improvement in all our processes, products, and services. Our success depends on our ability to learn from experience, to embrace change, and to achieve the full involvement of all our employees.

The other seven values are as follows:

- *integrity* in dealings with people inside and outside the organization
- *performance* to ensure a high return for shareholders
- *leadership* in markets, technologies, manufacturing processes, management practices and financial performance
- *innovation* in technology, products, markets and organization
- *independence*
- *the individual*, any one of the diverse employees contributing to Corning's achievements while developing their abilities and skills.

Consistent with Corning's purpose and values is its Total Quality policy, which focuses on the customer:

> It is the policy of Corning Incorporated to achieve Total Quality performance in anticipating and meeting the requirements of our customers. Total Quality performance means understanding who the customer is, what the requirements are, and meeting those requirements better than anyone else, without error, on time, every time.

This policy sends employees a strong message about standards: meet customers' requirements 100% of the time by delivering error-free products and services on time.

The emphasis in these communications on customers and employees is intentional. James R. Houghton, Corning's chairman and chief executive officer, points out: 'Performance ... is a result of putting our customers and employees first.'

Corning's six quality strategies

Corning's quality philosophy and policy lead to six strategies. Underlying these strategies is a set of assumptions about employees (assumptions that in many companies are not articulated):

1. Employees want to do a good job.
2. Most employees know a great deal about the job that they do and, in fact, may be experts.
3. Most people like to be recognized for what they are doing.
4. If people are unhappy or unproductive in their job, they got that way because of poor management, poor systems or poor communication.

Three strategies represent a framework for the company's support systems for Total Quality.

Provide visible, unquestioned leadership. Descriptions of successful quality initiatives stress the need for involved, committed leadership, and Corning is a case in point. Since the inception of Corning's quality process, Houghton has been its champion. He visits fifty company sites annually to reinforce the quality message. In meetings with employees, management, stockholders, community organizations, and the financial community, he can discuss the details of the company's quality journey.

Focus on customer results. When an organization undertakes a quality initiative and employees become involved in training and group activities, it is easy to lose sight of the customer. Corning initially focused on meeting the needs of internal customers, but quickly shifted attention to external customers – identifying and agreeing on their requirements and determining the appropriate metrics.

Provide a quality process and quality tools. Implementing an organization-wide, uniform process that presents quality principles and quality vocabulary in the same way is essential for achieving unity of purpose. At the operating-unit level, it is important to recognize that units may have differing needs, depending on environmental pressures, as well as the unit's experience with the quality process. As we shall see, Corning has developed a portfolio of quality tools that support uniformity of approach across operating units while also being useful at a unit's developmental level.

The remaining three strategies directly concern employees.

Train all employees to meet the requirements of the job. The driving force for quality comes from employees, and education focuses their energy. Corning offers training at three levels, in sequence:

- quality awareness,
- quality skills, and
- job-related skills.

Achieve and recognize employee participation. If employees are assuming responsibility for solving problems, recognition must be central to a quality process. Corning has many forms of recognition, most designed by employees at the unit level.

Communicate internally and externally about quality. Internal communication is two-way. First, leaders must listen to employees in formal and informal communication forums. Second, management must let people within and outside the organization know its intentions and plans for achieving Total Quality. External communication is the process of deciding how, when, and to what intensity the message and organizational intentions about Total Quality will be given to suppliers and customers.

As Corning's leaders formulated the philosophy of Total Quality and its strategies, they also considered the cultural change that needed to occur to make quality integral to the organization and developed a system to manage Total Quality.

THE CORNING TOTAL QUALITY MANAGEMENT SYSTEM

Also formulated in 1983, Corning's system of work, the Corning Total Quality Management System, endures because it provides a basis for understanding Total Quality, as well as a framework and structure for cultural change. Derived from the work of Philip Crosby, a leading quality consultant, the system is based on four principles and ten actions that guide the activities of Corning's employees.

The Four Principles

The four principles align with defining quality, setting a standard of performance for quality, identifying the management method for achieving quality, and measuring improvement effects.

Meet the requirements.   This principle recognizes that quality is defined by the customer, whether external (buyers of Corning's products and services) or internal (co-workers), and that clear communication is central to a successful customer–supplier relationship. Quality is achieved when the customer says that requirements are met on time and without error 100 per cent of the time.

Error-free work is the standard of performance.   Aimed at reducing waste, this principle focuses on developing an attitude of not expecting errors. As a result, attention has shifted to 'parts per million' from 'acceptable quality levels'.

Manage by prevention is the method.   This principle places a premium on planning, anticipating problems and taking preventive action, as opposed to taking action first and correcting later. The purpose is to build quality into the process rather than inspecting for quality.

Cost of quality is the measure.   There is a cost related to not doing things correctly the first time. Focusing on the cost of quality directs attention to problems, helps set priorities for error correction, and marks progress toward eliminating problems.

The Ten Actions

The actions which form a guide to behaviours consistent with the four principles. are:

- *Commitment*: Each employee pledges to act in support of Total Quality;
- *Teams*: In groups, manage Total Quality around processes that deliver to the customer.
- *Education*: Create awareness, and teach the skills and techniques required for Total Quality.

- *Measure and display*: Measure error rates, and use visual displays of those rates to show progress.
- *Cost of quality*: Identify the dollar cost of non-compliance to quality vs. the cost to detect and prevent errors.
- *Communication*: Continuously and consistently inform everyone about company and unit strategy and goals, and encourage employee ownership of this vision.
- *Corrective action*: Establish systems to identify and eliminate problems; management must respond to improvement suggestions (usually within seven working days).
- *Recognition*: Recognize individual and group participation in and contribution to Total Quality performance and results.
- *Event*: Hold gatherings of employees to celebrate achievements and recommit to Total Quality.
- *Goals*: Establish personal error-reduction goals.

Formulating the Total Quality Management System – and, more importantly, sustaining it as the foundation of the quality process – facilitated Corning's change in culture. Complementing the management system is a strong support system, described next.

CORNING'S CONTINUOUS IMPROVEMENT SUPPORT SYSTEMS

In a well-managed organization, employees understand and internalize its philosophy and policies. In the preceding section, we described how Corning's leaders established and continue to reinforce the quality imperative. Equally important is an organizational commitment to create the systems that assist employees in performing their daily work effectively and efficiently. Corning continues to invest substantial resources in developing quality-related systems to support employees at every level. These systems are the focus of this section: self-managed work teams, tools for Total Quality, and reengineering.

Self-managed work teams: Corning's partnership process[1]

Self-managing work teams make sense intuitively. What could be more effective than having employees use their skills and expertise to deliver value to customers? In many organizations, management has tried to institute self-managing teams by forming work groups – either by assigning employees or asking for volunteers – and waiting for improvements. Such efforts usually fail because management has not recognized that a cultural change is required to make customers *and* employees the focus of the business. Management must develop a culture in which participative decision-making – not autocratic control – is central to the culture.

    The success of Corning's self-managing teams follows from the spirit of partnership among employees as they focus on meeting the needs of customers. *Partnership* is the 'the relationship and interaction between two or more groups in attaining a common goal through full utilization of talents, experiences, and available resources')[2]. At Corning, partnership has six characteristics:

- *A clear vision, goals, and overall business plan* that are understood by everyone in the organization;

- *Shared information* covering all aspects of the business and contained in a common database;
- *Processes designed to fit systems and people resources*, which involves having employees who do the work analyse and document their work, eliminate steps that do not add value, and find a better way to do the work;
- *Self-managed, customer-focused work groups*;
- *Continuous improvement of people and processes*; and
- *A 'whole' organization approach*, which extends the partnership concept beyond manufacturing to all parts of Corning.

Corning has developed a model for the partnership process based on self-managing teams (see Figure 13.1). Although the model, which is iterative and dynamic, may be modified to fit a particular situation, the seven overlapping steps represent the approach used successfully in a number of Corning units, as well as in manufacturing, service and administrative functions.

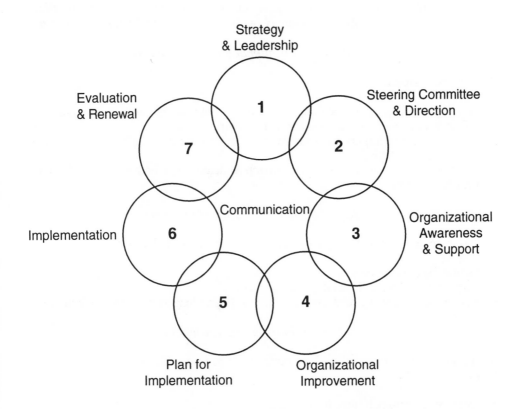

Figure 13.1   The seven steps of the partnership process

Step 1: Develop strategy and leadership

Key activities are to:

- Educate top leaders on partnership.
- Link partnership with business strategy.
- Identify the major strengths of partnership, as well as barriers to achieving it
- Involve union leadership and gain their support.
- Determine the scope of the initial effort.
- Identify the role of internal and consulting resources.
- Determine measurement criteria.
- Start developing leaders to support the initial effort.

Step 2: Appoint steering committee and determine direction

Comprised of representatives from a cross-section of the organization, the steering committee must organize itself to define its role, plan the scope of the change effort, lead the effort, delve into the issues identified in Step 1, and develop a communications and involvement strategy, with emphasis on leadership involvement.

Step 3: Build organizational awareness and support

Key activities are to:

- Develop a common database, including both quantitative and qualitative information, about the business and partnership.
- Formulate a continuous communication plan that includes training, meetings, site visits and newsletters.
- Develop an ongoing assessment approach to determine whether people understand the change effort.

Step 4: Begin organization improvement

At this stage, the teams of people closest to the work are established to:

- Gauge the environment.
- Analyse technical and social system processes.
- Recommend improvements, review them with unit leaders and other stakeholders.

Step 5: Plan for implementation

In this step, plans are developed to move each work team towards self-management. Key actions are to:

- Determine responsibilities for the plan.
- Develop the criteria for measuring success.
- Determine resource requirements to provide needed skills.
- Identify and plan for training and development.
- Identify needed changes in support systems.
- Formulate a continuous-improvement plan.

Step 6: Implement the plan

The recommended changes take place, with each work team refining changes to its work process and resources. Modifications are made in support systems, training and development, and performance feedback and recognition.

Step 7: Provide evaluation and renewal

This step builds continuous improvement for people and processes into the partnership process. Key activities are to:

- Compare progress with the change plan, and revise the plan, if appropriate, with teams tracking their own performance.
- Celebrate successes; Corning divisions set aside one per cent of budgeted salaries for cash awards, which managers and supervisors can give contributors (teams and individuals) on the spot, and plants hold quarterly recognition activities planned by employees.
- Plan for ongoing development of individuals and teams; as teams mature, team members evaluate each other's performance, and each person receives feedback and recommendations for development.
- Determine the appropriate level of support/resources needed.
- Develop the vision for the next level of partnership.

Corning has some tips to make the partnership process proceed more smoothly:[3]

- Take resistant employees on benchmarking visits.
- Older workers will support teams if they think their plant will improve as a result.
- Make the benefits of teams tangible to workers.
- Involve union management from the beginning.
- Skill-based pay allows the most experienced workers to replace low-level tasks by learning how to do high-level tasks.
- Keep company and union leaders' commitment to the partnership process visible in order to prevent relapses.

In implementing self-managing work teams, it is critical to plan for changes in supervisors' and managers' roles as coaching becomes central to their positions. These plans include training and development, as well as appraisal and reward systems. Some tips for supervisors and managers include:

- Communicate your support of the partnership process.
- Help each team understand your role as coach.
- Facilitate open communication within each group.
- Help to identify a team's needs, and work with the team to acquire the knowledge or resources needed.
- If you know that a decision will have a negative outcome, work with the team to obtain additional information so that they can solve the problem.
- As the group matures, stop attending every meeting so that they make decisions. Let the team know that you are available, and ask to be given progress reports.
- Find ways to improve your ability to participate fully in the partnership process.

Do self-managing teams work? Let's look at Corning's Erwin Ceramics Plant, where approximately 1000 employees produce industrial ceramics.[4] Results at this plant for fiscal 1991–92 showed that:

- Productivity increased 17 per cent (or an extra two months worth of production), with no lay-offs.
- Defective parts per million were down 38 per cent.
- Inventory space was cut by 60 per cent.
- On-time delivery was 99 per cent.
- Absenteeism fell to 1.6 per cent (from 7 per cent in the early 1980s).
- Operating costs were reduced by $350,000 in 1991 and by $850,000 in 1992.
- Overtime costs rose because training often takes place after hours; the annual training budget was $500,000.
- Employees initially spent 20 per cent of their time in training and 10 per cent-15 per cent as implementation proceeded.
- Sales remained steady (with Corning's personnel hoping that sales would increase as customers saw the benefits).

The success of the team approach may be observed in every Corning facility. One of the ways Corning supports self-managed teams is by providing employees with the tools to support their improvement efforts.

Corning's Total Quality Tool Box

During Phases I and II of Corning's quality journey, described earlier, employees learned about the basic tools of quality management, such as flow diagrams and control charts, and new employees receive similar training. Corning has built on this foundation by developing a set of Advanced Quality Tools that enable teams to go beyond making incremental changes to creating dramatic improvements (see Figure 13.2). These tools are the focus of this section: the Customer Action Planning System, IMPACT (process improvement), SOLUTIONS (problem-solving skills), the Innovation Process, Benchmarking, Key Results Indicators, World-Class Quality Assessments based on Baldrige and ISO 9000 standards, and the Supplier Total Value Process.

CUSTOMER ACTION PLANNING SYSTEM (CAPS)

CAPS is a four-phased methodology[5] for:

- obtaining customers' feedback about their perception of service-quality performance, and
- working with those customers to implement corrective action.

CAPS differs from many customer-feedback approaches because the built-in link between data and collaborative action yields an ongoing process for making customer-focused product and service improvements. In this section, we will describe CAPS' four phases.

Form a team to design a questionnaire. Customer feedback is solicited via a questionnaire based on the SERVQUAL model,[6] which defines five factors as critical to service quality:

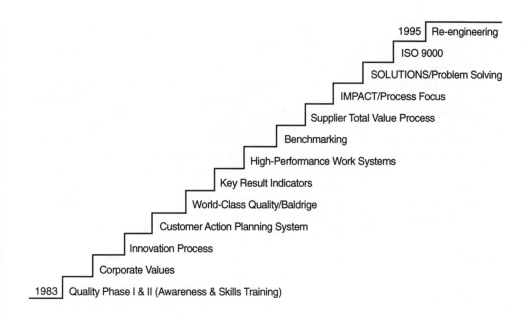

Figure 13.2 Corning's quality tools

- *responsiveness*: being helpful and prompt;
- *assurance*: being knowledgeable and courteous; inspiring trust;
- *tangibles*: physical setting, equipment, and employees' appearance;
- *empathy*: offering individualized, caring attention to customers; and
- *reliability*: performing the service promised dependably and accurately.

A cross-functional team, comprised of people who will participate in the improvement activities, designs the survey and determines which customer representatives will be asked to respond. A survey respondent describes each of the five factors in terms of world-class service and then rates Corning's performance on each factor. In addition, a respondent assigns an importance rating to each question. A typical survey has 20–25 questions and is administered annually.

Establish a dialogue with customers. A Corning team member meets personally with a customer respondent to explain the purpose of the questionnaire and to ask the respondent to:

- collaborate in the process by reviewing the results of the survey,
- verify the Corning team's interpretation of the results,
- help to set priorities for corrective action, and
- participate on or support the corrective action team.

Obtaining the customer's commitment early on is crucial to the success of the CAPS process. By establishing a collaborative, rather than an adversarial, relationship, discussions about priorities, costs, timing, and other potential constraints can be two-way, thus preventing any 'surprises' for the customer.

Analyse the responses.   The team analyses the responses, which consist of short-answer and open-ended questions. Especially important are the 'vital few' questions that customers rate as highly important but for which they assign Corning low ratings. Team members then formulate follow-on questions to obtain more in-depth information about these few questions through telephone interviews with respondents.

Develop a corrective action plan.   The Corning team forms a joint corrective action team with workers, supervisors, and managers from the customer organization. The joint team not only formulates the plan, but also implements it and monitors its progress. Integral to the plan is a communication plan to disseminate information within both companies about improvements made.

In use across a broad range of Corning units worldwide, the CAPS process is appropriate not only for external customers, but internal ones as well. Among the internal service units at Corning that have used CAPS are information services, engineering services and employee insurance.

The results of the CAPS process benefit both Corning and the customer. For example, service issues that a Corning team was unaware of were identified and addressed, and the ongoing close working relationship allowed this team to correct some long-standing misperceptions held by the customer's personnel.[7] For the individual Corning unit, the action-oriented CAPS tool helps employees meet and surpass the expectations of the individual customer about Corning products and services.

IMPACT

Time and money are equals in IMPACT (Improvement Method for Process Analysis of Cost–Time), a systematic, team-driven method designed to improve processes by mapping a key process and developing its cost–time profile. This set of tools targets reducing cycle time, eliminating steps that do not add value, and reducing sources of errors. The IMPACT process has seven steps:

- Commit to business improvement.
- Select a business and process.
- Determine the scope of the process and team.
- Target the improvements to be made.
- Analyse the current process.
- Redesign the process and measures.
- Implement the improved process.

In practice, a unit's leaders select a key process to be improved and form a permanent improvement team with a process owner. For example, Mailing Services used IMPACT to study the international mail process. The results indicated the need for a new supplier with computerized systems. With the new supplier, international mail reaches its destination in three to six days (instead of seven to eleven). Computerization allows an instant check on the progress of lost or delayed packages (compared to a six- to eight-week tracking period). Customer service improved; customers can drop off mail as late as 3.30 p.m. (instead of 2.30). And, perhaps best of all, the new supplier charges less for shipping.

After employees use IMPACT two or three times, this tool becomes part of every process improvement effort. In fact, Corning's management gives IMPACT high marks, and thousands of Corning processes have been mapped, including 300 in the finance area alone. Employees frequently use SOLUTIONS, another advanced tool, in conjunction with IMPACT.

SOLUTIONS

A rigorous, ration al approach to problem solving, decision making and opportunity analysis, this methodology provides tools for appraising a situation, analysing critical issues, and fixing problems permanently. Using this method, teams can:

- Identify, define, analyse and resolve problems accurately.
- Make the best, most productive decisions.
- Reduce the number and severity of potential problems.
- Maximize potential opportunities.

For example, at Corning-Asahi Video Products, eleven employees representing production, engineering, quality, customer service and maintenance teamed up to identify the requirements for a material to replace asbestos. The team identified 29 material requirements and categorized them into eight 'musts', five 'high wants', and sixteen 'wants'. As team members evaluated materials, they searched for one that would satisfy the 'musts' so that the material selected was the best choice. Later, they would use the list as a guide to improvements by chipping away at the 'high wants' and 'wants'. Some of these improvements may be made using Corning's Innovation Process.

Innovation process

Innovation characterizes Corning's technology tradition. The Innovation Process is used to develop ideas and create market-appropriate technologies, products and services. The six stages of the process are to:

- Generate new ideas.
- Build knowledge.
- Determine feasibility.
- Test practicality.
- Prove profitability.
- Commercialize.

Because this process is proprietary, we cannot describe its inner workings. But here is an example of how a team improved the Innovation Process through benchmarking.

Benchmarking

Corning employees continually search for best practices. To identify them, Corning has developed a benchmarking process, which consists of eight steps:

- Identify the process.
- Define the scope.
- Analyse the current process.
- Refine the current process.
- Design the benchmarking study.
- Collect data.
- Analyse the results of the study.
- Design and implement the improved process.

Consider an example. A Manufacturing Technology Research team investigated why some Corning groups had a great deal of success bringing ideas to fruition while others rarely succeeded. They found that good ideas often fail or falter because the inventor does not know how to move an idea through the funding/support maze. Using IMPACT, the team found that a clear, repeatable process for moving ideas through the first stages of Innovation did not exist. The team went on to benchmark the early stages of Innovation at such companies as Polaroid and Procter & Gamble, and determined that good ideas need wings if they are to fly. These wings include creating an innovation enhancement team composed of marketing, business planning, project management and manufacturing experts, all of whom assist the inventors.

Benchmarking also plays a role as business units establish world-class quality standards. These measurable standards become Key Result Indicators, a critical component of the Corning Total Quality Tool Box.

Key Result Indicators (KRIs)

Evidence of performance, a KRI is a measure of quality that focuses on one of three areas integral to achieving world-class quality:

- occurrence of a customer deliverable,
- what a process does, and how well, and
- satisfaction of customers and employees.

Let's look at an example, on-time delivery, which involves four processes: order entry, planning, processing, and shipping. Each process has its own KRIs. In the case of order entry, the KRIs are handling time, accuracy, and credit-check timeliness. In addition to the process KRIs, a customer satisfaction KRI is defined and measured by comparing actual on-time performance with the level agreed upon with the customer.

Figure 13.3 illustrates the important role of KRIs in the tool box. One key KRI is the difference between 'current performance' and 'customer requirements'. Equally important is the benchmark KRI, the difference between 'current performance' and 'world-class quality', established in the benchmarking process and representing the level at which customers will be delighted. KRIs provide a quality focus on the customer and process issues that customers value, particularly those that affect competitive positioning and customer satisfaction.

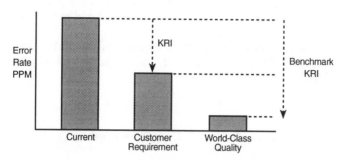

Figure 13.3 KRIs and benchmarking

Approximately 30 reporting areas have a total of 250 KRIs, which are reviewed quarterly at four levels – business/unit, division, group, and strategic leadership team. Each unit develops its KRIs as part of a quality-assessment process.

World-class quality assessments

How are the KRIs set by the operating units? Corning has developed an assessment process consisting of two components: a unit self-assessment and an independent assessment by a Corning team. This process helps each business unit measure and evaluate its performance against Baldrige and ISO 9000 world-class standards. The assessment process serves as the basis for establishing improvement plans, including the appropriate KRIs, built around the 'vital few' areas of most concern to customers.

Supplier Total Value Process (STVP)

Corning's customers also benefit from a process designed to pursue continuous improvements with Corning's suppliers. Corning developed this process so that the company could develop world-class customer–supplier relationships and so that its suppliers could:

- Sell on Total Value, not on price alone.
- Achieve the status of 'best' among Corning's suppliers.
- Obtain regular feedback from Corning.
- Use the advantages of the system with its own suppliers.
- Gain market share.

Each supplier is evaluated on four dimensions: performance in product quality, responsiveness, and customer service; quality systems, technology, contribution and pricing. Corning rates a supplier on each dimension and categorizes the supplier into one of five levels on the basis of the lowest score achieved. The levels, starting with the best, are as follows: preferred, certified, qualified, developing and new.

This collaborative and highly interactive process allows Corning and a supplier to:

- Establish and agree on requirements.
- Measure, track, and report progress.
- Score and reward achievements.

- Pursue continuous improvement, including reduction of cycle times.
- Pass the Total Value of improvements on to Corning's end customers.

Corning's 12-year quality journey – with its emphasis on cultural change, process and tools – set the stage for the extension of Total Quality to a major re-engineering effort, begun in 1994.

Reengineering: Corning competes

In most companies, when management mentions re-engineering, employees expect the worst: cost-cutting, job losses, more work for those remaining. In an initiative named Corning Competes, management undertook re-engineering to reduce costs after 1993 yielded a loss of $15.2 million, resulting from competitive pressures to reduce prices in Corning's basic markets.[8] Management expected reengineering to make Corning a stronger competitor and improve shareholder value through improved capabilities, profitable growth and permanent cost elimination.

To achieve these goals, management followed three strategies:

- Have a champion lead the initiative; as Chairman Houghton was and is Total Quality's champion, President Roger Ackerman assumed responsibility for reengineering and heads the strategic leadership team.
- Restructure key processes, as opposed to eliminating jobs.
- Build on Total Quality by involving employees directly in the work of re-engineering.

Following a strict timetable in 1994, the re-engineering groups completed the first three phases – Priority Setting and Team Launch; Opportunity Detailing, which focused on five key areas – innovation effectiveness, the roles of the corporate and line organizations, manufacturing effectiveness, purchasing and inventory effectiveness, and information technology; and Action Planning, during which 17 teams composed of 100 of the company's best employees worked full-time to redesign processes and reduce complexities.

In January 1995, implementation began. The focus shifted to the business units where champions, or service suppliers, coordinated recommendations with line employees. At some level, everyone in the organization is participating in re-engineering.

There are several lessons to be learned from Corning's experience with re-engineering thus far:

- Senior management leadership and stakeholder involvement are critical, a lesson consistent with the results of re-engineering efforts in many other organizations.
- Value is created and delivered through well-designed processes.
- Processes that are core to your key values and cost reduction in non-strategic areas warrant investment.
- Process analysis causes critical review of capabilities and competencies.
- Organize around processes and competencies.
- Focus redesign efforts on cross-functional activities.

Lessons concerning employees are not yet evident. Certainly as word spread about the negative experiences many companies have had with re-engineering, there was grumbling and grousing. Has this period been stressful for workers? Yes. Have jobs been eliminated? Yes, a small number of jobs have been eliminated as key processes have been redesigned. Most of the workers affected (including members of senior management) have opted for early retirement, but some employees have been reassigned when the redesign indicated the need for additional people. As we shall see in the Results section, Corning's financial performance improved in 1994, which reduced pressure at every level.

THE RESULTS OF TOTAL QUALITY

Has Corning's investment in Total Quality paid off? In this section, we will look at the results of Corning's Total Quality process from several perspectives. First, let's consider the three goals initially established for Total Quality:

- to improve Corning's competitive positioning,
- to increase profits, and
- to increase employee satisfaction.

With regard to competitive position, Corning has maintained its leadership position for such products as lens systems for projection television and flat glass for liquid crystal displays, which allows for larger displays in such products as the laptop computer. Moreover, Corning employees are fully using Total Quality tools in the product development and innovation processes. Corning's customers see the results of the Total Quality process. In 1994, more than 40 customers gave Corning citations and awards related to product and quality performance.

Corning's profitability has improved. From 1984 to 1994 (excluding accounting changes, one-time events, and extraordinary credits), Corning saw its net profit after taxes increase 15 per cent annually. Other financial indicators for the same period include the following:

- Operating margin: +22 per cent per year
- Earnings per share: +13 per cent per year
- Value increased from $1.4 billion to $6.8 billion
- Return on equity went from 9.1 per cent to 17.1 per cent

Comparing 1994 with 1993, sales were up 19 per cent, with net profits of $281 million.

The people who work at Corning say that they buy in to the need for quality and want to do more to make it work. This high level of business involvement is supported by a 1995 survey of employees in which 91 per cent agreed with the statement, 'I understand how the work I do contributes to the success of my business.' (In most employee surveys, 60 per cent is considered a high response.) In the same survey, 82 per cent reported that 'satisfying customers is the highest priority', and 76 per cent reported having 'the right skills to do my job'. At a recent meeting of customer service representatives from diverse businesses within Corning, over 50 per cent said that they had had a face-to-face meeting with a customer within the past week.

Another indicator that Total Quality has taken root is the pervasive use of Key Result Indicators to measure customer satisfaction, error reduction and process improvement. The adoption of these measures indicates that everyone at Corning looks beyond the financial statements.

Complementing these internal indicators is the recognition Corning has received from independent assessments. One external broad-gauge indicator, the Malcolm Baldrige National Quality Award, was won in 1995 by Corning's Telecommunications Products Division, the global leader in manufacturing optical fibres for short- and long-distance optical communication systems. The Baldrige complements Corning's citation as a 1994 winner of the National Medal of Technology, the country's highest technological award for excellence in innovation and commercialization. The company continues to be among the most admired corporations in America, ranking 18th in *Fortune* magazine's 1995 listing.[9]

We will leave it to the reader to assess these results while Corning employees continue their journey with the objective of making quality basic to everyday life across Corning's worldwide locations.

ACHIEVING WORLD-CLASS QUALITY

What are the hallmarks of Corning's quality journey thus far? Six elements, shown in Figure 13.4, characterize the process:

- *Four principles, 10 actions*: Corning's system of work, which guides employees' behaviours and activities, facilitated a shift in the corporate culture.
- *World-class quality assessments*: A self-evaluation process places responsibility on the operating units for identifying and making improvements.
- *Customer focus – KRIs*: A focus on customer requirements makes measurement critical in order to ensure that Corning's performance aligns with customer expectations.
- *Process understanding*: By mapping key processes, employees can make improvements that add value for customers and reduce sources of error.
- *Benchmarking*: Employees benchmark to determine competitors' strengths and to identify best practices.
- *Re-engineering*: Well-designed processes yield value.

Corning's quest for world-class quality will continue as its employees integrate quality into their business and personal lives. As shown in Figure 13.4, the integration phase will evolve into successively higher phases that are yet to be determined and that will take Corning closer to world-class quality. Although the objectives of these phases have yet to be clarified, one thing is certain: Corning employees will live the value of Total Quality.

REFERENCES AND NOTES

[1]This section is based on 'Partnership Teams', written by Robert S. Rider, a Corning employee, and included in Scheuing, Eberhard E., and William F. Christopher (1993), *The Service Quality Handbook*, New York: AMACOM, 302–311.

[2]Rider, p. 305.

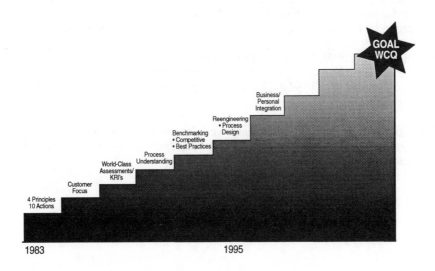

Figure 13.4   Corning's path to world-class quality

[3] The six tips are drawn from Liebowitz, S. Jay, and Kevin T. Holden (1995), 'Are Self-managing Teams Worthwhile? A Tale of Two Companies', *SAM Advanced Management Journal*, 60:2 (Spring), 11–17; this article describes Corning's and Motorola's approaches to self-managed teams.

[4] Liebowitz, Jay and Holden, 14–15. Op. cit.

[5] This section is based on 'CAP Off Your Quality Strategy with Customer Action Planning', *Quality Assurance Bulletin*, 1411, June 10, 1991, 1–3.

[6] Parasuraman, A., Leonard L. Berry, and Valarie A. Zeithaml (1988), 'SERVQUAL: A Multiple-Item Scale for Measuring Consumer Perceptions of Service Quality', *Journal of Retailing* (Spring), 12–40.

[7] Farley, John M., Carson F. Daniels, and Daniel H. Pearl (1990), 'Service Quality in a Multinational Environment', *1990 ASQC Quality Congress Transactions*, Milwaukee: American Society for Quality Control.

[8] For an expanded description of Corning's reengineering initiative, see 'Re-engineering, with Love', *The Economist*, September 9, 1995, 69–70.

[9] *Fortune*, 6 March, 1995, 66–7.

Additional sources

Bell, Chip (1994), *Customers as Partners*, San Francisco: Berrett-Koehler.

Hale, Roger L., Ronald L. Kowal, Donald D. Carlton, and Tim K. Senhert (1994), *Managing Supplier Quality*, Exeter, NH: Monochrome Press.
Lewis, Jordan D. (1990), *Partnerships for Profit*, New York: Free Press.

Parker, Glenn M. (1994), *Cross-functional Teams*, San Francisco: Jossey-Bass.

Scheuing, Eberhard E. (1994), *The Power of Strategic Partnering*, Portland, OR: Productivity Press.

Wellins, Richard S., William C. Byham, and Jeanne M. Wilson (1991), *Empowered Teams; Creating Self-directed Work Groups That Improve Quality, Productivity, and Participation*, San Francisco: Jossey-Bass.

FOURTEEN

GTE:

Aligning environment and technology with quality

ROGER HALLOWELL
AND
NANCY BURZON

FOURTEEN

GTE:

Aligning environment and technology with quality

In 1995, GTE was the largest single provider of local telephone services in the United States. The firm provided local telephone service in numerous geographically disparate markets across the country. GTE also (1) provided cellular telephone service in its local markets, (2) managed all telephone service in Venezuela and the Dominican Republic, and (3) owned subsidiaries that published telephone directories and provided telecommunications services to governments. In 1994, GTE had 111,162 employees and earned profits of $2.5 billion on revenues of $20 billion.

INTRODUCTION

This chapter describes how a largely decentralized company achieved quality performance by determining which elements of quality were universal to the company and which relied on each operating unit's environment and technology. Three areas of the company found particularly significant success with this approach: GTE corporate management (company headquarters), GTE Telephone Operations (a provider of US local telephone service), and GTE Directories (a publisher of telephone directories).

GTE's various operating units possessed distinct histories, cultures, capabilities, operating environments and technologies (with 'technologies' defined as the products and services delivered, as well as the processes and equipment used to deliver them). The differences in each operating unit's approaches to quality were striking. For example, GTE's Directories subsidiary (which publishes telephone directories) followed the criteria for the Baldrige award to such success that Directories received the 1994 Baldrige award for quality in a service company. In contrast, GTE's Telephone Operations subsidiary found success with a very different approach that combined radical process re-engineering and continuous process improvement.

Despite these vastly different approaches to quality, all business units at GTE shared a primary focus on using business processes to deliver low-cost, high-quality products and services. Other elements of quality found throughout the company included management's commitment to quality efforts, the implementation of measurement programs, improved education and training, a new focus on teamwork, and the implementation of meaningful recognition plans.

With this combination of independent and universal elements of quality, the GTE case offers insights into pursuing quality efforts in both decentralized corporate environments and single-line businesses. GTE's success exemplifies two basic concepts of quality: first, in order to succeed, a quality effort must be appropriate to the environmental conditions an organization faces and the technologies it employs; second, the effort must be supported by actions at a high level within the organization that in turn affect behaviour throughout the company, all the way to the front lines.

A PROVEN NEED FOR CHANGE

GTE launched its quality effort in 1982, both in response to negative publicity and to prepare for the impending deregulation of the US telecommunications industry. A series of newspaper stories and magazine articles in the early 1980s described the quality of the company's service as 'terrible.' A 1982 piece in *Business Week*[1] labelled GTE's California subsidiary 'the very worst telephone company in the U.S.', also stating that 'General Telephone appears to be faltering ... a victim of frail finances, continuing consumer hostility, and growing competition in its formerly cloistered markets.'

The article also described the company's customer service reputation as 'infamous'. For example, several of GTE's California switching offices had reported error rates of higher than 8 per 100 calls ('errors' meaning problems such as misconnected numbers and lack of a dial tone); customers occasionally had to wait more than a month for installation. Finally, the article quoted an industry expert as stating that GTE's executive management was so unprepared for deregulation that when it took place, they would 'not know what hit them'.

GTE responded to these reports in 1982 by initiating a several-year corporate benchmarking process called 'The Best Program'. Each GTE business unit was charged with identifying which of their competitors offered the best service and then comparing that company's service to GTE's. The results of The Best Program provided hard, quantified, *internally generated* data that indeed supported the negative claims made by the press.

By 1984, Executive Management had decided that the time for change had arrived, and that quality would be the company's approach to that change. GTE began this process by formally adopting a set of corporate values and a quality policy, stated below.

Corporate values:

- Quality
- Benchmarking
- Employee Involvement and Teamwork
- People
- Innovation
- Technology
- Market Sensitivity

---

[1] See 'General Telephone of California; trying to disconnect a bad image.' *Business Week.* Nov. 29, 1982.

Quality policy[2]:

GTE will pursue quality leadership with goals aimed at achieving error-free results that fully meet the needs and expectations of its internal and external customers.

From this policy, GTE set its 1994 goal of 'being the easiest telecommunications company to do business with'.

LAYING THE GROUNDWORK

With no structure for realizing these quality goals, GTE decided to hire a quality leader in 1984. After reviewing internal and external candidates, the Chairman selected Otis Wolkins, then president of a GTE subsidiary that manufactured microcircuits. Wolkins, however, had other ideas. He later recalled how he felt at the time:

> I'd come up through manufacturing. I didn't want a staff job, and I didn't want to leave the Southwest for the Northeast. Besides, my view of quality was that it was where the people who couldn't cut it on the line went – they were manufacturing rejects. I politely said 'no thank you'.

Yet in the end, Wolkins was the Chairman's choice. He spent the first six months in his new job learning about quality initiatives and travelling throughout the company and around the world, trying to understand why, as Wolkins put it, GTE was 'so bad'. Ultimately, he reached the conclusion that the problems stemmed from a gap in leadership. According to Wolkins, 'What the Chairman said about quality did not match his, and the organization's, behaviour.' When confronted, the Chairman acknowledged the need for change throughout the company and asked Wolkins to recommend a strategy. Having no background in quality or change management, Wolkins turned to GTE's management education staff, who suggested that Wolkins seek the advice of David Garvin, a Harvard Business School professor and an acknowledged expert on quality.

Garvin developed a program for GTE based on feedback from meetings with 20 GTE top executives. The program focused on two approaches to quality:

1. The basic quality literature, which Garvin used to introduce different approaches to quality and to illustrate some of the quality tools available. This presented quality as a *problem to be solved*.

2. The concept of quality as a strategic weapon, a way to differentiate an organization. This presented quality as an *offensive (as opposed to defensive) tool*.

The program was received so favourably that the Chairman asked every manager with the rank of vice president and above to attend future sessions. Those managers were then trained in leading the program, which they delivered to their management

---

[2] The quotation provided is an excerpt of GTE's quality policy.

teams. By the end of 1989, virtually every GTE employee had received an educational experience with roots in the Garvin program.

Garvin attributed the program's success to five factors:

- First, the right people attended. Participants were grouped in teams of *decision makers* from a particular operating unit. The head of each operating unit choose between four and twelve individuals to attend from that unit.
- Second, those individuals could be, and were, *held accountable* for delivering appropriate quality programs to their operations.
- Third, the education sessions included time for participants to *translate the ideas* to their specific operations. A workbook was developed for each team to facilitate this process.
- Fourth, the CEO showed a *visible commitment* to the program through actions such as changing incentive and evaluation programs to reflect quality goals.
- Finally, the program brought quality concepts to life for participants by *incorporating GTE materials*, such as quantitative data and a discussion of the strategic quality plan developed for one Telephone Operations market.

Garvin's education programme helped GTE begin to focus on quality through business processes in two basic ways: it fostered the commitment of corporate and operating management, and it began to disseminate quality tools throughout the organization. According to several GTE executives, this education laid the groundwork for management's current focus on quality as a tool to transform GTE into a telecommunications leader for the twenty-first century.

GTE CORPORATE MANAGEMENT: SETTING THE STANDARD

To build a framework for successful implementation of these quality concepts, GTE's corporate management set several policies that affected quality across all business units.

Quality and bonuses

One of the most significant of the corporate policies was the inclusion of quality measures in bonus determination. Senior managers and executives at GTE received approximately half of their potential compensation in salary and the other half as a variable bonus, up to 35 per cent of which was based on measures of customer satisfaction. According to Otis Wolkins, this compensation plan applied to between 5000 and 8000 managers, including corporate executives.

GTE corporate management used bonuses as incentives, rather than directives, to encourage business units to pursue quality. Said Wolkins, 'We never forced any business unit to adopt quality programs, but we did offer them education on quality, and told them that their bonuses would be based on it.'

The number of levels in each GTE organization where compensation was tied to customer satisfaction or other quality measures varied according to business unit. In some business units, all levels of management, from the president to each front-line supervisor, had some portion of their bonus tied to quality measures. While the portion of total compensation at risk declined as positions approached the front line, the amount of at-risk compensation tied to quality measures often increased to as high as 100 per cent.

GTE corporate management also recognized that in order for bonuses to affect behaviour, the bonus plan would require the commitment of senior management. The opportunity to demonstrate this commitment presented itself in the first bonus period after the policy took effect, at a time when management bonuses tended to be taken for granted. Management in one operating unit failed to meet their quality targets for this period, and as a result were to lose 35 per cent of their bonuses. When the managers realized this consequence, they asked the Chairman to pay a full bonus based on 'good faith' efforts, despite not achieving their quality objectives. The Chairman refused, setting a precedent for the compensation plan and showing a clear commitment to quality.

Quality and planning

Like many large corporations, GTE relied on an elaborate planning process. Since the late 1980s, planning at GTE has combined a strategic positioning dimension (related to the company's market sensitivity, described later in this chapter) with a quality dimension. Specifically, each GTE subsidiary's plan had to address both (1) where the subsidiary's services would be positioned in the marketplace relative to those of competitors (and potential substitute services), and (2) how the subsidiary would achieve its quality goals, which were driven by the corporation's quality policy and its overall goal of 'being the easiest telecommunications company to do business with'.

The inclusion of quality planning in the overall process, according to Otis Wolkins, had a dramatic effect on subsidiaries' attention to quality processes and enabled GTE to integrate quality and strategic planning. In the past, GTE's strategic planning process required a discussion of (1) how the environment in which operating units exist might change, (2) how the technology used might evolve (gradually or dramatically), and (3) what the financial results of an operating unit were likely to be. However, the process did not require an in-depth analysis of what an operating unit must do to either *create change* within itself or *cope with changes* in its environment. By adding quality planning to strategic planning in the planning process, GTE operating units had to declare both (1) what market position their services would hold, and (2) how the operating unit would achieve that position. Thus the quality planning process integrated strategic positioning, with a focus on business processes.

This integrated planning process enabled corporate management to evaluate operating managements' plans for the future and track operating performance against specified goals. As a result, this evaluative feature of the planning process ensured the attention of operating managements. Combined with the use of customer satisfaction data in the calculation of bonuses, GTE's planning process strongly encouraged operating management to focus on business processes to achieve quality performance.

Market sensitivity and leadership

After building quality into the bonus and planning processes, GTE corporate management began to add a new focus to its quality effort described by Otis Wolkins as 'market sensitivity'. Market sensitivity refers to an organization's ability to focus on understanding the needs and desires of customers so well that it can successfully innovate to meet those demands better than any other firm. Market sensitivity is somewhat akin to strategic positioning in that it requires an understanding of GTE's services relative to its competitors', as well as a prediction of how new and/or improved services will relate to those of competitors. When combined with GTE's quality processes, market sensitivity was designed to place GTE in a position to profit from the delivery of low cost, high quality services. Wolkins predicted that GTE's ability to anticipate new services and markets, combined with an ability to deliver services both cost-effectively and well as a result of the company's quality processes, would enable GTE to achieve 'market leadership', which in turn would yield the following results:

1. The ability to offer superior customer satisfaction (and thus value) to customers.
2. Improved customer retention.
3. Improved profit margins and maximized long-term total return for shareholders.

Wolkins explained some of the rationale for adopting market leadership as a goal:

> Quality is absolutely essential, but you can have quality products and services and still go broke. Quality, as it is often defined, is a backward looking activity. It measures the effectiveness of what was done in the past. Process yields, warranty costs, and customer satisfaction scores are measures of yesterday's activities.
>
> Leading companies require quality to look forward as well as measuring the past. Measurement of future customer needs is critical to this concept, which, of course, requires in-depth knowledge of customers coupled with an understanding of the changing technology available to meet their needs. Given the rapidly changing telecommunications environment, this is especially important for GTE.

A DECENTRALIZED APPROACH TO QUALITY

GTE corporate management encouraged its operating units to focus on business processes as a way to improve quality, primarily through customer satisfaction. It did not, however, require the operating units to adopt a particular approach to this end.

The freedom of each business unit to craft its own quality program largely reflects GTE's history as a conglomerate. Before the early 1990s, GTE owned subsidiaries such as Sprint, a long-distance telephone-service provider, and Sylvania, a manufacturer of lighting products and electronics. These subsidiaries represented distinctly different types of businesses that were managed relatively independently, making a centralized approach to quality unworkable in the GTE management model.

By the mid-1990s, GTE had focused on local telecommunications and related services, yet kept its highly decentralized approach to quality. As a prime example, GTE's corporate quality department had only one employee: Otis Wolkins. While the operating units had somewhat larger quality departments, they were intentionally smaller than those of equivalently sized corporations because, said Wolkins,

'Quality is everyone's job, and I don't want anyone thinking that someone else is in charge of it.'

The decentralized nature of quality at GTE is also evident in the dramatically different approaches to quality taken by subsidiaries in the early 1990s. An examination of the history, culture, and environmental and technological issues at two GTE business units – Directories and Telephone Operations – illustrates how the remarkably different paths these organizations took were appropriate, given their specific circumstances.

DIRECTORIES

Directories was, by GTE standards, a relatively small organization, employing fewer than four per cent of all GTE employees[3] in 1995. In the 1970s and most of the 1980s, Directories was considered highly successful, growing faster than any of its major competitors worldwide. One corporate executive described the business unit's culture as 'relaxed and open'. Yet Directories experienced slower growth in the late 1980s. Market research as part of an early quality effort suggested that customers were not as satisfied with the service they received as the company had thought. One manager recalled customer feedback from the research in which a customer described a typical visit by a Directories' salesperson as a 'drive-by shooting', suggesting that Directories had room for improvement in terms of customer relations.

By the early 1990s, Directories' operating environment was largely deregulated. Management at the subsidiary reported that 85 per cent of Directories' markets were served by at least one competitor in addition to GTE. While paperless, computerized telephone directories were technologically feasible at the time, few Directories end users had begun using this new technology, even though Directories itself had the capabilities to provide paperless service. Thus while the future of Directories' technology was somewhat uncertain, the pace of change was manageable given the business unit's capabilities and its relatively stable, though newly competitive, environment.

Under pressure from corporate management to improve both financial and quality results, in 1991 the President of Directories publicly announced that the business unit would apply for, and win, the 1994 Baldrige award. He backed his words by initiating quality improvement teams (QITs) throughout the subsidiary; by 1992, 100 per cent of Directories employees and managers participated in at least one QIT.

This ubiquitous involvement may have been influenced by several factors. First, participation in QITs became one of the measures on which employee and managerial performance was evaluated. In particular, middle managers (a typical source of resistance to change) were evaluated on the quantity and quality of their participation. Second, the President set a clear directive to implement almost all QIT recommendations. Managers estimate that fewer than three per cent of these ideas were rejected, noting that 'if you rejected a QIT recommendation, you had to be prepared to defend that rejection to the President'.

These two factors reinforced each other, since management participation in QITs encouraged recommendations that would be acceptable. In addition, participants

---

[3] GTE does not release separate financial data on Directories.

openly stated that many QITs initially targeted relatively simple goals, or 'low-hanging fruit', to illustrate the programme's success and gain the buy-in of more sceptical individuals. The combination of these three factors created an environment that encouraged continuous process improvement. Benchmarking, training in process evaluation and teamwork, and team-based incentives and recognition programs also helped Directories' employees and managers focus on developing business processes designed to deliver customer satisfaction. As a result, Directories fulfilled the President's prophecy by receiving the 1994 Baldrige award for quality in a service company.

A number of Directories' managers described winning the Baldrige award as 'thrilling'. Several also reported the phenomenon known as Baldrige Blues, which was the sense of directionlessness an organization can experience after achieving a significant milestone and then asking, 'Where do we go from here?'. The Baldrige process alleviated this symptom to some degree by requiring winning organizations to serve as national quality advocates. In addition, Directories further addressed the problem by increasing its focus on employee issues as precursors of customer satisfaction. This renewed focus reflected Directories' belief that it must actively manage the processes throughout its value chain, including those delivering internal service quality, employee satisfaction and employee capability[4].

TELEPHONE OPERATIONS

Telephone Operations, responsible for all GTE wire line (traditional telephone) service within the United States, was GTE's largest operating unit. In 1994, it employed 69,000 people and provided 88 per cent of total profit and 80 per cent of total revenues at GTE. Unlike Directories, Telephone Operations had a history of troubled quality performance, as noted earlier in this chapter. Before quality efforts began to affect the unit in the late 1980s, its culture was, according to managers:

- Typical of a regulated monopoly.
- Slow, bureaucratic.
- An employment agency, where a job was for life, and if you didn't shoot someone you'd be promoted as long as you waited for the person at the desk you wanted to move up or die.

In response to GTE's corporate quality initiatives in the mid-1980s, Telephone Operations implemented continuous process improvement in 1988. These efforts had a dramatic effect, raising the level of GTE customer satisfaction to just above the average of the regional Bell operating companies (RBOCs, such as Bell Atlantic or NYNEX, which provide local telephone service to a specific, geographically contiguous market). To reduce costs, the previously decentralized regional Telephone Operations offices were consolidated into a single national headquarters, enabling Telephone Operations to eliminate thousands of jobs and create significant cost reductions[5].

Despite these service and cost improvements, research conducted for GTE in 1991 indicated two ominous facts. First, customer loyalty was low. A high percent-

---

[4] Employee capability is an employee's perception of his or her ability to serve customers.
[5] Many employees were offered (and accepted) early retirement, others were retrained, and some were terminated.

age of customers indicated that if another telephone service provider offered them equivalent service at a somewhat lower price, they would accept it. More striking, a moderately high percentage of GTE customers indicated that they would accept equivalent service at the *same* price, if offered by another telephone service provider.

Second, research indicated that Telephone Operations' costs were not competitive. Management stated that on a 1991 'controllable' cost base of approximately $6 billion, Telephone Operations was approximately $1 billion higher than the average RBOC would be.

From 'Budget, Build, and Bill' to 'Choose, Use, and Pay'

Had Telephone Operations existed in its traditional, protected marketplace, these research results would have caused only moderate concern. However, given the recent and forthcoming shifts in its operating environment, and the dramatic changes in technology being adopted by customers (such as cellular and other wireless services), management at Telephone Operations recognized that sustaining trends in financial performance (and thus GTE's stock price) would require dramatic reductions in costs, coupled with equally significant improvements in customer service.

In the early 1990s, Telephone Operations' environment was shifting dramatically due to pressure from two directions. First, pending deregulation of the telecommunications industry meant that retail customers soon would be able to choose their local telephone supplier. Potential competitors included (1) cable television operators, who could offer telephone service at a low additional cost through existing networks, and (2) suppliers of telecommunications services that employed alternate technologies, such as cellular. Service problems at cable TV companies and the high costs of cellular providers made it unlikely that either group would dominate the entire local telephone market in the short term. However, alternative service providers and other competitors would have the opportunity to selectively capture some of Telephone Operations' best customers, or 'skim the cream', as one manager stated.

Second, and of more immediate concern, long-distance carriers such as AT&T (described as Telephone Operations' largest supplier, customer and potential competitor) were pressuring Telephone Operations for lower prices in providing access to local telephone lines. Long-distance carriers paid Telephone Operations an access fee whenever their customers placed long-distance calls that either originated on, or were placed to, a GTE local telephone line. RBOCs received similar fees. In this way, long-distance telephone charges to the end user subsidized local telephone rates.

In 1991, Telephone Operations received a higher price than the RBOCs for such access, which caused concern among long-distance carriers. This disparity had been justified in the past by the greater geographic distances GTE Telephone Operations had to wire and service, given many of its markets' rural locations. This situation had not changed. What had changed was the balance of power between Telephone Operations and long-distance carriers that resulted from deregulation and the advent of new technology.

By the early 1990s, it was possible for long-distance carriers to circumvent local carriers, such as Telephone Operations, for high-volume customers and in densely populated areas, the most profitable segments of local telephone service. This ability gave long-distance carriers, such as AT&T, more leverage in their negotiations with Telephone Operations, forcing a reduction in access fees. Telephone Operations management attributes the timing of AT&T's action to the increased competition AT&T faced from the growth of its primary competitor, MCI.

The magnitude of the effect of these reductions in long-distance carrier access fees can be seen in Telephone Operations' essentially flat revenues since 1991, despite of the fact that *usage* (minutes of use) and *number of lines added* had each grown at approximately nine and three per cent, respectively, on an annual basis. This effect presented the first tangible evidence of a dramatic paradigm shift in Telephone Operations' industry. Managers described the regulated, monopolistic past as 'Budget, Build, and Bill'. In other words, the business unit managed by negotiating with regulators, which enabled the company to budget for changes, build those changes (generally infrastructure), and then bill the user for them. Managers described the new industry paradigm as 'Choose, Use, and Pay', a testament to the power consumers now had and the need for service providers to compete.

Radical changes

In 1991, Telephone Operations decided to use radical process re-engineering as the vehicle to drive the enormous change necessary for it to compete. Management set two broad goals for the re-engineering effort: (1) improved service quality and (2) a $1.5 billion reduction in costs.

Unlike continuous process improvement, which works to continually improve an existing process, radical process re-engineering attempts to redesign a business process, starting from the premise that the old process should be ignored and a new process developed to replace it completely. The new process's design is limited only by the goal of delivering high-quality, low-cost service to the customer.

Radical process re-engineering is predicated on the notion that business processes develop by adding bits and pieces to existing processes over a period of years or decades, and as a result are often inefficient. Despite the deficiencies in existing processes, both managers and employees tend to become trapped in the mindsets these processes create, making it difficult for those involved with day-to-day work to 'think outside the box' in which they operate. As a result, process re-engineering teams tend to be led by individuals not associated with the process being re-engineered. These teams often comprise individuals from a variety of functional disciplines, as well as at least one person who understands the existing process.

Telephone Operations established eight re-engineering teams, based on eight fundamental processes that represented the vast majority of the business unit's daily operations: Customer Contact, Network Operations, Network Provisioning, Billing, Systems, Staff and Administration, Inter-exchange Provisioning, and Operator Services[6]. Telephone Operations also decided to attack all eight fundamental processes simultaneously, rather than consecutively. Three factors supported this approach. First, initial estimates suggested that each process would require eighteen

---

[6]These eight had been modified substantially by the end of the re-engineering process as the teams discovered that these initial categories were more functionally oriented than business-process oriented, especially as viewed from the customer's perspective.

months to re-engineer. Management believed that the organization could not wait eighteen months for each of the eight processes, an effective span of twelve years.

Second was the recognition that processes do not exist in isolation, that changes in one might lead to alterations in another, and that aligning processes could be beneficial. Simultaneous re-engineering could therefore result in a whole greater than the sum of its parts. Third, management acknowledged that radical process re-engineering would (1) eliminate thousands of jobs and (2) create significant discomfort for employees who remained, as a result of changes in both corporate culture and specific job tasks. By re-engineering processes simultaneously, Telephone Operations sought to minimize this still considerable pain by facing it relatively quickly.

Re-engineering at Telephone Operations involved mapping the eight processes as they existed, benchmarking best practices of similar processes at leading firms, redesigning the processes from the ground up, and implementing the redesigned processes. As of early 1996, all eight fundamental processes had been mapped, benchmarked and redesigned, and approximately 50 per cent of the redesigned processes had been implemented throughout the business unit. Based on extensive pre-implementation testing, managers were confident that the remaining 50 per cent of the implementation would progress relatively smoothly.

To facilitate the final implementation process, all eight of the re-engineered processes were implemented at an alpha site created in one of GTE's markets. This enabled Telephone Operations to work out many of the bugs in the new processes and create a working model of the business unit's new, re-engineered, way of life. The creation of the alpha site fostered both management and union commitment to the change programme as it enabled each to see what the re-engineered Telephone Operations would look (and to some degree feel) like before final implementation.

The role of teamwork at Telephone Operations

The re-engineering process at GTE relied extensively on teamwork. All process mapping, benchmarking and redesigning of processes was done in teams. Teams were also developed to keep the organization customer-focused and efficient through continuous process improvement that would follow the re-engineering. In addition, teamwork helped to strengthen Telephone Operations' relationships with its two unions, as front-line employees (union members) were involved in re-engineering from the beginning. Finally, through broad-based communication, Telephone Operations attempted to bring the entire business unit onto the 'team'. Communication was considered tremendously important during the development and implementation of the new processes, as one manager noted:

> Communication has been open and honest. We've given people notice that jobs were going to change as soon as we knew it, as much as 18 months in advance of the actual changes. This has helped people who want to transition to the new working environment to do it, and enabled many of those who don't to find jobs elsewhere and to get new training.

Thus teamwork existed between those involved in the re-engineering efforts as well as those affected by them, even in the dissemination of sensitive, and for some individuals, bad news.

UNIVERSAL ELEMENTS OF QUALITY AT GTE

Despite the dramatic differences in quality approaches at Directories and Telephone Operations, several elements were common to both. Above all, both approaches reflected a focus on business processes.

Perhaps the single most important element of quality at GTE in the mid-1990s was its simultaneous ubiquity and invisibility. Quality was everywhere at GTE, yet was not specifically mentioned in a great deal of the corporate organization's literature. This condition arose because the premier goal of the organization was to deliver quality service, which enabled management and employees to *talk less* about quality and spend more time *achieving* it. Consider Figure 14.1, showing the leadership process at GTE. While 'quality' appears in none of these leadership topics, every one of them is related to GTE's quality processes.

Management commitment

GTE management has shown more than simply verbal commitment to quality. Since the mid-1980s, management has taken specific actions to prove its commitment, reinforcing the meaning and importance of quality throughout the organization.

The translation of verbal commitment to action may have begun when David Garvin delivered the education programme described earlier in this chapter. Garvin delivered the first programme to GTE's senior executives. During the session, he illustrated a startling contrast by pointing to six flipcharts covered with quality improvement efforts already initiated at GTE, while simultaneously reading the results of a recent employee survey stating that only a third of GTE's employees believed that the company was serious about quality. 'What's going on?', Garvin asked the group, emphasizing the distance between what were effectively words (the list of quality efforts) and genuine action backed by management commitment. Chuck Lee, the current CEO, later described the session as 'a life-changing experience'. The visible commitment of senior corporate management began that day and has remained strong since.

An early sign of this commitment appeared when operating unit management attended the Garvin-designed education sessions in teams. On the first day of the sessions, each team received a memo from the corporate executive to whom its members reported. The memo stated that quality processes were so important to GTE going forward that the team was to deliver an implementation plan for their quality process 60 days after the end of the education session. This willingness to ask for a specific implementation plan represented a high level of commitment on the part of corporate executives and created accountability among the operating managers.

Another early demonstration of management's commitment to quality was the inclusion of quality measures (specifically customer satisfaction) in bonus calculations, as described earlier in this chapter. The Chairman's personal involvement in enforcing this policy sent a clear message throughout GTE that quality was now an

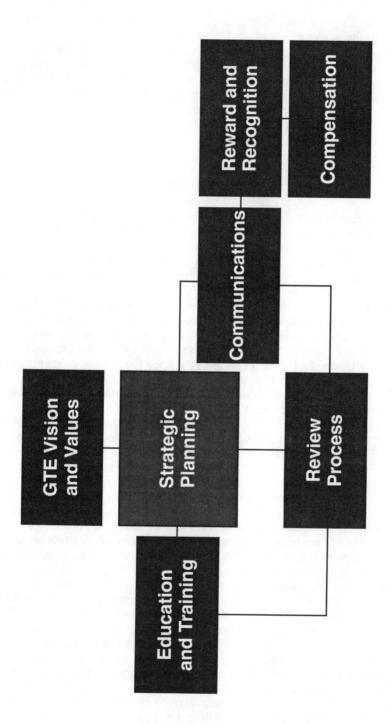

Figure 14.1 The leadership process at GTE

integral part of performance. Corporate management also demonstrated its commitment to quality by including it in the planning process, thus tying additional evaluation to the achievement of quality goals.

In 1995, a seemingly superficial event at Telephone Operations further demonstrated management's commitment to implementing quality at the operating level. The then recently appointed President of the organization changed the dress code from formal to 'business casual'. This act sent a signal to anyone still in doubt that the President wanted the culture of the organization to change, in alignment with the re-engineering changes being implemented.

Measurement

As GTE operating units conducted independent quality programs, few measurements of quality applied to them all. However, every operating unit measured customer satisfaction as one of its most important quality indicators. While customer satisfaction was measured in different ways at the various operating units, the existence of a single conceptual measure for the entire company made an important statement about GTE's goals.

An example of the effect this single conceptual measure had can be seen at Directories where the measurement of customer satisfaction resulted in a new operating direction for the subsidiary. By listening to customers through individual interviews, focus groups, competitive surveys and other communications devices, Directories developed a list of seven 'performance factors', or elements of customer satisfaction: (1) value, (2) business relationships, (3) customer service, (4) sales approach and sales support, (5) quality of documentation, (6) quality of Yellow Pages product, and (7) ad content.

These seven indicators of customer satisfaction provided the basis for what Directories referred to as 'marching orders', which guided their operating business decisions. Directories took the measurement process one step further by developing an algorithm to weigh the different elements of customer satisfaction, recognizing that they are not equal in importance. While this technique advanced their understanding of customer desires well beyond those of most organizations, Directories had yet to create a mass-customization approach, enabling them to measure and act upon the specific service desires of individual customers.

GTE also used benchmarking operations and employee satisfaction as important quality tools across the organization. Directories conducted comparisons of (1) industry operating statistics, (2) service quality, (3) employee satisfaction, (4) operational and support services, (5) human resources, and (6) marketing information, among others. The subsidiary performed comparisons against competitors, best practice organizations, and other GTE operating units. In addition, Directories worked with a number of external benchmarking organizations, such as the Hackett Group Consortium, the Saratoga Institute, and various human resource consortiums.

Directories also measured specific operational performance factors, such as increases in productivity, reductions in cycle time and improvements in customer responsiveness. These operational factors were linked to customer satisfaction and financial data in order to estimate their effects on organizational performance. In this way, Directories began the challenging process of developing quantitative measures linked to its quality processes. This critical part of the quality process would eventually enable Directories to understand the effect of quality on performance, thus supporting current and future quality efforts with hard data.

Telephone Operations also used benchmarking as part of its measurement programs, including particularly interesting measures of customer satisfaction. The business unit polled the customers of other telephone companies (primarily the regional Bell System companies, such as NYNEX or Bell South) to establish their level of satisfaction with the service they received. GTE also delivered the same questionnaire to its own customers to determine their satisfaction, and then compared the scores.

By benchmarking in this external way, rather than only against previous internal satisfaction levels, GTE could determine how its service compared to that of its competitors, as opposed to simply how it changed over time.

Education and training

Education and training at the corporate level followed what Nancy Burzon, Director of Quality Education, called a 'leave no fingerprints' philosophy. This approach recognized that the actual quality programs and processes adopted must fit with each subsidiary's culture, technology and environment. This has made the role of corporate education and training at GTE subtle, yet essential.

Following the initial quality education designed by David Garvin and conducted throughout the company, corporate education and training focused on its role as facilitator. The resulting programmes guided the adoption of fundamental approaches to quality, while enabling the operating units to determine which specific quality process to adopt. This occurred through a focus on quality training including, strategic quality planning, Malcolm Baldrige workshops, benchmarking workshops and process management workshops. All of these were (1) team based, (2) action learning oriented, and (3) focused on real problems from the operating units.

At the operating unit level, education and training focused on both the particular quality process adopted by the unit and the specific business needs of the individual employee. For example, Directories offered the following primary education and training programmes:

- Quality improvement training
- Initial sales training
- Systems training
- Sales management development training
- Local and by-request courses and self-study materials
- On-the-job departmental training
- Combination classroom and on-the-job training for
- technical skills
- Customer relations training

As this list illustrates, Directories acknowledged the necessity of both job-specific and process-specific training in implementing quality processes. In addition, some forms of job-specific training (such as customer relations training) emerged from the quality process when they were identified as necessary to increase employee sensitivity to customer needs.

Training was also developed to help managers learn to work in teams. Teams were defined as both horizontal teams of peers and vertical teams of subordinates and superiors. According to Nancy Burzon, before the use of quality processes at GTE:

> There was little need for teamwork. People tended to work independently. That has all changed now. Quality processes require the use of teams, both horizontal and vertical.

Teamwork training focused on individual and group dynamics, as well as management style. Managers were encouraged to think about their individual styles – did they manage as police, or did they manage as coaches? Teamwork training also focused on why the use of teams benefited quality processes, in order to facilitate the development of teams in the operating units.

Innovation

Innovation in quality at GTE could be viewed from two perspectives. The first is inherent in what this chapter described as the 'corporate' design of quality at GTE. The corporate strategy required quality as an output of the operating units, yet allowed the units to determine the specific processes to adopt in pursuit of the required outcome. This strategy created enormous flexibility to ensure an appropriate process/business-unit fit while still maintaining accountability for the outcome. Given the diversity of the environments in which GTE's business units operated, this strategy increased the likelihood of successful design and implementation of appropriate quality processes, whether they were established or innovative.

The second view of innovation is to consider how quality processes changed over time at GTE. Telephone Operations offers an excellent example of innovation in the quality process. The business unit began its quality process in the mid-1980s, committed to continuous improvement as the vehicle for organizational change. However, within a few years, Telephone Operations management recognized that the unit's operating processes were antiquated and insufficient in their ability to deliver high-quality, low-cost service to customers. In fact, management came to the conclusion that given the rate of change in their industry and the current condition of their operating processes, it was likely that a continuous improvement strategy would never enable them to achieve parity with (let alone superiority over) their competitors.

Management's recognition of this situation led them to a major innovation, adding process re-engineering to their quality programme. While re-engineering and continuous improvement are often portrayed as opposite ends of a spectrum, GTE saw them in a more unified light, as two different paths to the same goal of delivering superior value to customers. The two processes coexisted within Telephone Operations. In general, the relationship could be characterized by stating that after a process was re-engineered, it became subject to continuous improvement in order to maintain its efficiency and (internal or external) customer focus.

Through the use of process re-engineering, Telephone Operations made dramatic strides toward its goal of changing the way customers were served. This was exemplified by its stated objective of being able to serve every customer call within 'two touches' (with no more than one 'hand-off' to another area). GTE decided that expert systems (in this case, computer systems designed to analyse relevant information and deliver it to front-line employees) would play a role in enabling front-line service providers to serve their customers without multiple transfers and delays.

Telephone Operations' adoption of process re-engineering may appear obvious and uncontroversial. Yet some quality paradigms developed by distinguished experts argue that continuous improvement is the only process that will ultimately deliver quality output consistently. In this light, GTE's willingness to adopt re-engineering and combine it with continuous process improvement is significant. In addition to supporting the company's innovativeness, this action illustrates GTE's focus not just on quality (process for the sake of process), but also on delivering value for the customer and, ultimately, the shareholder.

Recognition of achievements

Rewards and recognition were critical elements of quality processes at GTE, both at the corporate and operating levels. As noted, the inclusion of quality measures in all managerial bonus calculations was mandated for all operating units, making rewards a corporate-wide initiative. Recognition, however, occurred at the operating-unit level, in a variety of forms.

For example, Telephone Operations developed an elaborate recognition program culminating in 'The President's Leadership Awards', described by individuals who had attended as a three-day annual ceremony resembling a cross between the Academy Awards and the Mary Kay sales-leadership ceremonies[7]. Hundreds of individuals and teams at Telephone Operations competed for President's Awards nominations each year. Winners were sent to Dallas for the entire ceremony, receiving both performance recognition and a brief, all-expenses-paid vacation. In addition, a photograph of each year's recipients went on permanent display at Telephone Operations' headquarters in Dallas.

The President's Awards themselves were cash and trophies, yet the trip itself emerged as the main prize. Otis Wolkins stated, 'Everyone loves the cash and the trophy, but they really remember the event. That's the heart of the recognition.'

In contrast, Directories approached recognition by offering smaller, but more, prizes. Like Telephone Operations, Directories rewarded teams based on competitions. Directories sometimes held unusual contests, such as one for the best-decorated office space. The Directories legal staff turned their offices into a jungle, complete with tropical trees and stuffed gorillas. Nancy Burzon commented on their exceptional work:

> The entire space took on the look of a jungle. The jungle theme reflected their vision of the world in which they operate. Morale – and productivity – in the office was extremely high. The decoration reflected the creativity of Directories – it is a very fast-moving, fun, creative culture. The kind of competition they have is in contrast to what you might see at another operating unit.

---

[7] The Mary Kay Cosmetics company holds what are generally acknowledged to be the most elaborate, awe-inspiring recognition ceremonies in the USA. They are designed to acknowledge sales leadership among the independent consultants comprising its sales force.

Whether flying employees to Dallas or boosting morale in the office, GTE operating units built successful systems of reward and recognition by tailoring them to their specific environments. Yet despite the differences in implementation, the importance of employee recognition remained constant throughout GTE.

CONCLUSION

GTE made remarkable achievements in quality in the 1990s as measured by excellence of process focus, changes in customer satisfaction levels, and reduction in costs. (Corporate Management estimated that 20,000 jobs had been eliminated by improvements in business processes since the late 1980s at GTE. Note that this was at a juncture when only 50 per cent of the re-engineering at Telephone Operations had been implemented.) By giving the operating units the freedom to select their own approaches to quality while creating incentives to adopt quality processes that deliver customer satisfaction, GTE corporate management dramatically transformed the entire organization.

GTE's quality programmes have enabled the company to deliver its products and services in dramatically different, and superior, ways. In short, quality has delivered GTE to the strategic position it has chosen to hold. Few firms can claim as much.

However, GTE is not *guaranteed* the ability to successfully manage the enormous environmental and technological transition it faces, particularly in Telephone Operations. At this writing, the question remains as to whether GTE's strategic position, or that of *any* of its major competitors in the provision of local telephone service, is optimal. Given the scope and pace of change in the industry, it is difficult (at best) to predict what constitutes an optimal strategic position. Ultimately, GTE's lasting organizational success will rely on the effective implementation of quality processes *and* their successful integration with optimal strategic planning.

INDEX